On Her Their Lives Depend

Friday Nov. 6th
Center City 1:45

On Her Their Lives Depend

Munitions Workers in the Great War

Angela Woollacott

UNIVERSITY OF CALIFORNIA PRESS
Berkeley · *Los Angeles* · *London*

University of California Press
Berkeley and Los Angeles, California

University of California Press, Ltd.
London, England

© 1994 by
The Regents of the University of California

Library of Congress Cataloging-in-Publication Data

Woollacott, Angela, 1955–
    On her their lives depend : munitions workers in the Great
War / Angela Woollacott.
        p.   cm.
    Includes bibliographical references and index.
    ISBN 0-520-08397-0 (alk. paper). — ISBN 0-520-08502-7
(pbk. : alk. paper)
    1. World War, 1914–1918—Women—Great Britain.
2. Weapons industry—Great Britain—Employees.   I. Title.
D639.W7W66   1994   93-20667
940.3'41'082—dc20.   CIP

Printed in the United States of America
9 8 7 6 5 4 3 2 1

The paper used in this publication meets the minimum
requirements of American National Standard for Information
Sciences—Permanence of Paper for Printed Library Materials,
ANSI Z39.48-1984. ⊚

For my parents,
whose love of reading history
was my first inspiration

Contents

Illustrations

Tables

Acknowledgments

For the study of British women's work in World War I, the outstanding collection of documents is that of the Women's Work Collection at the Imperial War Museum. This collection, assembled by the Women's Work Committee of the then National War Museum, which was commissioned in 1917 but not opened until after the war, is testimony to the foresight and indefatigable efforts of that committee of women. Its formidable resources, covering women's involvement in all aspects of the war effort, remain as yet largely unexploited by historians. This collection, along with the oral histories recorded and preserved by the Sound Records Department also in the Museum, provided the backbone of the research for this study. The records of the Ministry of Munitions, housed in the Public Record Office at Kew, are another rich source. Other important sources include the Institute of Personnel Management papers and the YWCA papers, both at the Modern Records Centre at the University of Warwick; the Gertrude Tuckwell Collection at the Trades Union Congress Library; and volumes of newspaper clippings at the Fawcett Library. I am grateful to the staffs at all these institutions for their assistance.

This book began life as a doctoral dissertation under the supervision of Alfred Gollin. I would like to thank all members of my doctoral committee for their help and advice, especially Patricia Cline Cohen. I am grateful to the University of California, and especially the history department at Santa Barbara, for the various fellowships that supported both my research and myself.

In the spring of 1990 I was extremely fortunate to hold a fellowship at the Dartmouth College Humanities Research Institute on Gender and War. The institute gave me the perfect opportunity to think through some of the issues at the heart of this book. I would like to thank the institute benefactors and organizers, and all the participants for their provocations, insights, and comments. Miriam Cooke has been an especially generous and inspiring colleague and friend.

I would like to thank my colleagues in the history department at Case Western Reserve University who read the manuscript: Michael Grossberg, Lois Scharf, David Van Tassel, and Ann Warren. Michael Altschul read it at various stages, and Carl Ubbelohde gave me invaluable help with editing. I have benefited greatly from Philippa Levine's help and advice. I am grateful to the readers for the University of California Press for their suggestions, to editors Sheila Levine and Monica McCormick for their support of the manuscript and gracious guidance, and to Elvin Hatch for having steered me to them. Dore Brown and Scott Norton skillfully clarified my writing and translated my Australian English into American.

It is not possible to list adequately all the ways in which I am grateful for Carroll Pursell's help and support. He has been an ideal partner at every stage of this project, from research assistance to helping formulate ideas and sentences to cooking more than half the meals. May every feminist scholar be so lucky.

Introduction

The decade 1910–20 saw not only an advance in the position
of women, unparalleled in any similar period, throughout the
civilized world; it saw also an entire reversal of the public
attitude towards their claim to equal citizenship. Yet this is
true only of the second half of the period. . . . It was only the
outbreak of the World War which brought about that great
and sweeping reform in the position of women which had
been accomplished by 1920.

Encyclopaedia Britannica, *1922*

On 4 February 1916, *The Pioneer and Labour Journal* of Woolwich
reported that "Elsie Mary Davey, aged 17 years, who has been missing
from her home at Fleet-road, Hampstead, since January 10, has been
found engaged on munition work in a factory at Woolwich. In trying to
obtain assistance from the Marylebone magistrate on Monday, the mother—
a widow—said the girl was 'mad on munitions.'" In this account, which
is reminiscent of that of a boy's running away to sea, munitions work
figures as an alluring wartime adventure for girls and young women. It
offered them a means of escape, if escape they wanted, a way of legiti-
mately moving to distant places around the country. Because the wages
were at first livable and later lucrative, munitions work proffered independence, a reliable income, and even an improved standard of living.
Financial independence, mobility around the country, and some disposable income either to save up or to use for immediate pleasure were
attributes that had characterized men's work before the war far more than
the low-paying jobs available to women of the working class.

This book offers an examination of the experience of women munitions
workers in Britain in World War I. Munitions factories were the arena in
which British women's experiences of the Great War were most comparable to those of working-class men, of "Tommy." The numbers of women
in munitions work were far larger than those in any other wartime role;
indeed, they constituted the army of women who were most directly
involved in supplying the forces and thereby conducting the war on the

1

home front. They were the first stage in the production line of death that ended at the front; they were well aware of the lethal nature of their manufactures and believed themselves to be essentially involved in the conduct of the war.

I focus on the approximately one million women who worked in munitions factories in a variety of capacities, ranging from unskilled assemblers to skilled fitters and turners. In spite of their celebration by the wartime press, middle- and upper-class women munitions workers were a tiny fraction of the whole. Thus at times, unless they are of particular significance, they are overlooked in my assessments in order to reach a class specificity appropriate to the dominant portion of the group. However, British women who worked in munitions factories in World War I came from all classes and all strata within each class, as well as all regions of Britain (including some from the dominions). They worked in factories all over Britain, in very different jobs, and earned wages with sizable discrepancies. A matrix of class, age, and other factors of difference underlies this whole book and I have sought to illuminate these factors wherever possible.

This study includes the middle-class women who held quasi-professional jobs such as welfare supervisors, factory inspectors, and women police and patrols, as well as reform and religious association workers, insofar as they dealt with women munitions workers. In a context in which women availed themselves of unprecedented employment opportunities created by the massive dislocation of the war, the interaction between women of different classes on the shop floor and in other venues associated with munitions factories failed to create cross-class gender bonding. Instead, this interaction exacerbated class tensions to a degree that would significantly affect postwar reconstruction.

The testimony of the articulate upper and middle classes, so powerfully recorded in the novels and memoirs of the war, can answer questions about the gendered experience of those women. Although a small proportion of the educationally and economically privileged participated directly as nurses or workers in the war effort or gained work as professionals, they more typically took newly available clerical jobs or confined themselves to charitable works. Clerical work offered middle-class—and some working-class—young women both financial and social independence. Yet it was mostly working-class women who learned new skills with machinery and experienced sharp increases in pay. For the women munitions workers who were able to do "men's work" for the duration, their jobs often involved challenge and the excitement of operating powerful equipment. Women who were trained as oxyacetylene welders enjoyed the creative satisfaction of their trade. Women drove electric cranes, locomotives, and trucks at a time when a woman driving a car drew social comment. Women who were trained as fitters and turners were made well aware that they were privileged to join a trade normally the preserve of men.

Many women munitions workers found themselves in unfamiliar surroundings. They commonly moved across the country to take jobs at new factories, and even those who travelled lesser distances often found themselves in new towns, or at least new domestic situations, surrounded by other women workers in large hostels, or boarding with local women and their families. Being away from their own homes and families frequently meant greater social freedom: even in the relatively controlled situation of hostels, women workers could still exercise some discretion about what they did in the evenings and on Sundays off, with whom and until when. In this way too they were thwarting conventions of women's social behavior that had affected women of the working class as much as, or perhaps more than, women of the middle and upper classes.

During the war the woman munitions worker became a powerful symbol of modernity. She challenged the gender order through her patriotic skilled work and control of machinery, and she undermined class differences through her increased spending power. Robert Graves and Alan Hodge later claimed that at the end of the war "the 'modern girl' was still the popular heroine that she had become when working on munitions in factories."[1] British society was well primed to perceive and discuss changes in women's roles and behavior. Not only had the years immediately prior to the war been the culmination of the largest and most dramatic phase of the suffrage campaign, but at the same time feminists had broadened their agenda and raised issues such as female sexual pleasure, homosexuality, and birth control.[2] In the same years, experimental cultural modernism was so powerful that many believed an important transformation had taken place.[3]

1. Robert Graves and Alan Hodge, *The Long Week-End: A Social History of Great Britain 1918–1939* (1940; reprint, New York: Norton Library, 1963), 43.

2. Susan Kingsley Kent, *Sex and Suffrage in Britain, 1860–1914* (Princeton: Princeton University Press, 1987), 22. On the significant developments in American feminism in the 1910s, see Nancy Cott, *The Grounding of Modern Feminism* (New Haven: Yale University Press, 1987).

3. David Harvey, *The Condition of Postmodernity: An Enquiry into the Origins of Cultural Change* (Oxford: Basil Blackwell, 1989), 28; Modris Eksteins, *Rites of Spring: The Great War and the Birth of the Modern Age* (Boston: Houghton Mifflin, 1989). On the connections

The word "flapper" came to signify the modern young woman on the eve of the war and implied physical and social liberation as well as changing sexual mores that crossed class boundaries.[4] The expansion of regulating agencies during the war was central to the experience of women workers. The social and sexual behavior of women workers was observed, decried, and regulated by the government, military authorities, and voluntary middle-class women's groups, a reflex of a society in great fear of losing control. There is insufficient evidence concerning the intimate aspects of women munitions workers' lives to say whether they experienced the war as sexual release, despite contemporary accusations that the working class created huge numbers of illegitimate "war babies." As before the war, many women workers aimed to live by the tenets of respectability. The interaction between women workers and the mostly middle-class women police, patrols, welfare supervisors, and social workers should be seen as a process more complex than class conflict or social control. With new opportunities for women of all classes, class relations among women adapted to new circumstances, but interclass tension continued.

For many women of the working class, the war offered escape from jobs of badly paid drudgery. Compared to domestic service, work in munitions factories was free of servility and far better paid. Elsie Bell recalled that her wartime job at Pirelli's cable works was "very nice" after domestic service "'cause you had more freedom and you were amongst more people," on top of the fact that she was earning around three pounds a week compared to her previous half crown (two shillings and sixpence).[5]

Not everyone reacted the same way. After all, a job in a munitions factory was usually physically exhausting, protracted work in an unpleasant and even dangerous environment. Lottie Barker's overwhelming feeling at the Armistice was relief that she could quit her job as a crane driver at the Chilwell shell-filling factory and leave "the confines of the factory, that had held us captive for three years with never one single moment to relax."[6] But a widely shared sense among munitions workers that they had proven themselves able and hard workers, and deserved to

---

between Futurism, Expressionism, and the outbreak of the war, see George L. Mosse, *Fallen Soldiers: Reshaping the Memory of the World Wars* (New York: Oxford University Press, 1990), 54–59.

4. Graves and Hodge, *Long Week-End*, 43–44.

5. Imperial War Museum (hereafter IWM), Department of Sound Records (hereafter DSR), 7435/01.

6. Lottie Barker, "My Life as I Remember It, 1899–1920," TS, 62, Brunel University Library.

be considered so, drove them to large, angry demonstrations against their demobilization at the end of the war. It was not that they thought they could or should continue to make the munitions of war, but they demanded that their hard work be recognized by a public commitment to their continued employment in industrial work. They vehemently resisted returning to the servility, low pay, long hours, poor conditions, and lack of autonomy of domestic service.

Contemporary observers hailed the benefits of women's wartime opportunities. Flora Annie Steel's assessment of women's situation at the time of the Armistice was one of apocalyptic optimism:

> Verily and indeed, if we women have done something in this war, the war has done more for us women. It has taught us to recognise ourselves, to justify our existence. Ideas that for the most part were but the baseless fabric of a dreamer's vision have taken form and the world is fresh and new for womanhood. Why, our very carriage is different, as anyone with eyes can see! As Kipling puts it, we walk now as if we owned ourselves, and we stand closer to each other.[7]

Working-class women benefited from the war in the gender-specific ways of increased employment opportunities, higher wages (up to three times their prewar rates of pay), and a chance to learn new skills. Not all women experienced greater gender consciousness during the war, but the evidence suggests that, at least for some women, wartime work created gender-related growth in self-esteem and assertiveness. The gender consciousness that existed among women munitions workers was not, however, an identity that cut across class lines. Rather, their sense of themselves as women was constructed around options available to them as members of the working class.

"ON HER THEIR LIVES DEPEND"

The massive recruitment of civilians for the total effort of the Great War opened up direct war participation far beyond the bounds of the regular armed forces. In the process, the gendering of patriotic involvement became negotiable. While the primary, heroic, mythical figure of the soldier remained resolutely male, the introduction of women's paramilitary organizations raised questions about the precise nature of the mas-

7. Flora Annie Steel, "Woman Makes a New World," *Daily Mail,* 12 November 1918. See also H. M. Principal Lady Inspector of Factories, *Annual Report of the Chief Inspector of Factories and Workshops for the Year 1916,* Cd. 8570, 1917–18, vol. 14, 161, 7.

culine domain of soldiering. As women approached the battle zone in their supportive roles, clerical and transport functions were no longer exclusively masculine preserves. Physically distant from the battle zone but directly involved in propagating the war, women's role in making the munitions of war transgressed notions of war as a masculine enterprise. Much as the working men of Britain were expected to join up and go off to fight for king and country, and to lay down their lives if necessary, so working women were expected to do their share by taking over the critical jobs in industry. The poster that proclaimed "On Her Their Lives Depend" sought to draw women into munitions factories by glamorizing the munitions worker's patriotic importance. But its message became a commonly held belief, particularly in the wake of the May 1915 "shells scandal" in which the Northcliffe press attacked the government for hampering the army with an inadequate supply of munitions.[8]

The woman munitions worker, dubbed a "munitionette," was also nicknamed "Tommy's sister." A standard term for the representative British private soldier, "Tommy" originated in nineteenth-century War Office manuals. Thomas Atkins was the name used in sample entries instructing soldiers how to fill out their forms. It was said that the Duke of Wellington had chosen the name in honor of a soldier who had been exceptionally brave.[9] Tommy Atkins became a national folk hero through Rudyard Kipling's verse of the 1890s, in which the poet paid homage to the ordinary, working-class soldier who was treated with contempt in time of peace and then put on the front line in time of war.[10] With the same amalgam of class condescension and genuine appreciation, in 1916 Hall Caine paid tribute to Tommy's sister:

> They are in the factories now, five hundred thousand of them all over the country, a vast army of female soldiers, who stand for British womanhood. . . . We talk of the British Tommy and his unconquerable light-heartedness, as if he were a peculiar type, but the Cockney girl is Tommy's own sister, with the same humour and the same tameless blood in her. . . . Tommy's sister in the munition factories, like Tommy in the trenches, lives in the last moment, now joking, teasing, laughing and wriggling, and then fuming and flaming and weeping over her troubles as if the world were coming to an end.[11]

8. R. J. Q. Adams, *Arms and the Wizard: Lloyd George and the Ministry of Munitions 1915–1916* (London: Cassell & Co., 1978), 31–35.

9. Ralph Durand, *A Handbook to the Poetry of Rudyard Kipling* (New York: Doubleday, Page & Co., 1914), 26–27.

10. See, for example, "To T. A." and "Tommy," in *The Complete Barrack-Room Ballads of Rudyard Kipling* (London: Methuen & Co., 1973), ed. Charles Carrington, 29–33.

11. T. Hall Caine, *Our Girls: Their Work for the War* (London: Hutchinson & Co.,

The image of a female counterpart of Tommy Atkins has also been invoked to emphasize the significance of the war experience of the Women's Army Auxiliary Corps (WAAC), through which women entered into the military forces in Britain in World War I, albeit in clerical and service positions. Thus when one WAAC chose to publish her letters home at the end of the war she called them *The Letters of Thomasina Atkins*.[12] Similarly, the World War I image of "the girl behind the man behind the gun" has been taken to apply to members of the WAAC, although during the war it was used in posters aimed at recruiting women into munitions factories.[13] But the number of WAACs was a small fraction of the women who entered the munitions factories.

My point here is not to make invidious distinctions between various women's roles in the war in order to claim that women munitions workers were more critical to the war effort or that they sacrificed more. Nurses and women ambulance drivers behind the lines in France knew the dehumanization and numbing terrors of the war zone as those in Britain could never know them.[14] Yet nurses, the Florence Nightingales of World War I, performed the maternal, nurturing role of healers, those who worked to restore life to the decimated, emasculated victims of war.

In contrast, women munitions workers, besides being numerically more of an army, were the first stage of the production line of war: they made the guns, shells, explosives, aircraft, and other matériel that "made" the war at the front. They could not consistently partake of the pacifist opposition to war that was available to, and subscribed to by, some nurses, members of the Voluntary Aid Detachments (VADs), and ambulance drivers. Women munitions makers were utterly implicated in the "making" of war. It is probable that most of them were at least morally comfortable with their direct involvement in the propagation of war; those on the home front who opposed the war were a vilified minority in every class.

1916), 66–70. See also Deborah Thom, "Tommy's Sister: Women at Woolwich in World War I," in *Minorities & Outsiders,* vol. 2 of *Patriotism: The Making and Unmaking of British National Identity,* ed. Raphael Samuel (London: Routledge, 1989), 144–57.

12. *The Letters of Thomasina Atkins* by "Private (W.A.A.C.) on Active Service" (New York: George H. Doran, 1918).

13. Elizabeth Crosthwait, "'The Girl Behind the Man Behind the Gun': The Women's Army Auxiliary Corps, 1914–18," in *Our Work, Our Lives, Our Words: Women's History & Women's Work,* ed. Leonore Davidoff and Belinda Westover (London: Macmillan Education, 1986), 161–81.

14. See, for example, Lynn Knight, introduction to *We That Were Young,* by Irene Rathbone (New York: Feminist Press at CUNY, 1989), xv.

In many ways, they were subject to a militaristic regimen. The hostels built to house them near the factories had a barracks atmosphere. Women munitions workers put in long hours on regular shifts six and sometimes seven days a week, were disciplined by various agents of authority, wore uniforms, and were continually urged to work hard, to increase production, and thus to help to win the war. At least at Woolwich Arsenal, women workers were known to the office by their number rather than their name.[15] All over Britain, the factories in which they worked were deafeningly noisy, full of noxious fumes, often unheated, and usually located either in the industrial parts of cities or in the remote countryside, surrounded by fields of mud.

Like the men in the trenches, women munitions workers received public acclamation for their part in the war effort. For example, the *Daily Mail* proclaimed: "Only those who are daily risking their lives and safety, flying over the scenes of strife and warfare, can fully comprehend how much they owe to the women aeroplane makers. For in the skill and care of the hands that construct the machine the lives of the men are held."[16] The burden of doing what their country needed and expected was lightened for women workers by the respect and gratitude expressed in the press and in a few public ceremonies. A number of women munitions workers received the Order of the British Empire for bravery during explosions or accidents and for injuries they suffered.[17] On 20 April 1918, a special service for London munitions workers was held at St. Paul's Cathedral, during which the "Last Post" was played for those who had died.[18] They were recognized in the charitable works of middle- and upper-class women, who knitted for the troops and sold flowers in order to build huts for women workers.

It was commonly believed that women munitions makers worked for reasons beyond the high wages, that in fact their ambitions were fired by the patriotic cause of war. Newspapers, frustrated by the censorship that limited their coverage of the war at the front, seized on munitions factories as scenes of the war at home. In March 1917, *The Englishwoman* published a one-act play, "The Munition Worker," the dramatic tension of which

15. Caroline Rennles recalled that this made her feel "like a soldier." IWM, DSR, 000566/07, 16.

16. G. Ivy Sanders, "Women Aeroplane Builders," *Daily Mail*, 11 August 1916.

17. For example, "Blind Heroine's Medal Presentation at Brighton," *The Times*, 17 May 1918, 3; "The Empire Medal: Remarkable Record of Brave Deeds by Women & Men," *Sheffield Weekly Independent*, 12 January 1918, 2.

18. "Service for Munition Workers," *The Times*, 9 March 1918, 3.

centers on Tina, a skilled shell worker who is dying of a consumptive complaint but refuses to be placed in a rest home by the factory matron and doctor. She explains that when she heard she could work in a munitions factory,

> God was talkin' to me, and He'd never done that before, 'cos of course I'm too poor for the likes of Him, and He said, 'Tina, you must go along and make shells for your country, and never think you won't have the strength,' He says, 'I'll give you the strength,' and to this day He's given it to me, Matron, and there's nothing you can say to me—nothing—for my country wants me![19]

The doctor and matron urge Tina to take a spell at the rest home for munitions workers, but she refuses because there is nothing in the world she wants to do more than keep on turning out as many shells as possible, and thus help the men at the front to kill Germans. Finally, they resign themselves to the fact that she "will die as surely on the battlefield as any of our heroes" but comfort themselves with the thought that Tina's "spirit is the spirit of a whole nation soaring towards Heaven."[20]

Although their deaths were only a fraction of those of the armed forces, a significant number of women and men munitions workers laid down their lives for their country as surely as did the troops. Of the women who worked in munitions factories in World War I, many (certainly hundreds, perhaps upward of a thousand) were killed and others maimed, poisoned, or injured in the processes of making explosives, filling shells, and working with fast, heavy machinery.[21] Of course, this is not to suggest that their sacrifices or suffering approached those of the men who were physically or psychologically scarred by or killed in the war.[22] Nevertheless, suffer and die women munitions workers did. When their deaths were publicly announced, they too were called noble; but for reasons of security and national morale, these factory injuries and

19. Alec Holmes, "The Munition Worker: A Play in One Scene," *The Englishwoman* 33 (March 1917): 264.

20. Ibid., 255–70.

21. David Mitchell estimated that "several hundred women" died in munitions factory explosions during the Great War. *Women on the Warpath: The Story of the Women of the First World War* (London: Jonathan Cape, 1966), 248. Other writers eschew attempting to guess the number. My own estimate that the number was well into the hundreds and perhaps over a thousand is derived by assessing the prevalence of the explosions for which there are records and extrapolating to include those that are likely to have gone unrecorded.

22. J. M. Winter asserts that the "best estimate" shows that 722,785 British servicemen died in the First World War. *The Great War and the British People* (Cambridge, Mass.: Harvard University Press, 1986), 71.

fatalities were covered up as far as possible.[23] Numerous accounts tell of women who witnessed or were close to a fatal explosion and who returned to work as soon as the dead and wounded had been removed and the debris cleared. Munitions workers also knew that their factories were targets of the zeppelins and airplanes that bombed coastal areas and London—one hit would have an exponential effect.

According to public mythology, the male experience of war included patriotic service, being under fire, and heroism to the point of dying for one's country. Insofar as women munitions workers' experience of war shared some of the features of this mythological construct, they too were publicly praised and a few given militaristic honors. When they sought by their own agency to control and shape that experience to their own ends, however, they were harshly and publicly condemned, were considered threatening by male coworkers, and were widely criticized for exhibiting autonomy in their social behavior and the ways they chose to spend their increased income. They were accused of sexual promiscuity, drunkenness, and wanton extravagance and were subjected to the surveillance of newly created women police forces. Because women's experience of war was constituted by the opening up of a temporary liminal gender space between normal expectations of feminine and masculine behavior, in which women appropriated masculine roles and characteristics, it posed a threat to the hegemonic gender order of peacetime.

Despite the comparable dimensions of the experiences of Tommy Atkins and Tommy's sister, the lives of World War I women munitions workers have not become part of the fabric of British culture. Paul Fussell has described the ways in which the trench warfare experience has permeated literary culture since the war.[24] In response to the exclusion of women's experience of the war from Fussell's book, Claire Tylee has sought to recapture women's cultural memory of the war through their writing.[25] Yet the factory-floor experience of Tommy's sister has attracted little scholarly attention, in part because few written records were left by the women involved. Further, women's factory experience, lacking warriors, battles, and other traditional components of war, has usually been

23. Short notices of some explosions did appear in the press, but not for all explosions, nor were they given the prominence they warranted. It was only when an explosion was inescapably known to the public that it received detailed coverage.

24. Paul Fussell, *The Great War and Modern Memory* (London: Oxford University Press, 1975).

25. Claire Tylee, *The Great War and Women's Consciousness: Images of Militarism and Womanhood in Women's Writings, 1914–64* (Iowa City: University of Iowa Press, 1990).

viewed by historians as an aberration from normal employment patterns rather than as involvement in war. To the extent that feminist scholars have shared pacifism and belief in the interrelationship between feminism and pacifism, we have had ideological difficulties with evaluating women's work in munitions factories. I do not claim that making the munitions of war was a liberating or inherently good process for women or that women's increased participation in war is a feminist goal. Rather, I argue that munitions making needs to be seen as a sphere of activity within the war effort replete with its own moral problems, dangers, and discomfort. I hope a female experience of war, a war endured and fought in the close, grinding confines of the factory, can be recuperated and retained as part of Britain's cultural memory of the Great War.

HISTORICIZING EXPERIENCE

This study is not a narrative of the policy decisions and attitudes of the government and male trade unions that allowed the wholesale entry of women into areas of work from which they were previously excluded. My aim, rather, is to discover and interpret the experience of being a woman munitions worker in Britain in the Great War. My understanding of experience as a category of historical analysis is that people's responses to changes and events in their own lives and circumstances reconstitute their self-identities and their understanding of their positions in relation to others. Women's experience of World War I, therefore, was a composite of how they responded to the changes in their class- and gender-defined circumstances as the demands of total war opened up a liminal space between gender roles as they had normally operated before the war.

By the term "experience" I mean both women's individual lives and their shared circumstances as munitions workers during the war. The term implies not only that women workers were exposed to new realities but also that they recognized and responded to them.[26] My intention is to historicize the experience of women munitions workers in World War

26. Clifford Geertz emphasizes the dimension of individual response in human experience, which he says makes all experience construed experience. *The Interpretation of Cultures: Selected Essays* (New York: Basic Books, 1973), 405. My use of the term "experience" here is similar to that proposed by Mary Jean Corbett, *Representing Femininity: Middle-Class Subjectivity in Victorian and Edwardian Women's Autobiographies* (New York and Oxford: Oxford University Press, 1992), 8–9. See also Ruth Roach Pierson, "Experience, Difference, Dominance and Voice in the Writing of Canadian Women's History," in *Writing Women's History: International Perspectives,* ed. Karen Offen, Ruth Roach Pierson, and Jane Rendall (Bloomington and Indianapolis: Indiana University Press, 1991), 79–106.

I by identifying the shared dimensions of the lives of that group and searching for the ways in which, as a cohort, they constructed the meanings of being a woman munitions worker. But at the same time as seeking the commonality of their experience, it is critical to be aware of the diversity among the women who were munitions workers and the very different ways in which munitions work shaped their lives.

World War I women munitions factory workers in Britain, despite their diversity, formed a cohort that acquired new jobs and in many cases new skills.[27] They gained public recognition for the national importance of their work, a recognition that led to greater self-esteem for many workers. Together they shared the exhaustion of long shifts and the dangers inherent in many areas of munitions work. A subgroup among them bore the visible emblems of yellow skin and orange hair, effects of the poisoning induced by working with TNT. For many, the experience of working in a large factory with so many other women was novel, a significant contrast to their cramped or isolated working quarters before the war.

The vast majority of women munitions workers were of the working class. When they confronted the hostility of some male coworkers and the efforts of male trade unionists to exclude them from postwar industry, they were brought face to face with their subordination as women within their own class. But when they dealt with middle- and upper-class women war workers and with the middle-class women who served as welfare supervisors, police, and club leaders, they sharply confronted their status as members of the working class. Thus women munitions workers knew that they could not identify simply either as workers or as women. Their increased income, newfound discretionary control over disposable money, and the industrial assertiveness that led to their increased union membership all challenged their subordination as women both at home and in the labor movement. Probably few working-class women ever believed that they could overcome class differences sufficiently to form any kind of class-blind feminist movement. As Florence Bell noted in 1919, while ruminating about the likelihood of women of different classes understanding one another in the postwar world,

27. This study shares, unfortunately, in the English bias of much of so-called British history. Although munitions factories in Scotland and Wales are within its parameters, the bulk of the evidence on which it is based deals with factories in England. There were munitions factories in Ireland; they receive bare mention in the sources I have used. Irish women who moved to England to work in factories during the war receive more attention than the Irish factories.

The working class have always known a very great deal about the well-to-do; many of them have been in domestic service themselves, or have associated with domestics, and the domestic class obviously have a very intimate knowledge of the daily life of their employers. The employer has not always the same intimate knowledge of the daily life of the woman at the works; although most of the well-to-do now know a great deal more about the working class than they did before. Public opinion requires them to do so.[28]

The few middle- and upper-class women who worked in munitions factories gained a detailed appreciation of the daily lives of the working class. But wartime cross-class interaction did nothing to persuade working-class women that there was any significant newfound sympathy or understanding on the part of their more fortunate colleagues. Without hope of meaningful or lasting bonding with women above their own station, but strengthened by their employment, income, skills, and patriotic status, women munitions workers gained autonomy as women within the limits imposed on them by class.

Another reason for salvaging and interpreting women munitions workers' experience is to further the feminist scholarly project of probing the intersections of gender and war.[29] Gender is disrupted, constructed, and reconstructed during war.[30] Such gendering and regendering occurs in state policy and in all arenas and media of wartime discourse. Essential to the gendering of war is the meaning that both male and female participants give to their roles. Interpreting the meaning for women munitions workers of their own experience in war thus becomes a project crucial to the deconstruction of wartime gendering. To find this meaning, we must look at all dimensions of their experience both as it was represented in wartime discourse and as it can be constructed from the records of what they did and when, where, and how they did it throughout the war.

This book is founded on the premise that it is not only possible but

28. Florence Bell, "Women at the Works—and Elsewhere," *Fortnightly Review* 106 (1 December 1919): 911.

29. For further discussion of the intersections of gender and war, see Miriam Cooke and Angela Woollacott, "Introduction," *Gendering War Talk,* ed. Cooke and Woollacott (Princeton: Princeton University Press, 1993). Other volumes concerned with the interconnections between gender and war are Margaret Randolph Higonnet et al., *Behind the Lines: Gender and the Two World Wars* (New Haven: Yale University Press, 1987) and Helen Cooper et al., *Arms and the Woman: War, Gender and Literary Representation* (Chapel Hill: University of North Carolina Press, 1989).

30. By "gender" I mean the social and cultural construction of ideas of femininity and masculinity, which are linked to but distinct from biological differences between women and men.

crucial to study a period on its own terms rather than in the light of later issues or concerns that subsequent decades might cast backward.[31] The war was a searing epoch unto itself that no one who lived through it could forget. As Samuel Hynes opens his account of how the war transformed culture: "The First World War was the great military and political event of its time; but it was also the great *imaginative* event. It altered the ways in which men and women thought not only about war but about the world."[32] For the women who made the munitions of war, it was their war, a war in which they had been caught up and were centrally involved. So much was changing about the world that it was not unreasonable for them to hope that, especially given their hard work and dedication to the war effort, they might have a significantly better position in industry when the war was over.

The debate among the current generation of historians about the effects of World War I on women in Britain has been waged in terms of changes that can be seen to have outlasted the war, that is, through the lens of the postwar period. The first position in this debate was taken by several social and political historians who saw the war as an apocalyptic liberation for women because of their novel roles, their newly won partial right to vote, and a greater assertiveness, all of which, it was contended, had lasting impact.[33] The response to this position, the argument that the war changed nothing for women, has been called both "the new feminist pessimism" and "the revisionist interpretation."[34] Those who take this position argue that the war was a victory for patriarchy, which

31. Lizabeth Cohen has argued for the importance of assessing the historical meaning of a period on its own terms rather than by subsequent developments. *Making A New Deal: Industrial Workers in Chicago, 1919–1939* (Cambridge: Cambridge University Press, 1990), 367. E. P. Thompson similarly issues a warning against reading history "in the light of subsequent preoccupations, and not as it in fact occurred. Only the most successful . . . are remembered. The blind alleys, the lost causes, and the losers themselves are forgotten." *The Making of the English Working Class* (1963; reprint, Harmondsworth: Penguin, 1980), 12.

32. Samuel Hynes, *A War Imagined: The First World War and English Culture* (London: The Bodley Head, 1990), ix.

33. Arthur Marwick, *The Deluge: British Society and the First World War* (London: The Bodley Head, 1965), 93–94. Mitchell, *Women on the Warpath,* xv–xvi. Adams, *Arms and the Wizard,* 112.

34. Sylvia Walby calls this position "the new feminist pessimism." *Patriarchy at Work: Patriarchal and Capitalist Relations in Employment* (Cambridge: Polity Press, 1986), 156. In an essay on the effects of World War II on women in Britain, Penny Summerfield has proposed that it is time to go beyond what she labels the "revisionist" historical interpretation that war changed nothing for women. "Women, War and Social Change: Women in Britain in World War II," in *Total War and Social Change,* ed. Arthur Marwick (New York: St. Martin's Press, 1988), 95–118.

resisted the challenge of women performing a multitude of different roles and tasks by in fact hardening the distinction between "men's work" and "women's work."[35] Underlying this debate are common assumptions that the war was a powerful force that bore on women's roles, women's experience, and attitudes toward women.[36] The historiographical debate about women and war reaches well beyond the impact of World War I on women in Britain.[37]

My study is a conscious attempt to move beyond the terms of this entire debate to look for what was of significance to women munitions workers during the war. I consider women's work during the war not as an aberration in the pattern of women's employment in the early twentieth century—a view in which its importance is gauged by what did or did not change—but as women's participation in the war. The women who worked in munitions factories believed themselves to be directly engaged in the war effort, as well as earning their living. They believed they deserved whatever wages they could earn, and they tolerated extraordinary working shifts and conditions because of the demands of the war effort. It is critical to view their wartime lives from their perspective (rather than those of the government, the employers, and the male trade unions) and to recognize their awareness that their employment was dictated by the war. For Tommy's sister, munitions making was just as much an experience of war as being in the armed forces was for Tommy. There are multiple

35. The most important articulation of this view is Gail Braybon, *Women Workers in the First World War: The British Experience* (London: Croom Helm, 1981; reprint, Routledge, 1990). In this pioneering book, Braybon examines men's attitudes toward women working in World War I and presents an overall picture of the shifts in women's employment during the war. Braybon's conclusions were a needed antidote to the apocalyptic tone of previous writers because they underscore the systemic power of patriarchy. In a second book coauthored with Penny Summerfield, *Out of the Cage: Women's Experiences in Two World Wars* (London: Pandora, 1987), Braybon, in contrast, emphasizes the positive, liberating aspects of the war for women.

36. See also Deborah Thom, "Women and Work in Wartime Britain," in *The Upheaval of War: Family, Work and Welfare in Europe, 1914–1918,* ed. Richard Wall and Jay Winter (Cambridge: Cambridge University Press, 1988), 317. A body of unpublished research also exists: Marion Kozak, "Women Munition Workers During the First World War with Special Reference to Engineering" (D.Phil. thesis, University of Hull, 1976); Deborah Thom, "Women Munition Workers at Woolwich Arsenal in the 1914–1918 War" (M.A. thesis, University of Warwick, 1975); Antonia Ineson, "Science, Technology, Medicine, Welfare and the Labour Process; Women Munition Workers in the First World War" (M.Phil. thesis, University of Sussex, 1981); Sallie Heller Hogg, "The Employment of Women in Great Britain 1891–1921" (D.Phil. thesis, Oxford University, 1967).

37. The essays in Higonnet et al., *Behind the Lines,* cover different aspects of women's work and lives in various countries in both world wars and are linked by the premise that gender definitions shifted through both.

experiences of any war that frequently belie the traditional binary conception of the male warrior and the passive female onlooker (for whom the war is purportedly fought). While women's paramilitary forces were a groundbreaking development of the latter stages of the Great War, women's active participation in the war effort, both in numbers and in the understanding of contemporaries, was most importantly that of making munitions.

CHAPTER ONE

The Army of Women

Munitions Factories and Women Workers

I was thinking of the women bending over those endless rows of machines, of how they would go home not at sunset, but at sunrise. I was thinking that I had seen a wonderful thing, not only good labour and pride in work, not only one of the little armies of the big war, but a little army 3,000 strong, and of women.

> *"English War Workers: An American Point of View,"*
> The Times, *11 May 1916*

WOMEN ENTER MUNITIONS FACTORIES

The armed forces' demands for supplies in World War I, combined with their constant bleeding of the work force, created industrial jobs that women eagerly filled.[1] According to the Board of Trade, the total number of women in paid employment increased from 5,966,000 in July 1914 to 7,311,000 in July 1918 (while the total female population went from 23,721,000 to 24,538,000).[2] The number of nonprofessional positions for women and girls increased by 1,590,000; 891,000 of these jobs were in "industrial occupations."[3] After initial trade disruption and unemployment, between April and July 1915 women were taking jobs at the rate of 21,700 a month.[4] Conversely, they were laid off gradually before the war was over, beginning in late 1917. The Great War produced a proportional leap in the employment of women that took them from

1. World War I claimed 5,500,000 men from the U.K. for the fighting forces, out of a total male population in July 1914 of 14,350,000. Humbert Wolfe, *Labour Supply and Regulation* (Oxford: Clarendon Press, 1923), 2.

2. *Report of the War Cabinet Committee on Women in Industry,* Cmd. 135, 1919, 80.

3. Ministry of Reconstruction, *Report of the Women's Employment Committee,* Cd. 9239, 1919, 8.

4. *Report of the Intelligence and Record Section,* Public Record Office (hereafter PRO), MUN 2/27, 12 February 1916.

being 26 percent of all those employed in the United Kingdom in July
1914 to 36 percent in November 1918.[5]

There is no exact statistic of the number of women employed in
munitions work in World War I. Probably the most useful figures were
those compiled by the War Cabinet Committee on Women in Industry,
which was commissioned in 1918 and reported the following year. It
calculated that the number of women employed in industry *increased*
between July 1914 and July 1918 by 792,000 from 2,178,600 to 2,970,600.
We can presume that the bulk of these women went into munitions
industries because they were the only ones expanding during the war,
but women left some industries (such as textiles) for other industrial
work, so it is not a complete figure. The committee's statistics are broken
down by industry: metal, chemical, textile, clothing, and so on. We can
assume that most of the women in the metal industry (594,000 in July
1918) and the chemical industry (104,000 in July 1918) were at work
on munitions. All of the 223,000 women classed under government
establishments (arsenals, dockyards, etc.) were at work on munitions, but
so also were a significant proportion of the 79,000 women classified
under wood and aircraft trades. Although the 1,000,000 total of these
figures is an overestimate because not all in each category were munitions
workers, we must also take into account the fact that a proportion of the
827,000 women working in textiles in July 1918 were working on
government contracts for the armed services, as were some of the 568,000
working in clothing, the 235,000 working in food, drink, and tobacco,
and the 43,100 working in leather.[6]

The Secretary to the Minister of Munitions publicly announced in
May 1918 that there were 1,000,000 women working in munitions
industries. Another 1918 source refers to "more than a million" women
employed on munitions work, while the *Encyclopaedia Britannica* of 1922
states that the total number of women and girls employed in July 1918
in "government work" in industries including metals, chemicals, textiles,
clothing, and the government establishments was 1,302,000.[7] The *History
of the Ministry,* however, claimed that the "production of munitions

5. G. Evelyn Gates, ed., *The Woman's Year Book 1923–1924* (London: Women Publishers
Ltd., n.d.), 329.

6. *Report of the War Cabinet Committee on Women in Industry,* 80–81, 85–96.

7. "Women Help More In War," *New York Times,* 24 May 1918, 3; National Council of
Women of Great Britain and Ireland, *Annual Council Meeting in Harrogate, 8th, 9th, &
10th October 1918.* Occasional paper no. 80:15; *Encyclopaedia Britannica,* 12th ed., vols.
31–32 (1922): 1048. See also the *Employment Report of the Board of Trade,* PRO, MUN 5/
71/324/34.

occupied ultimately at least 700,000 women and girls and 250,000 boys";
this suggests that the *History* counted workers in metals and chemicals
only, rather than using a broader definition of munitions.[8] In July 1918
women and girls constituted 25 percent of the work force in metals
industries, 39 percent in chemicals, and 47 percent in government establishments.[9] Yet the public impression of the vast replacement of men by
women in all areas of the industrial manufacture of munitions was such
that one observer claimed, "In 1918 ninety per cent. of all the workers
in every branch of munitions manufacture were women."[10]

Compared to these figures, only a small number of women became
nurses or joined the Voluntary Aid Detachment (VAD), the Women's
Land Army, or other paramilitary organizations during the war. One
source states that there were about 40,000 women employed as VADs in
Britain by January 1918, 17,596 women officially enrolled in the Women's
Land Army during its existence, and some 80,000 women in the various
war service corps by the time of the Armistice.[11]

Apart from the village women who worked locally on the land part-
time and the greater part of the WAAC, the women who joined the
Women's Land Army, the VAD, and other paramilitary organizations
were predominantly from the upper and middle classes. In some of the
corps, such as the First Aid Nursing Yeomanry (FANY), which provided
ambulance drivers for the front, women actually paid their own expenses
in order to carry out war work for their country. Thus both numerically
and in the relationship between their needs and motivations for their
wartime role, these women stood in contrast to the working-class women
who comprised the bulk of munitions workers.

WOMEN WORKERS BEFORE THE WAR

Most of those who constituted the great increase in the number of women
in industry during World War I worked not simply for patriotic motives
but because they needed the money; they therefore came from elsewhere
in the general work force. For some women it was their first job after
leaving school. A good proportion of them, however, were married

8. *History of the Ministry of Munitions,* 12 vols. (1918–23; reprint, Sussex: Harvester
Microform Press, 1976), pt. 5, no. 3, ch. 1:2.

9. *Report of the War Cabinet Committee on Women in Industry,* 81.

10. Iris A. Cummins, "The Woman Engineer," *The Englishwoman* 46 (April 1920): 38.

11. Gates, *Woman's Year Book 1923–1924,* 326. See also *Encyclopaedia Britannica,* vols.
31–32 (1922): 1055–58; Crosthwait, "'Girl Behind the Man,'" 181.

women who needed to support their families because their husbands, sons, and fathers were off fighting. Although women were entitled to separation allowances from their male breadwinners' army or navy pay, some were refused these allowances, and even those who received allowances often found them insufficient. Before the war, there was a pervasive social prohibition against the employment of married women, except in the Lancashire textile industries, in which it was not uncommon for women to have more steady work than men.[12] The reality of life for the working class, however, was such that married women often had to work in one way or another despite the taboo, taking low-paying temporary or part-time jobs, piecework, or seasonal work. Thus, for many of these women, wartime meant not so much the fact of working as doing so in regular, full-time, and relatively well-paid jobs.

Many of the women who took up industrial work during the war came from domestic service, a fact encapsulated by a *Punch* cartoon on 23 May 1917. Entitled "The Servant Problem," it depicts the lady of the house seated at her writing desk and interviewing a well-dressed, haughty-looking young woman. Fishing around to find out why the prospective servant left her last position, the lady finds that the words "mistress" and "employer" cause offense, and on inquiry is informed that, rather, the young woman calls those in whose service she is engaged her "clients."[13] The "servant problem" caused so much anxiety among the middle and upper classes that a government inquiry into the matter was held in 1916. The wartime unpopularity of domestic service was a dramatic episode in the long, slow decline of that occupation. The *Woman's Dreadnought* noted in February 1917 that "before the War, the number of women willing to occupy the position of 'servant' to a 'mistress' was on the wane. War has accentuated the process of evolution in this matter."[14]

Domestic service had long been the bulwark of employment for working-class women. Yet according to the 1911 census, women in industry outnumbered those in domestic service 2,047,700 to 1,734,040.[15] While the total number of women in paid employment had increased slightly over the thirty years to 1911, in fact the 1911 figure was slightly less than the total in 1861. The proportions of women working hardly

12. For 1911 census figures for England and Wales see Ministry of Reconstruction, *Report of the Women's Employment Committee,* app. 9:110.

13. *Punch,* 23 May 1917, 342.

14. *Woman's Dreadnought,* 10 February 1917, 671.

15. British Association for the Advancement of Science, *Draft Interim Report of the Conference to Investigate into Outlets for Labour after the War* (Manchester 1915), 22–23.

changed in the late nineteenth and early twentieth centuries, but the female labor force was significantly redistributed during this time from the industrial sector to the tertiary or service sector.[16]

Of women in industry in July 1914, 863,000 worked in textiles and 612,000 in clothing. The metals industries were in the next level down, with 170,500 women. Male craft unions in metals and engineering had jealously excluded women in the nineteenth century, but after the turn of the century that exclusion weakened in areas of semiskilled work.[17] Women's work in the metals industries before the war included tin-plating; wire-drawing; the making of chains, nails, bolts, nuts, screws, rivets, and springs; light castings and allied trades; both general and electrical engineering; and cutlery and metal smallwares (needles, pins, etc.). In general engineering, they operated capstan lathes on small repetitive processes, worked power and hand presses, did plating, soldering, enameling, assembling, and polishing. The armaments industry, in Birmingham and Newcastle, employed women on small arms ammunition. In electrical engineering, they were employed on electric meters, dynamos, lamps, fittings, and switches.[18]

The women who entered wartime factories came from most occupational categories. Some became munitions workers because the factory in which they worked switched to munitions contracts. One incentive for changing jobs, in addition to better wages, was the shorter work day. Although munitions workers usually put in long hours, barmaids, like domestic servants, worked even longer. Before the war in London, licensed premises were open nineteen and a half hours per day on weekdays, nineteen hours on Saturdays, and seven on Sundays; those in country areas were open nearly as long.[19] A twelve-hour shift in a factory could be a relatively inviting prospect.

Prior to the war, Grace Bryant worked as an assistant in a penny bazaar, before becoming the sole assistant in a haberdashery shop where she worked 8:30 A.M. to 8 P.M. Monday to Thursday, 9 A.M. to 9 P.M. Friday, and 9 A.M. to 10 P.M. Saturday, doing the sweeping and cleaning of the shop and the window dressing as well as the sales work. For this she earned 7s. 6d. a week and received threepence discount on a pound.

16. Louise A. Tilly and Joan W. Scott, *Women, Work and Family* (New York and London: Methuen, 1987), 150–51.

17. Walby, *Patriarchy at Work*, 134–35, 142–43.

18. *Report of the War Cabinet Committee on Women in Industry*, 10–11.

19. Joint Committee on the Employment of Barmaids, *Women As Barmaids* (London: P. S. King & Son, 1905), 12–13.

When the war started, Grace's mother "thought this wasn't sufficient when the girls were getting big money out in factories" and made Grace hand in her week's notice.[20] At age 16, she took up a wartime job at the Southampton Docks as an inspector and cleaner of guns brought back from the front, and later became a machine operative at the Canute aircraft factory.

Wartime factory workers were also drawn from among laundresses. Despite the increasing mechanization of laundries just before World War I, laundry work was still arduous, an area of segregated and low-status work.[21] Munitions work lured laundresses and others in part because it held out the chance of better working conditions. Workers left their jobs in villages, towns, and cities alike. The Reverend Andrew Clark observed in Essex in September 1915: "Braintree industries have begun to be disorganised by the rush to munitions works.—Williams, fishmonger, has closed shop and gone as a munitions worker. Four of the Hope Laundry women left their work this morning to go 'munitioning.'"[22]

The national munitions factory built during the war at Gretna in Scotland, close to the English border, attracted women workers from southern Scotland, northern England, and farther afield. The factory management calculated from its records of these women workers (totaling 11,576 in July 1917) that, out of every hundred, thirty-six had formerly been in domestic service, twenty had lived at home, fifteen had already worked in munitions elsewhere, twelve had worked in other kinds of factories, five had been shop assistants, and the remaining twelve had been laundry workers, farmhands, dressmakers, schoolteachers, or clerks.[23]

HARD TIMES EARLY IN THE WAR

Britain entered a state of war with Germany in the late evening of 4 August 1914, after Germany's refusal to withdraw its troops from Bel-

20. IWM, DSR, 7433/02. Grace Bryant was interviewed by the Southampton Oral History Project.

21. See Patricia E. Malcolmson, *English Laundresses: A Social History, 1850–1930* (Urbana: University of Illinois Press, 1986); Arwen Mohun, "Women, Work and Technology: The Steam Laundry Industry in the United States and Britain 1880–1940" (Ph.D. diss., Case Western Reserve University, 1992).

22. James Munson, ed., *Echoes of the Great War: The Diary of the Reverend Andrew Clark 1914–1919* (Oxford: Oxford University Press, 1985), 85. Entry for Tuesday, 21 September 1915. Rev. Clark was rector of the village Great Leighs in Essex and kept his war diary for the sake of posterity. It is now in the Bodleian Library.

23. IWM, Women's Work Collection, Mun. 14/8.

gium. The economy was immediately thrown into turmoil. International trade was disrupted, and those who could normally afford consumer and luxury goods curbed their purchasing in order to ensure financial security. Straightaway, workers in consumer goods industries were laid off. The Women's Trade Union League later reported: "Within a few days of the declaration of war tens of thousands of women were without work: in the middle of August whole trades, including the cotton trade of Lancaster, were at a standstill: a fortnight later it is probable that a majority of women in all industrial occupations were affected, and to the number of victims there were heavy daily additions."[24]

The number of women employed in industry dropped from 190,000 in September 1914 to 139,000 in October, 75,000 in December, and 35,000 in February 1915. In the five weeks up to 16 April 1915, 89,577 women and 20,815 girls registered at the Labour Exchanges, while employers listed only 37,607 jobs for women and 12,215 for girls.[25] A 1914 YWCA report on the homes they ran for young working women lamented the hardship caused by this sudden bout of unemployment:

> As a community they have been hit very hard by the war. It is not easy for any one to immediately change their calling; therefore, as these Homes have received and housed a large number of dressmakers, milliners, tailoresses, typists, etc., it has been heart-breaking to observe how so many of such employees have had to suffer through lack of employment. If fortunate enough to obtain work their wages have been terribly reduced in most cases— sometimes to even one half their customary earnings ere the war commenced. Many able workers have had to accept eight, nine, or ten shillings per week. Some even less![26]

The instability of the economy was a two-edged sword: alongside unemployment, the cost of living rose abruptly. The *Woman's Dreadnought* monitored this crisis. On 23 January 1915 the paper announced that the cost of living had risen 25 percent since the previous July and complained that although the government had recognized this by raising the billeting allowance for soldiers, separation allowances for soldiers' wives and children had remained the same.[27] This hardship culminated in a protest demonstration in Trafalgar Square on 28 February, in which trade union-

24. Women's Trade Union League, *Fortieth Annual Report . . . September, 1915* (Manchester, 1915), 3.

25. G. D. H. Cole, *Labour In War Time* (London: G. Bell and Sons, 1915), 229.

26. YWCA, *Homes for Working Girls in London: The Work of the Year 1914* (London: n.d.), 11.

27. *Woman's Dreadnought,* 23 January 1915, 183.

ists, socialists and suffragists demanded that the government import foreign wheat cheaply and fix prices for food and other "necessaries."[28]

The lack of other jobs and the rise in the cost of living, which made regular work an even more desperate necessity, were two major attractions of munitions work when it became available from mid-1915 onward. In March 1915 the government established a national Register of Women for War Service, planning to have a centralized list from which it could draw for industrial and agricultural workers if necessary, but in fact women who took jobs in munitions work, if they registered anywhere, had done so on the ordinary register at the Labour Exchanges of the Board of Trade. Ironically, the industries that had so quickly laid women off at the start of the war found trouble getting sufficient women laborers when, by 1916, their trade had picked up; this trouble was ascribed to the "patriotic glamour" of doing "men's work" as opposed to the "feminine occupations" of dressmaking and millinery, but wage rates were surely a significant factor (see figure 1).[29]

WOMEN'S WORK DURING THE WAR

The munitions industries of World War I produced the metals, chemicals, weapons, ammunition, textiles, food, and other equipment required by the armed forces. These industries included the government-owned arsenals, dockyards, and factories as well as private firms both small and large, some of which came under national control during the war. British industry not only manufactured the vast quantity of equipment required by the British and imperial armed forces but also supplied the armies of Britain's European allies. By the end of the war, British industry had produced more than 4,000,000 rifles, 250,000 machine guns, 52,000 airplanes, 2,800 tanks, 25,000 artillery pieces, and over 170 million rounds of artillery shells.[30] Despite the fact that sometimes "munitions" was and is taken to mean only engineering and chemical industries, the term included more than military hardware. As labor leader Susan Lawrence put it: "Tents are munitions; boots are munitions; biscuits and jam are munitions; sacks and ropes are munitions; drugs and bandages are munitions; socks and shirts and uniforms are munitions; all the miscel-

28. Ibid., 6 March 1915, 205.

29. Statement by a chief woman inspector of the Board of Trade Labour Exchange, *The Times,* 15 September 1916.

30. John Stevenson, *British Society 1914–45* (Harmondsworth: Penguin, 1984), 66.

TABLE ONE. Number of Females Employed in Different
Industries, 1914–18 (counted in July of each year)

Industry	1914	1915	1916	1917	1918
Textiles	863,000	905,000	897,000	884,000	827,000
Clothing	612,000	634,000	603,000	574,000	568,000
Food, Drink, & Tobacco	196,000	209,000	224,000	226,000	235,000
Metals	170,000	203,000	370,000	523,000	594,000
Paper	147,500	138,500	145,500	143,500	141,500
Wood	44,000	48,000	56,000	68,000	79,000
Chemicals	40,000	48,000	87,000	109,000	104,000
Mines	7,000	6,500	11,000	12,000	13,000
Building	7,000	7,500	6,000	20,000	29,000
Govt. Est.	2,000	6,000	72,000	205,000	225,000
Other	89,500	104,500	121,500	138,500	150,500

SOURCE: Public Record Office, MUN 5/71/324/34. Figures taken from diagrams based on Section C of the employment report prepared by the Board of Trade in January 1919.

laneous list of contracts which fill up three or four pages of the Board of Trade Gazette, all, all are munitions."[31]

Definition mattered because industries that were classed as munitions came under the control of the Ministry of Munitions, the government department created in May 1915 to oversee the production of munitions. The ministry enforced legislation and regulations governing wages and conditions of employment, among its other functions. The spectacular growth of munitions industries created by the insatiable demands of the armed forces in the first years of the war, plus the combing out of men from these industries by recruitment and conscription, made these areas in which the employment of women was required in large numbers. But women were employed in other industries also.[32]

The government establishments (including government-owned arsenals, dockyards, and factories), metals, and chemicals categories shown in table 1 all clearly fall within the definition of munitions, but growth in the other categories listed must be at least partially attributed to the

31. A. Susan Lawrence, "Women On War Work," *Labour Woman* 3 (August, 1915): 315.
32. For a general survey of women's employment during the war, see Gail Braybon, *Women Workers,* and Braybon and Summerfield, *Out of the Cage.*

war effort. For instance, growth in the textiles and clothing industries in the first year of the war was due to the uniform requirements of the armed forces. Growth in the food, drink, and tobacco category reflects in part the supply demands of the armed forces and in part the taking over of men's jobs by women; the increase of women in the wood, mines, and building industries reflects the greater entry of women into jobs considered "men's work." Until women were prohibited from working in mines by the Mines and Collieries Act of 1842, they (and children) had been extensively involved in the mining industry. After 1842, they were allowed to work above ground at "the pit brow," but in the later nineteenth century they were partially pushed out of this work by jealous male unionists and other reformers. The war, however, increased the numbers of "pit-brow girls," who "re-appeared in Lancashire. It is said there are 2,000 working at the surface of the pits." In Wales their reappearance provoked a protest by the miners' association in Swansea, which asserted that it did not want women near the collieries and would rather have "foreigners."[33]

The war also stimulated a vast expansion of the numbers of women working in the civil service; in banking, finance, commerce, and other business as clerks, typists, and secretaries; and in retailing, both as shop assistants and in warehouses. In professional occupations such as medicine, law, and engineering, although there were no great numerical jumps, the presence and acceptance of women were boosted. A few professional positions in military-related work were filled by women: women chemists conducted experiments for the air force on how rubber was affected by heat and light; and women mathematicians and draughtswomen performed calculations related to aircraft design for the air force and the Royal Naval Air Service.[34]

In the railways and municipal tramways, too, the numbers of women employees leapt dramatically.[35] Women took over driving bakers' vans and other delivery vehicles and were chauffeurs for officers in the armed forces: driving was such a symbol of independence that the mere fact of women drivers attracted much social comment. As noted above, despite resistance by the chiefs of the armed services in the first years of the war, women formed their own paramilitary organizations, including the WAAC,

33. "Women's News," *Modern Woman,* 8 January 1916, 207.

34. IWM, Women's Work Collection, Mun. 15/—.

35. From July 1914 to November 1918 the number of females employed in the railways leapt from 12,000 to 66,000 and in municipal tramways from 1,200 to 19,000. Gates, *Woman's Year Book 1923–1924,* 330.

the Women's Royal Naval Service (WRNS), the Women's Royal Air Force (WRAF), and FANY, while the already established VAD expanded. These organizations mostly attracted upper- and middle-class women wanting "to do their bit," although the WAAC accepted working-class women who needed to earn money and chose this as a way of also participating in the war effort. For all classes, these organizations proffered adventure, although only a small proportion of women were sent abroad. The Women's Land Army was deemed an important patriotic effort because of the shortages of food and the need for agricultural laborers. Although the Women's Land Army remained numerically small, it received much public and press attention; that and the freedom and fresh air were the members' main rewards, for their work was arduous and poorly paid.

THE FACTORIES

In World War I modern technology revealed both its power and its inhuman monstrosity. Machine guns, huge shells, gas and chemical weapons, tanks, airplanes, and great battleships made this the first war among industrial states, a war in which men were slaughtered in masses with mechanical efficiency, a production line of death. The technological revolution was manifest at the battlefront, but its power originated with the capability of the belligerent nations and their allies to manufacture rapidly these weapons and ammunition in vast quantities, especially the shells that were expended during the war in astronomical numbers. In Britain this industrial capacity included new, quickly built munitions factories; dockyards, private munitions companies, and old government arsenals that were expanded; and a miscellany of industries that were converted into war factories.

The "dilution" of the labor force, as the wartime employment of women and unskilled men in areas of skilled work was called, was facilitated by technological innovation in the machines that manufactured weapons, specifically to make processes more automatic. The Ministry of Munitions played a critical role in offering incentives and advice to manufacturers willing to convert their firms. Sheer profit, particularly in an economic climate in which trade in many goods had dropped, was a powerful incentive for capitalists to convert their businesses, but there was an element of risk involved in committing capital to machinery to produce weapons that would be superfluous whenever the war ended.

The diversity of workshops that had undergone conversion by 1916 astounded the writer Boyd Cable on a tour of munitions factories. He reported that, for example, a tobacco factory had turned to making shells, a gramophone works was making shell-fuses, and a magneto-maker, a piano factory, and a coach-builder had turned to the manufacture of one or another kind of munitions, all within the same area. Similar conversions were happening around the nation, such that "the whole country is one seething munition factory."[36] It is obvious that arms manufacturers thrive in time of war, and World War I was no exception, despite the Ministry of Munitions' limitations on the profits of individual companies. While munitions-factory owners were reaping their profits, for managers it was a time of great strain and effort. Journalists and writers, the traveling observers for society at large, were sometimes struck by how arduous their workload was. Rebecca West, after she toured a munitions factory, responded with a burst of gratitude to the employers: "To our generation, hypnotised by an interest in trade unionism into minimising the importance of the employer, any glimpse of the life of an armament manufacturer in wartime is a revelation. This manager was one of many who think themselves well off when they get five hours' sleep. . . . And every minute of this long working-day is eaten up by hard mental work."[37]

The already established government arsenals and dockyards underwent dramatic expansion to cope with the war. The royal arsenal at Woolwich in southeastern London had been founded in the mid-seventeenth century, grown steadily but slowly in the eighteenth, and expanded fitfully in the nineteenth century, with peaks created by the Napoleonic campaigns and the Crimean War. It reached its maximum size and importance in World War I, expanding first at the outbreak of war, again when the Ministry of Munitions was formed and assumed control, and yet again in early 1917. The arsenal was a vast, cluttered maze, sprawling over an area approximately three and a half by two and a half miles on the south side of the Thames, with its own sizable internal railway. It was made up of several parts, including laboratories, small arms ammunition factories, shell filling factories, chemical shell factories, gun and carriage factories, fuse factories, and others. Women had been employed in the arsenal during the nineteenth century, if not earlier, but the numbers of them in the ordnance factories alone rose from 125 in August 1914 to 24,018 in

36. Boyd Cable, *Doing Their Bit: War Work At Home* (London: Hodder and Stoughton, 1916), ch. 2.

37. Rebecca West, "Hands That War," *Daily Chronicle*, 1916, in Jane Marcus, ed., *The Young Rebecca: Writings of Rebecca West 1911–1917* (New York: Viking Press, 1982), 384.

August 1918.[38] The arsenal's maximum wartime employment occurred in November 1917, when there were 28,000 women, 4,200 men, and 6,500 boy workers.[39] All other government arsenals, dockyards, and naval bases around the country expanded in a similar fashion.

Two munitions-industry dynasties had been founded in England in the first half of the nineteenth century, Vickers in Sheffield and Armstrong's in Newcastle. By the end of the century, these two firms had taken over their competitors, thus entrenching themselves as the foremost suppliers of arms to the British government.[40] During the war, Vickers' naval yards and shops at Barrow-in-Furness, gun manufactories at Erith and Crayford, and other works in Birmingham and Dartford all expanded enormously. Armstrong's original base at Elswick on the Tyne similarly expanded, as did the Manchester operation acquired from Whitworth.[41] Private companies, besides expanding their own works, were asked by the Ministry of Munitions to enter joint ventures with the government to build new munitions factories. National projectile factories were established for the manufacture of heavy shells: six in Glasgow, including three under the management of Beardmore's, two in Sheffield, one in Nottingham, one in Dudley, one at Hackney Marshes in London, one at Birtley managed by Armstrong Whitworths and employing only Belgian refugees, and one at Lancaster run by Vickers.[42]

National factories for filling shells were established in a like manner. One, the Scottish Filling Factory, was organized by a group of Glasgow businessmen. It was built in 1915 on the river Gryfe in Renfrewshire, not far from Glasgow, a site with "excellent fishing and boating." Lloyd George visited the factory soon after it was built, and "so delighted was he with the sylvan picture of smiling fields and leafy hedgerows in the neighbourhood, and with our fine array of bonnie lasses—not to mention the splendid trout he succeeded in catching," that he graciously agreed that the factory might be renamed "Georgetown."[43] National factories

38. O. F. G. Hogg, *The Royal Arsenal: Its Background, Origin, and Subsequent History* (London: Oxford University Press, 1963), 977 and passim.

39. Deborah Thom, "Women At The Woolwich Arsenal 1915–1919," *Oral History* 6 (Autumn 1978): 59.

40. J. D. Scott, *Vickers: A History* (London: Weidenfeld and Nicolson, 1962), 46.

41. David Dougan, *The Great Gun-Maker: The Story of Lord Armstrong* (Newcastle: Frank Graham, 1970), 168.

42. IWM, Women's Work Collection, Mun. 19/4, 1.

43. "The Story of Georgetown," *Georgetown Gazette* 2, no. 11 (August 1918): 331–35.

for the making of smaller shells were established in scattered places: thirty-four in a wide distribution around England, one in Scotland, and six in Dublin.[44] Aircraft factories were another new area of industry. Some were privately owned, and some government owned, such as the Royal Aircraft Factory built at Farnborough, and the former Dunlop aircraft factory at White City, Shepherd's Bush, which was taken over by the Royal Naval Air Service.

All of this massive expansion of war-related industries depended on the use of women workers. Women were taken on in factories small and large, old and new, privately and government owned, all around Britain. In December 1917 the Women's Work Sub-committee of the planning operation for the National War Museum (opened after the war as the Imperial War Museum) approached firms employing women on munitions engineering work to contribute specimens for the permanent exhibit that would show "the proficiency attained by women in work of an engineering nature."[45] Part of their acquisition scheme was to compile a list of various firms employing women on different engineering jobs and to write to each firm for particular specimens. The draft list they composed included forty-eight factories, with a mixture of small and large, private and government.

WOMEN'S WORK ON MUNITIONS

In late 1918, the *Daily Chronicle* reported that the work performed by the "800,000 women" in wartime munitions factories had been divided as shown in table 2. These figures probably underrepresent the total employment of women in munitions industries. Moreover, at least some of the workers listed in areas other than the Ministry of Munitions were covered by the ministry's orders and regulations. Yet the figures provide a good indication of the breakdown of women workers among the various occupations in munitions industries, particularly weapons manufacture. Women entered areas of work that were strictly male preserves before the war, and many became skilled or semiskilled workers.

The Intelligence and Record Section of the Ministry of Munitions regularly produced internal reports on the progress of "dilution," giving

44. "Intramural Work in National Factories," IWM, Women's Work Collection, Mun. 18.9/4.

45. "Permanent Memorial to Women's Work on Engineering Munitions," *The Engineer* 124 (7 December 1917): 496.

TABLE TWO.   Breakdown of Women
Munitions Workers by Area of Work

Area	Number of Workers
Ministry of Munitions	
Shell manufacture	183,000
Filling shells	64,500
Ordnance	18,900
Rifles, machine guns	8,800
Small arms ammunition	31,800
Trench warfare	24,900
Explosives, chemicals	35,900
Aeronautical supplies	63,700
Mechanical warfare	3,500
Railway material	3,100
Optical munitions, glass	3,800
Mechanical transport	18,400
Iron, steel	30,100
Nonferrous metals	10,800
Construction engineering	26,100
Machine tools	6,600
Gauges, tools, screws, etc.	20,100
Inspection	40,600
Subtotal	594,400[a]
Admiralty	114,800
War Office, misc.	60,400
Other government work	39,500
Work for Allies	5,700
Total	814,800[b]

SOURCE: "The 800,000 Women: How the Munitioneers Were Employed," *Daily Chronicle,* 21 December [?] 1918.
[a] Subtotal should be 594,600.
[b] Total should be 815,000.

details of the work usually considered "men's work" that women were now successfully performing—in tones that were both proud and patronizing. On 16 December 1916 the section reported:

> *Ship Breaking.*—Messrs. Hughes, Bolckow, and Co., Limited, iron and steel merchants of Blyth, are successfully employing women in their ship-breaking department. At present 13 women are doing light labouring and the disman-

tling of light parts of battleships. As an experiment the firm propose to start women on the actual work of ship-breaking. This has been permitted by the Ministry, provided the women do not have to use hammers exceeding 5 lb. in weight.

Keys and Locks.—The firm of Messrs. Samuel Baker and Co., Limited, makers of padlocks and cabinet locks, of Moat Field Works, Willenhall, are employing women as key filers. This is stated to be a skilled occupation. Women also are filing and riveting on locks.

Metal Rolling.—At the works of Dugard Bros., Limited (Birmingham), 2 girls are being instructed in the rolling of metal for brass and copper rods. The girls are proving quite successful at this work.[46]

Some women were trained to do exactly the same jobs using the same machinery as the men, while others were taught only a component of a skilled man's job or were trained on new machinery. One wartime industrial development was the advent of new machinery introduced partly to help women substitute for men and partly to improve efficiency. In full and animated style, *The Engineer* reported developments such as those at the Austin Motor works outside Birmingham, where "practically all the machining work is performed by females, special overhead lifting tackle having been provided for each lathe." Further, "we could devote many pages to a description of the novel and ingenious machines and devices for expediting the production of shell which Sir Herbert Austin has devised. . . . We were particularly impressed with the method of cleaning and varnishing the insides without handling the shell."[47]

For the women who were allowed to learn skilled or semiskilled work, the war offered novelty and greater self-esteem, albeit on a temporary basis. The many women trained to do oxyacetylene welding must have felt satisfaction at being admitted into a previously male club, as well as the constructive pleasure inherent in this craft, particularly in airplane building. Other women enjoyed operating machine tools. Joan Williams, a middle-class woman who worked as a turner and fitter at Messrs. Gwynne's new airplane engine works in Chiswick from 1916 to 1919, recalled after the war how exhilarated she had sometimes been by the work she did: "I don't think any worker can have enjoyed their work more than I did, even though they attained to a higher degree of skill and did far more important work. When I was on an interesting job it

46. PRO, MUN 2/27, 16 December 1916, 7. See also, for example, 13 January 1917, 7 and 10 February 1917, 7.

47. "Birmingham and the Production of Munitions," *The Engineer* 125 (5 April 1918): 288–89.

was nothing to leap out of bed at 5.15 on a frosty morning and I almost danced down Queen's Road under the stars, at the prospect of the day's work."[48]

Women who drove trucks and electric locomotives, or ran large electric motors in factories, must have felt a sense of empowerment, of doing work usually considered privileged and masculine.[49] In factories that used electric overhead cranes to maneuver material from one place to another, women took over the jobs of driving these and often found it exciting, though dangerous, work (see figure 2). Beatrice Lee was a crane driver at the copper works in Leeds: "We sat in these cranes, we'd climb up ladders to get in, there was a control at one side for carrying ropes, and a driving control on this side and we used to drive all around the factory. . . . [I]t was a very interesting job. . . . [I]t was a very happy life."[50]

Unfortunately, the majority of women workers were not in this lucky group but instead performed boring, repetitive, or strenuous tasks. Lilian Miles's first munitions job was at White and Poppe's in Coventry, where she was in one large factory with "hundreds of girls" under the same roof, standing at a long bench doing repetitive work on trays of detonators: "I never thought it was much of a job."[51] A large proportion of women workers were engaged in making and filling shells and cartridges. Miss O. M. Taylor recalled her job in a filling factory: "The filling was a boring and labourious [sic] task. A large amount of powder stood by each shell, and this had to be rammed into the shell using a piece of wood & wooden hammer. Often it seemed impossible to ram in any more powder but with the mallet and stem another small hole had to be made into the powder & more inserted."[52]

While some women in airplane factories may have been excited about welding, probably more were employed on sewing and doping the plane's body. Doping—varnishing the covered plane body—was dangerous work because the varnish was highly poisonous. Sewing the linen that covered the plane like a skin was not only like traditional "women's work," it also involved eye-strainingly fine mending and examination over electric light of voluminous quantities of linen. Similarly, many women were employed

48. Joan Williams, "A Munition Workers' [sic] Career At Messrs. Gwynne's—Chiswick. 1915–1919," IWM, Department of Printed Books (hereafter DPB), 63.

49. "Women in Munition Factories," *The Engineer* 126 (12 July 1918): 30. Barbara McLaren refers to a woman with "no technical experience whatever" operating a 900-horsepower motor in *Women of the War* (London: Hodder and Stoughton, 1917), 66.

50. IWM, DSR, 000724/06.

51. IWM, DSR, 000854/04, 5–6.

52. IWM, Department of Documents (hereafter DD), 83/17/1.

to sew the huge, cigar-shaped airships, which involved crawling under the belly of the ship. Another sewing job was making bags for the powder to be used with some shells; this occupied many women but was monotonous, mostly low-paid work. An incident occurred at the end of the war that showed how exploitive this work could be: the Social and Legislation Department of the YWCA heard from a worker in a factory sewing small "trotyl bags" that the workers, nearly all married women with children, had been doing overtime by taking the bags home with them as outwork. When they were dismissed at the end of the war, however, the firm refused to pay them the bonus rates they had earned on top of their meager wages. Quite uncharacteristically, the YWCA pushed the case of these workers until the firm agreed to arbitration, which the workers won.[53]

This story points up not only the unscrupulous behavior of this particular firm but also the fact that some munitions work was being done in the ill-paid, nonunionized mode of outwork or homework, an exploitive practice that labor organizers were trying to stamp out and that had in fact been declining before the war. Another instance of outwork came to light through a court case in Woolwich: two sisters were disputing the right to occupy a certain house. The defendant argued that she needed to stay in that house because she and her mother, who was over seventy, were both employed making bags on munitions work, and the house was near Woolwich Arsenal, from which she fetched the bags.[54] None of the many published or archival accounts of work done at Woolwich Arsenal, nor those of any other factory, acknowledge this outwork, yet it is not surprising that employers would resort to this form of employment, which had long been performed by poor women, especially those tied down with children.

For some women, replacing men workers was not so much glamorous as sheer hard work. Olive Castle recalled that when the two last men on hydraulic presses were called up for military service from the cordite factory where she worked, "I was ordered to be the press-hand myself,—dreadfully heavy work with those heavy cylinders to haul about all the time, and as I was on the smallish side—5' 3 1/2" tall, that wasn't much help. Those cylinders weighed 1 1/4 cwts., *empty* and had to be packed by hydraulic pressure ready for the actual press to make the moist cordite into cords. For doing this job I was given another 1/2d. per hour."[55]

53. "Our Arbitration Case," *Our Own Gazette* (YWCA) 37, no. 6 (June 1919): 15.

54. "The House Famine," *The Pioneer,* 18 May 1917, 5.

55. Mrs. Olive Castle, "First World War Reminiscences," IWM, DD, misc. 61, item 948.

Even worse than boring or heavy work was dangerous work, which included more than doping airplane bodies. A large number of women munitions workers handled explosives while filling shells with lethal substances such as TNT (trinitrotoluene) and lethal gases, or with other chemicals. Of the 11,576 women (69.5 percent of the work force) employed at the national filling factory at Gretna in July 1917, 6,654 were employed in making cordite (a powder made of nitroglycerine and guncotton), 1,803 in the nitrocotton section, 1,096 in the nitroglycerine section, and 297 in acids.[56]

Miss G. M. West joined the Women Police Service during the war and was sent to police four different munitions factories employing women, each of which she described in her diary. At the government factory at Queen's Ferry outside Chester, which made sulphuric acid, nitric acid, guncotton, TNT, and oleum, her strongest reaction was to the middle section where sulphuric acid was turned into nitric acid and nitric acid into oleum (a corrosive, oily solution):

> The particles of acid land on your face & make you nearly mad, like pins & needles only much more so; & they land on your clothes & make brown specks all over them, & they rot your handkerchiefs & get up your nose & down your throat, & into your eyes, so that you are blind & speechless by the time your hour is up & you make your escape.

Her next assignment was to a factory at Pembrey, a little coal-mining village in South Wales, where TNT, guncotton, cordite, and ballistite were being manufactured:

> The ether in the cordite affects the girls. It gives some headaches, hysteria, & sometimes fits. If a worker has the least tendency to epilepsy, even if she has never shown it before, the ether will bring it out. . . . [I]f they stay on in the cordite sheds, they become confirmed epileptics & have the fits even when not exposed to the fumes. Some of the girls have 12 fits or more one after the other.[57]

These instances were not exceptional. Rather, it was in the nature of ammunition that it should be dangerous to produce as well as to inflict on the enemy.

In World War I, munitions industries in Britain expanded to gargantuan proportions. As hundreds of thousands of jobs opened up in industrial occupations, women were recruited into areas of work previously consid-

---

56. "Women and Their Work at Gretna," IWM, Women's Work Collection, Mun. 14/8.
57. Diary of Miss G. M. West, 5 January 1917, 10 March 1917, IWM, DD, 77/156/1.

ered "men's" in huge numbers (see figure 3). To appreciate the dimensions of this experience for women workers is only to begin to understand it. Most women in munitions industries performed new jobs, many of which involved training to acquire new skills. The rapidity and technological innovation with which the government and employers facilitated women's entry into these areas of work exposed the degree to which their previous exclusion had been due to custom and prejudice rather than practicality. Women's eager filling of munitions jobs showed their preparedness to do "men's work" but also the attraction of munitions wages and the lack of other options. Some of these jobs were empowering, others were repetitive and dangerous. As the following chapters will consider, by enhancing women's geographical mobility, their exposure to others and to novel circumstances, their income and standard of living, their working conditions, their social lives and recreational pursuits, and even their general health, munitions work profoundly impacted the lives of the women involved and constituted their distinct vantage point of the war.

CHAPTER TWO

The Heterogeneity of Women Workers

Mixing and Mobility

Quite lately the wife of an officer, coming home from Egypt, decided to volunteer; her maid, who had travelled with her, followed her into the works, and now the two go to work of a morning together and return together at night.

Queen, *10 February 1917*

FACTORS OF DIFFERENCE

The danger of a phrase like "Tommy's sister" is that it implies a homogeneity among women munitions workers that simply did not exist. The women who made up this cohort were a mixture of ages, classes, sexualities, races, ethnicities, and regional and national origins and represented enormously varied standards of living, cultures, and political views. They themselves probably had little idea of the complete extent of their diversity, despite the diversity within any one workplace. One of the most salient features of munitions workers' experience was the fact of being members of a large group in a big factory, in contrast to the relative isolation they had known in domestic service, shop assisting, and working in sewing establishments or at home. Being one of many allowed each greater opportunities for socializing, making friends, and developing a feeling of unity. The length and intensity of the hours they spent together in close working environments facilitated friendships, camaraderie, and even a degree of sisterhood. Reports indicate the existence and significance of this workplace bonding. However, the evidence we have of relationships among women munitions workers suggests that they did not always overcome the factors of difference among themselves, and tensions not only existed but at times ignited.

For a start, their ages ranged enormously (see figure 4). Even before the war, it had been normal in the working classes (especially in industrial areas) for fourteen-year-olds, both boys and girls, to be out of school and working. The disruption of family life and society at large wrought by the war, combined with the wages available in munitions, brought to munitions factories large contingents of adolescent and teenage workers, some even younger than fourteen. Touring a factory that was probably Woolwich Arsenal, Hall Caine came across an eleven-year-old, who had earned five shillings for her first week's work, but did not appear to find her an oddity.[1]

Older women also undertook munitions work, for a variety of reasons. Some needed the money because they had lost their breadwinners, some wanted to do what they could for the war effort, and some joined in the factory workforce with their daughters. One observer at a shellmakers' training school noted that "one sees elderly women submitting to instruction like schoolgirls."[2] In Woolwich Arsenal at night, Caine found several women boiling lead in huge vats: "older, and, perhaps, coarser women . . . engage in this labour, and, as you approach the tents, and see the scaly gray liquid ladled out, you find it impossible not to think of the Witches in 'Macbeth,' especially when the hair of one of the workers falls from its knot, and, in lifting her ladle, her gaunt figure sways across the light."[3]

Despite this range in ages, the recruiters for women workers addressed themselves to those "between the ages of eighteen and thirty-five years."[4] One training school reported that the average age of its pupils was twenty-seven.[5] Without statistical evidence, relying rather on the testimony of reports and photographs, the average age was definitely toward the lower end of the scale: there were more teenagers and workers in their twenties than there were women over forty.

A good number of Irish women crossed the sea to England and Wales to work in munitions factories, drawn by advertisements of wages significantly higher than those being paid in Irish munitions factories. The Ministry of Munitions oversaw a scheme by which skilled tradesmen from the dominions of the British Empire came to the metropolitan country to supplement the ranks of workers in vital industries. No such scheme existed for women workers, but some women from the dominions

1. Caine, *Our Girls,* 71.
2. "Shellmakers in Six Weeks," *Weekly Dispatch,* 21 May 1916.
3. Hall Caine, "Feeding the Arsenal," *Nottingham Guardian,* 28 October 1916.
4. "Women Engineers," *The Engineer* 124 (28 September 1917): 279.
5. *Daily Mirror,* 4 May 1918.

came of their own volition and, among other occupations, entered the factories. Munitions workers included women from Canada, Australia, South Africa, and Belgium. There cannot have been a large number of women from these latter countries, yet their presence is attested to in several accounts.

While we have clear evidence of class and age differences among women workers, and of the fact that they included women from Ireland, Belgium, and the dominions, we know far less about racial differences among them. Britain's far-flung empire had made it possible for a small number of West Indians, Asians, and Africans to arrive on British shores and to form scattered communities. We have the following evidence that munitions workers included at least a few women of color. Policewoman G. M. West described the mixture of regional culture, language, and race among the workers at the cordite factory to which she was assigned at Pembrey in South Wales:

> There are about 3,800 women workers in all sections on both shifts. Some of these come from the little sheep farms in the mountains, & speak only Welsh, or a very little broken Enlish [sic]. Then there are the relatives of the miners from the Rhondda & other coal pits near. They are full of socialistic theories & very great on getting up strikes. . . . A number of the girls are from the Swansea docks, a different type from the others, with a good deal of German blood with a large admixture of other races, including blacks. There is one girl here, half negress, who is a most extraordinary mimic. . . . There was a trio of very rough lots on my shift. The worst of these was a very dark handsome gipsy woman.[6]

We know little enough about racial differences in the work force in the early twentieth century, but we know even less about another factor of difference, that of sexuality. Lesbian sexuality among privileged women during this period has been well documented, but comparable evidence about working-class women is extremely elusive and has yet to be compiled. We cannot know how many munitions workers were lesbian, but we do have the story of Ellen Harriet who cross-dressed, called herself Charles Brian Capon, and was a wireworker until her sex was discovered when she was forced to register at the recruiting office; she had been "walking out with a young woman."[7] The story is valuable because, isolated though it is, it alerts us to the fact that there is still much we do not know about women workers' sexual choices.

6. Diary of Miss G. M. West, 10 March 1917, IWM, DD, 77/156/1.
7. "Girl's Masquerade: Two Years as a Male Worker," *The Times,* 21 January 1918, 3.

CLASS AND ETHNIC TENSIONS

Not all the dynamics operating among women munitions workers were amiable. One widespread dynamic was the tension, even hostility, generated when middle- and upper-class women, doing "their bit for the war effort," mixed with working-class women. When women of different classes rubbed shoulders in the dense, noisy, and often grimy atmosphere of munitions factories, they cooperated as necessary to facilitate the work, but antagonism thrived.

By 1916, middle- and upper-class women became the object of propagandist advertisements run by the Ministry of Munitions to draw them into munitions work. The great appeal of these women in the eyes of the ministry and employers, besides their assumption that better educated women would learn skilled work more quickly, was that these women would be pleased to hand their jobs back to returning soldiers at the end of the war. Working-class women, they knew, would be more likely to resist dismissal and demand to be kept on.

The ministry employed several methods to coax more privileged women into the munitions factories. One was the promise that women who acquired firsthand experience of factories in this way would be useful in the process of postwar reconstruction because of their knowledge of "the conditions under which their working sisters live."[8] Another tack was to point out their duty arising from the fact that "better-class ladies" simply made better forewomen because they knew how to "rule a household." Further, working-class women were said to prefer "better-class" forewomen because, "like Tommy, they prefer not to follow their own class."[9]

Many observers were delighted by the social incongruity of ladies working in factories. G. M. West (before she joined the women police) noted in her diary her curiosity when she was assigned two helpers for her canteen at Farnborough who were "two dashing young ladies. . . . [T]hey are covered with paint & powder, & smoke cigarettes." When she asked them to peel potatoes and onions, they "attacked the job with shrieks & chuckles of glee." Puzzled, she commented on their behavior to one of her workmates, who pointed out that, being nieces of the Duchess of Wellington, they probably had not done that sort of job before.[10]

8. "The Demand For Women Workers," *Argyll Herald*, 23 September 1916.
9. Mrs. Alec-Tweedie, "The War of Liberation: The Woman's Army," *English Review* (January 1917): 40.
10. Diary of Miss G. M. West, 17 January 1916, IWM, DD, 77/156/1.

Accounts written by middle- and upper-class women who became munitions workers for the duration usually express affectionate condescension toward their less-privileged coworkers. Brenda Erwin, for example, joined the Women Relief Munition Workers' Organisation established by Lady Moir and Lady Cowan in mid-1915 to enable women factory workers to take weekends off without the machines being shut down. Describing her wartime experience, she ended by saying that she would never part with her overalls because they brought to mind

> so many precious memories. Auburn haired Florrie with that new 'boy' every week. Edie with her sweetly pretty face; shy Mary; high spirited Sal; all making you welcome, ready to help you at every turn, gay through the longest night, brave through the hardest day. When the originators of the scheme gave us the opportunity to make shells we felt they had given us something. [I] am not sure that they did not give us something bigger when unconsciously they gave us the opportunity to understand the heart of the factory girl.[11]

Joan Williams, middle-class fitter and turner at Gwynne's, Chiswick, was more aware than most of the political tension integral to the class relationship between herself and her workmates. She commented:

> I came up against very little class feeling either from men or women and found as a general rule you were accepted on your merits and treated according to your own behaviour. A good many of the workers, whose former work had always been in factories, had never come up against the upper classes at all and had very exaggerated ideas about them, fostered I suppose by labour papers and meetings. Most 'ladies' were to them people who "drew away their skirts" on encountering any working people, so I was very glad when they found out it was quite possible to make friends with the despised class.[12]

"Making friends" must have been a circumscribed activity, partly due to Williams's attitude about socializing with her workmates (notably her disinclination to go on an all-day outing with them), and partly due to the favoritism she reported receiving from the manager: he gave her especially interesting pieces of work, kept her from being put on night shift because he preferred to have her around during the day, showed off her work to the boss, and arranged a substantial raise for her.

Naomi Loughnan, another "war worker" who took the opportunity to record her brush with life among the working classes, revealed the difference she believed to exist between herself and those she considered her

11. Brenda Erwin, "Our 'Blue Overalls,'" IWM, DPB, Women's Work Collection, Mun. 17.2/8.

12. Williams, "Munition Workers' [sic] Career," IWM, DPB, 46–47.

social inferiors. Proud of her patriotic "roughing it," she described the leveling she felt occurred in the factory: "Inside the gates we are all on a level. Duchesses or coster-girls, we are crammed into earth-coloured overalls, and hustled and jostled, winked at and sworn at in the most indiscriminate and realistic manner. Any attempt to be lofty about a wink is usually met by yells of delight and a most fearful aggravation of the offence." Yet when she turned to describing the work carried out by her workmates, her belief that the lower classes were characterized by lesser intelligence was suddenly revealed: "The ordinary factory hands have little to help them keep awake. They lack interest in their work because of the undeveloped state of their imaginations. They handle cartridges and shells, and though their eyes may be swollen with weeping for sweethearts and brothers whose names are among the killed and wounded, yet they do not definitely connect the work they are doing with the trenches."[13]

It was not the case, however, that the middle and upper classes were the only ones whose prejudice prevented an all-encompassing sisterhood from developing among munitions workers. Gradation occurred at all social levels. Within the working class as in the other classes, levels of income, modes of behavior, and areas of residence were all variables that created classes within a class. Having a skilled trade, for one thing, elevated a worker over unskilled coworkers, but there was also a self-conscious distinction made by workers who believed themselves to be "respectable" rather than "rough." One social commentator described the power of the status of respectability a few years before the war:

> The workers of one factory will refuse to recognise those of another in the same street, and one workroom will ignore another, where the work done is dirtier or heavier; while the warehouse girls will not know the girls in the factory proper. The finest shades and distinctions are observed among these girls, and this from no less worthy motive than the passionate desire "to keep herself respectable." It is the ruling power of their lives. . . . Respectability is for them a thing to be fought for, to be fiercely protected, to be boasted of, to be kept and nurtured at all hazards. They cannot afford to risk association with those whose standards are less high than their own.[14]

13. Naomi Loughnan, "Munition Work," in Gilbert Stone, ed., *Women War Workers* (New York: Thomas Y. Crowell Co., 1917), 28, 33.

14. M. Mostyn Bird, *Woman at Work: A Study of the Different Ways of Earning a Living Open to Women* (London: Chapman & Hall, 1911), 16–17. For a discussion of the religious and cultural origins of the morality of respectability for the working class, see Elizabeth

Shirley Howes of Southampton, who had left school at fourteen and been apprenticed in ladies' tailoring, took a munitions job when tailoring work dried up during the war. She was one of the first wartime recruits in her company. Although she found the job enjoyable enough at first, later in the war, as the scale of the work grew, the company took on many more women workers: "But I left . . . when they took on a lot of girls, I didn't like it then. . . . I don't want to say I'm nasty or anything like that, but the type of girls that came into the factories later were not like they were when they first started, and I didn't care for it at all." Howes was reticent about explaining this aversion, but presumably she found her new co-workers distasteful because of both their socioeconomic backgrounds and their social behavior.[15]

At times tensions erupted into fighting. Lilian Bineham recalled with great animation how she exchanged "smacks round the mouth" with a "rough girl" from Silvertown who accused Bineham of talking about her in the shiftinghouse: their fight was resolved by a week's suspension meted out by Lilian Barker, the "lady superintendent" at Woolwich Arsenal.[16] Regional or ethnic differences could also become violent. One description of a munitions factory in "the North" noted the competition between shifts of women workers in the form of lyrics they invented for popular tunes, and that such competition sometimes spilled over into "fisticuffs," which the writer attributed to "the old 'Border' warfare still carrying on between the clans."[17] West was one of the policewomen who had to intervene when rioting broke out between English and Irish women workers at the shell-filling factory at Hereford in August 1917. She recorded the events in her diary:

> Some time ago several lots of Irish girls were taken on to work in the Amatol. There has been a lot of bad blood between them & the English. The Irish sang Sinn Fein songs & made offensive remarks about the Tommies. The English replied in kind. Each side waxed very wroth. The Irish wore orange & green, & the English Red white & blue. This went on for weeks. . . . Last week during the dinner hour, an English girl accused an Irish girl of stealing her dinner. The Irish girl replied by spitting in the English girl's face. There

---

Roberts, *A Woman's Place: An Oral History of Working-Class Women 1890-1940* (Oxford: Basil Blackwell, 1984), 5-6.

15. IWM, DSR, 7445/01. Interview conducted by Southampton Oral History Project.

16. IWM, DSR, 8778/2.

17. Beatrice Heron-Maxwell, "Our Munition Girls of the North," *Daily Mirror,* 22 June 1917.

was a battle, all the others standing round & cheering on the combatants. We were called in to separate them. . . . Next evening scenting trouble 8 or 9 of us went down to see the shift train off from Hereford station. A tremendous battle ensued on the platform between about 20 Irish & the rest of the shift.[18]

The trouble was only settled by the Irish women being sent back to Ireland the following day. Political, class, and language differences as well as differences in customs, religious beliefs, and modes of social behavior created divisions among women munitions workers.

FRIENDSHIP AND SISTERHOOD

Some of the unskilled processes in which large numbers of women were engaged entailed working closely at a large table or bench with perhaps fifteen or twenty other women. Such proximity, hour after hour and day after day, must have promoted a closeness that, although not necessarily always amicable, involved some feeling of comradeship. Amy May, who worked at Woolwich Arsenal from March 1917 until after the war was over, recalled how she and the other women would sing "all the old war songs" while they worked, how they talked and laughed, and how her coworkers would "tell all their experiences with their boyfriends, some of them would, and all that sort of thing." She and her friends used to spend their breaks at the YWCA hut at Plumstead, having tea or coffee and "learning the dances." As a final consolidation of friendship, May married the brother of one of her workmates when he returned from being a prisoner of war.[19] The constant companionship that such women shared was not unlike that shared by troops in the armed forces.

According to a Weybridge printer, who was appealing before a conscription tribunal to allow him to keep his "last man" in July 1918, it was impossible for him to obtain female labor because "girls will not work anywhere except in munitions, where they can sing, dance and play."[20] Apparently, he failed to consider that wage levels in munitions had anything to do with the predilections of women workers. Journalists were responsible, in good part, for this public image of women munitions workers, proffering descriptions of munitions factories such as the following one of the scene during a dinner hour:

18. Diary of Miss G. M. West, 30 August 1917, IWM, DD, 77/156/1.
19. IWM, DSR, 000684/05.
20. *The Pioneer,* 12 July 1918.

Away in one corner of the yard are two lines of merry dancers, their arms linked, dancing their favourite "Knees up, Mother Brown," while sturdy women, obviously picked for their strength and size for heavy machines, stand by with folded arms and nod to each other with a smiling "It-does-your-heart-good-to-see-them" look.

Some there are who "keep themselves to themselves," and sit apart with a chosen friend and crochet antimacassars. Others have precious letters to be read again and again, even perhaps read out. . . .

On the staircase is a moving stream of gay-coloured overalls, for the munition girl loves brightness, as the old deaf flower seller who sits outside the works has discovered, and in many breasts are bunches of fresh primroses.

The procession pauses while its leaders gaze over the rail and throw a laughing word at a self-conscious group who are being photographed—very trying this, for the interruption has sent Elsie off into hysterical giggles again. But no matter, for Mrs. Bunce, who has worked her heavy lathe for "three years come May" and who means to send this group, with herself as the central figure, to a certain stalwart sergeant, father to seven small Bunces, has soon silenced her with a peremptory "Don't act so silly!" and the required fixed look has returned to all faces.[21]

Even allowing for the journalist's license at work here, the impression emerges of bonds developed over time, amounting to sisterhood. That some munitions workers did feel such sisterhood was eloquently revealed in two separate instances, both of which were women munitions workers' weddings, settings in which they could express their sense of unity. In December 1916 in Elstead, Surrey, a munitions worker married her soldier. The bride's workmates demonstrated their pride in their munitions jobs, as well as their sisterhood: "The bride was attired in 'overalls,' and a party of the bride's girl friends also wore their working dress."[22] Two years later, in September 1918, a remarkably similar event occurred when "twenty-four munition girls in white smocks and trousers attended a munition worker's wedding at Ealing and pulled the taxicab from the church to the bride's home."[23] Pulling a taxicab was a feat of strength that demonstrated their physical capability. This scene, too, suggests both pride in their munitions work and a sense of group identity. Perhaps, in fact, the two went hand in hand: the pride in being munitions workers and the common experience of working at the same factory, doing the same jobs, taking the same risks, enhanced any basic sisterhood that women workers shared.

21. *Daily Mail*, 10 April 1918.
22. "Bride in Overalls," *Banbury Guardian*, 21 December 1916.
23. *The Pioneer*, 20 September 1918, 5.

THE MECHANICS OF MOBILITY:
TRANSPORT AND HOUSING

GETTING TO WORK

Women, who had been less mobile than men before the war, experienced the war as greater freedom to move around the country, live in different circumstances, and mix with others beyond their prior experience. In all these ways, they partook of adventures previously more available to men. The locations of munitions factories were determined not by the local supply of workers but rather by security considerations or the availability of an engineering factory that could be transformed and expanded. The labor force for munitions factories had to be recruited from all around the United Kingdom. In consequence, women migrated from their homes to munitions factories at unprecedented rates: in early 1917, they were being transferred through labor exchanges at rates of between four and five thousand a month.[24]

When factories were built, converted, or expanded in cities or other industrial areas, there was a labor supply on hand. Frequently, however, the local labor supply proved inadequate and women were attracted from all parts of the United Kingdom to supplement it. When factories were built at remote locations, such as at Gretna and East Riggs in southern Scotland, the entire labor force had to be brought from elsewhere. Thus an immediate problem was the attraction and transportation of workers. Labor exchanges, run by the Board of Trade in cities and towns around the nation, were a crucial source of prospective workers. During 1916 well over two million women registered at labor exchanges as willing to enter munitions or other war-related work.[25] Newspaper advertisements and even some recruiting drives, notably in Ireland, were also used to round up sufficient numbers.

Because the government had taken control of the railways for the national emergency, it was relatively easy to implement schemes by which workers traveling from their homes to factories could use free rail passes, for both the first long trip from home for migratory workers and the daily trips for commuters. The Welfare Department of the Ministry of

24. U.S. Dept. of Labor, "Migration of Women's Labor Through the Employment Exchanges in Great Britain," *Employment of Women and Juveniles in Great Britain during the War: Reprints of the Memoranda of the British Health of Munition Workers Committee* (Washington: Government Printing Office, 1917), 68.

25. "Women in Munition Works," *The Engineer,* 11 January 1918.

Munitions made arrangements with the Travellers' Aid Society to provide help for the migrants, who would often arrive at their destination hungry, penniless, and without a place to stay. The Georgetown factory made an arrangement with the Caledonian Railway Company providing for special trains between Glasgow and Georgetown, as well as for building a Georgetown station and for enlarging Houston Station, and further decided to pay the fares of all workers to attract labor. At first it instituted a system by which each worker carried a "zone" ticket, but as numbers increased it needed greater efficiency, so it introduced a system in which each train was limited to eight hundred passengers, each worker carried a pass stamped with the number of her or his train, and the trains were scheduled in fifteen- to twenty-minute intervals. Workers' starting times were staggered accordingly.[26]

To cope with the increased volume of passengers going to work at Woolwich Arsenal, the London County Council increased the supply of tramcars in and to Woolwich. Instead of the 975 cars arriving at the same stop each day before the war, the number rose to 1,595, an increase of more than 63 percent. At the same time the number of passengers rose from a prewar peak hour of 4,094 to a wartime peak hour of 13,688, a jump of over 234 percent.[27] The provision of trams came to be so important to the production of munitions that on 6 September 1916 the tramways themselves were declared munitions work and brought under the provisions of Part I of the Munitions of War Act of 1915, which prohibited strikes and authorized the leaving certificates that prevented workers from easily quitting munitions jobs.[28]

Traveling in such crowded conditions was often a trial. Joan Williams found that on the whole she could endure hard work and long hours, but

> there was one thing that to the end enabled me to keep a small feeling of 'roughing it' and that was the daily struggle with the busses and trams. . . . [T]he trams were a nightmare and a purgatory the whole three years. A nightmare when you lost them, owing to their pleasing habit of sailing off the moment they saw the tube lift opening, and a purgatory when you caught them, especially on a bad morning when you either had to freeze on a damp seat outside, or step into the oppressive interior which had just disgorged a load of heated humanity and be gradually squashed flat during the journey.[29]

26. Ministry of Munitions, *Official History of the Scottish Filling Factory No.4 (National), Georgetown, Renfrewshire* (Glasgow, 1919), 110–11.

27. "L. C. C. Trams and the War," *The Pioneer,* 4 August 1916.

28. "Trams and Munitions," *The Pioneer,* 20 October 1916, 5.

29. Williams, "Munition Workers' [*sic*] Career," IWM, DPB, 26.

Some women, notably in Southampton, rode to work every day on their bicycles, a relatively recent advance in women's (and men's) mobility. The various technologies of transport, and their cooptation by the munitions factories in need of a work force, enabled women workers to go farther to work than many had ever previously gone.

FINDING LODGINGS

Housing for workers became one of the interwoven wartime crises, a problem the Ministry of Munitions hoped would prove tractable to the various schemes it brought forth. The natural result of the enormous influx of workers into munitions areas was an overcrowded situation in which less scrupulous landlords stood to make sizable profits. In a November 1916 case in Woolwich, a woman munitions worker with four children whose husband was away in the army was given one month's notice of eviction when she fell behind in paying her rent after the landlord raised it. She had sought alternative lodgings in all the surrounding neighborhoods for a fortnight, but landlords did not want her because of her four children, apparently a common prejudice.[30] The overcrowding caused by the concentration of munitions workers usually occurred in the areas that had been most densely inhabited before the war: the slums or poor areas where industrial workers lived.

As competition for lodgings increased and rents went up, the standard for lodgings at the lower end of the scale dropped to levels considered unacceptable before the war. When two members of the Advisory Committee on Women's War Employment (Industrial) toured Coventry in late 1916, they found "houses condemned and closed by the Corporation now reopened and inhabited owing to the shortage of dwellings," one of which "contained a girl lodger working at the Rudge Whitworth Factory." They were also told by a town councilor that a malt house had been "hastily adapted so as to give temporary shelter to whole families who were found practically camping out."[31]

It was common for beds to be used in shifts, an arrangement known as "box and cox." Lilian Miles recalled the lodgings she and her sister found when they were working at the ordnance factory in Coventry. The

30. *The Pioneer,* 3 November 1916.
31. Adelaide M. Anderson and Violet R. Markham, "Report on Industrial Welfare Conditions in Coventry," IWM, Women's Work Collection, Emp. 42, 15 November 1916, 3.

lodgings situation in Coventry was bad because "girls were all over the place there, and a lot of Irish girls there. And it seems as if they bundled in and didn't bother, you know. They just didn't seem to bother. There were six sleeping in that one bed, six, you know. And there was me and my sister got this single bed. I shall never forget it. It was a filthy place."[32] Fortunately, they soon found better accommodation with their foreman and his wife.

By September 1915, the Ministry of Munitions was aware that landlords around munitions works were increasing their rents. In November the ministry decided to take action, and the Increase of Rent and Mortgage Interest (War Restrictions) Act was passed.[33] Rents were stabilized at their prewar levels and increases were allowed only when landlords' local tax rates were increased. Rent control was a drastic and effective government intervention. Another such measure was the Billeting of Civilians Act in 1917.

Lodgings lists and registers had been initiated in most areas by diverse agencies from virtually the beginning of the war. At Woolwich, for example, the Board of Trade and the Home Office set up the Woolwich Advisory Committee on Women's Employment. One of its first tasks was to compile a register of available lodgings. The committee contacted the local press, trade unions, cooperative guilds, and social and religious organizations, propagating the idea that people who offered lodgings to munitions workers were making a noble gesture toward the war effort. Voluntary workers then went to inspect all lodgings offered. From May 1916 to May 1917, 1,347 lodgings were investigated, 500 of which were approved and placed on the register.[34] Part of the operation was a separate register kept of lodgings suitable for women supervisors and overlookers, a quiet affirmation of hierarchy and class.[35] Such efforts to help workers obtain lodgings were replicated around the country to greater or lesser extents.[36] These lodgings registers frequently were administered by local labor exchanges.

Lodgings lists were also considered part of the duties of welfare supervisors in many places, particularly where there were "outside" or

32. Lilian Annie Miles, IWM, DSR, 000854/04, 10.

33. *Parliamentary Debates, Commons,* 5th ser., 76 (25 November 1915): 428–29.

34. *The Pioneer,* 26 May 1917; "Woolwich Advisory Committee on Women's Employment," *The Pioneer,* 1 June 1917, 5.

35. "Woolwich Advisory Committee on Women's Employment: Lodgings for Munition Works," *The Pioneer,* 7 July 1916.

36. Anderson and Markham, "Industrial Welfare Conditions in Coventry," IWM, Women's Work Collection, Emp. 42, 4.

"extramural" welfare workers. These welfare supervisors were charged with the responsibility of compiling lists of available lodgings, inspecting them, meeting newly arrived women workers at the railway station and helping them to find lodgings from the list.[37]

Supervision of this aspect of welfare work radiated from the extramural subsection of the Welfare Department of the Ministry of Munitions in 1917 and 1918.[38] Beyond compiling lists of lodgings, part of this welfare work was the provision of "clearing hostels," where newly arrived women workers could stay until they found permanent lodgings. By May 1917, there were sixteen clearing hostels around the nation.[39]

Despite lodgings registers, the housing shortage continued, growing in proportion to the growth of munitions factories and the burgeoning numbers of workers. The Billeting Act of May 1917 created the Central Billeting Board, set up in August 1917. This board oversaw the implementation of compulsory billeting for munitions workers, a step that was familiar if resented in the case of soldiers, but unprecedented for working civilians. The board worked through local committees of employers and workers, often under the direction of town mayors, and employed local billeting officers who were supposed to use persuasion in lieu of compulsion. The board also laid down standard rates for lodgings in each district, which was a boon to workers.[40] The success of the board was reflected in the fact that, although the residents of Barrow and Hereford had been adamant that "there was no further accommodation even for a stray cat," it found additional billets for nine hundred people in Barrow and twelve hundred in Hereford.[41]

HOSTELS FOR MUNITIONS WORKERS

Finding and securing lodgings was only one part of the Ministry of Munitions' efforts to provide accommodation for munitions workers. In conjunction with charitable organizations and employers, the ministry built large numbers of hostels close to factories. Where necessary, the Lands Branch of the ministry acquired land for hostels by taking it under

37. "Instructions to Outside Welfare Officers," PRO, MUN 5/93/346/100.
38. "Welfare & Health Department: Staff, December 1917," PRO, MUN 5/94/346/39.
39. "First Report on Hostels, May 1917," PRO, MUN 5/93/346/131.
40. Wolfe, *Labour Supply and Regulation,* 192–93.
41. L. K. Yates, *The Woman's Part: A Record of Munitions Work* (New York: George H. Doran Co., 1918), 58.

the Defence of the Realm Regulations.[42] The ministry also undertook projects of building houses for workers, but they were almost exclusively for men workers and their families.

Before the war, there had been sixteen hostels for women workers and six hostels for men workers in England, and eleven for women and three for men in Scotland. Some of these were in fact boarding houses, some were hostels run by private companies for their workers, and others were hostels run by charitable organizations with moral and religious purposes. Whereas boarding houses were available to men workers or to "educated working women," institutional hostels run by, for example, the YWCA and the Girls' Friendly Society catered specifically to working women who held less well paid jobs, often in industrial work, many of them young women who had arrived in the city from the country.[43]

Because of the need to house munitions workers, however, by May 1917 there were 494 hostels for workers in 206 different locations in Britain: 276 were for women, 216 for men, and 2 for boys. Built and run by government, charitable organizations, private firms (especially the large munitions firms such as Vickers), and individuals, they accommodated 24,000 women workers and 22,800 men.[44] By January 1918, the total number of hostels had risen to 524, and the number of workers housed in hostels had grown disproportionately because of their higher level of occupancy.[45]

Not all hostels were newly built. Under clause 2(a) of the Defence of the Realm Regulations, the ministry could take over "unoccupied premises" for the housing of workers.[46] Hostels were frequently converted from buildings that were available and suited to the purpose. When Vickers had to devise means of housing its greatly increased work force at Crayford, Dartford, and Erith in Kent, the Ministry of Munitions assisted them by inveighing the Defence of the Realm Regulations against any owners reluctant to rent out their nonessential properties to the company. In this way, Vickers acquired two hundred houses and institutions in the district around its works. The company then spent significant amounts of money converting the buildings into hostels. Its first expectations and designs were that men would want separate cubicles,

42. For example, PRO, MUN 5/96/346.2/15, 3 February 1916. Correspondence re the construction of hostels for workers at the Thames Ammunition Co., Erith.
43. "First Report on Hostels, May 1917," PRO, MUN 5/93/346/131.
44. "Existing Hostels and Their Distribution," no. 4, ibid.
45. "Second Report on Hostels, January 1918," ibid.
46. "Housing and Construction," no. 7, 18 December 1915, PRO, MUN 2/27.

whereas women would be content with dormitory accommodation. In fact, its experience was the reverse. Providing adequate lavatory accommodation was found to be difficult and expensive, "the arrangements of many country houses in this respect being extraordinarily primitive. In the majority of cases, in fact, only cesspools were employed."[47]

Where Monica Cosens spent a short period as a munitions worker, which may have been at Vickers in Kent, the factory management converted "a board-school, a charitable institution, a workhouse, and practically all the empty houses in the neighbourhood" into hostels for their women workers. The food was prepared in a central depot and brought around by "motor wagons," and her bedroom was one screened-off section of a large classroom "fitted with a black iron bedstead with a number pasted on the foot of it, a washstand and a dressing-chest."[48]

In 1916, a journalist who toured the "wooden bungalow huts" that had been built as a hostel for six hundred women workers at one munitions works was impressed with their cleanliness and coziness. Each room had an electric light, and there were numerous bathrooms with a constant supply of hot water. For a weekly bed-and-board rate of 13s., each woman had her own cubicle: "Little rooms they are, simply furnished but complete, each with a well-sprung, comfortable bed, a locker, washstand, and looking-glass." The general decoration scheme was simple, "comprising a dado of dark brown boards with a rich cream plaster above." However, the journalist noted that many a "tiny room [was] transformed into a cosy den by various feminine touches and trifles," and "in almost every room I peeped into there was the photograph of some dear one—husband, father, sweetheart, son, or brother—wearing the uniform of the King. Too many, alas! were hung with black crepe or ribbon."[49]

Most hostels could not boast of numerous bathrooms. At the Ministry of Munitions' hostel at Gloucester, for example, there were two baths for thirty-eight tenants, and at Lancaster one bath for twenty-one tenants.[50] Nevertheless, commentators claimed that wartime hostels for both women and men were more comfortable than prewar ones. This comfort supposedly originated in the improved facilities in the later hostels, and in

47. J. E. Hutton, *Welfare and Housing: A Practical Record of War-Time Management* (London: Longmans, Green and Co., 1918), 26–30.

48. Monica Cosens, *Lloyd George's Munition Girls* (London: Hutchinson & Co., 1916), 118–20.

49. "Homes for Munition Girls: What the Government Is Doing," *Daily Mail,* 4 August 1916.

50. "Number of Baths," no. 4, PRO, MUN 5/92/346/40.

their superior planning and daily administration, which was mostly due, according to the ministry, to the policy of employing "educated women" as hostel matrons with responsibility for the housekeeping.[51] The matron had to be sufficiently tactful yet practical to handle, for example, the delousing of any workers who needed it (a problem that occurred at hostels around the country), their segregation into separate sleeping quarters, and the steam-cleaning of their clothes.[52] Under the matron, each hostel had its staff of maids and kitchen hands. Women police and patrols were employed at some of the larger hostels to keep order, a role the ministry considered "valuable work," although it also admitted that their "employment must be considered as an emergency precaution rather than a part of an ideal form of management."[53]

Just as separate lodgings registers were kept in some places for overlookers, welfare supervisors, and other women considered to be of a superior class, so too was there hierarchy in hostels. At Woolwich, for example, there were two classes of hostels for women. Ordinary women workers lodged at the Joan of Arc Hostel, which could accommodate 750 women, although it was usually less than full, and the larger Eltham Hostel and Well Hall Hostels, which also had rooms for men. The Queen Mary Hostel, however, which could accommodate only 250, was reserved for "the better class . . . ladies working in the Arsenal." The "ladies" at the Queen Mary included voluntary canteen workers, welfare supervisors, and middle- and upper-class factory workers who came from around the country or from the dominions. The weekly charge at the Queen Mary was higher, but residents received better meals there than at the other hostels, such as a choice of dishes for breakfast and a three-course dinner.[54]

Similarly, the recreation room at the Queen Mary was furnished as a lounge on a scale unknown in the hostels for ordinary working women. Agnes Foxwell, an overlooker of women workers in the arsenal, extolled the recreation room's attributes, which included "plenty of really comfortable chairs and sofas. Windows are on three sides, fireplaces at intervals on either side of the room. There is artistic colouring, and the mode of decoration is similar to an old manorial hall, the arched roof composed

51. "First Report on Hostels, May 1917: 6. Effect of the War in the Pre-war Hostels," PRO, MUN 5/93/346/131.

52. "Cleansing of Clothing and Bodies," PRO, MUN 5/92/346/40, 2.

53. Ibid.

54. Lady Henry Grosvenor's testimony to the Committee for the Organisation of Women's Service, 23 November 1916, IWM, Women's Work Collection, Mun. 2:18.1.

of oak beams; electric lights are suspended from them by chains, and silken shades of warm tones add a charming touch of colour." The lounge was always graced with plenty of fresh flowers. Especially at teatime, Foxwell felt, when residents clustered around fireplaces and made toast and chatted, it was just like their college days.[55] In other munitions centers also, separate hostels were allocated to welfare supervisors, women police, and any other women considered to be above the level of the ordinary working woman.

Charges for the average weekly hostel bed-and-board were around 12s. in 1916, but rose to something like 17s. 6d. later on.[56] They varied from place to place and were correlated to wages, so that where wages were higher so were hostel charges. Particularly later in the war, these charges drew some comments in the press. In October 1917, *The English-woman* condemned hostel charges at Woolwich as "scandalously expensive." With weekly hostel charges at 16s. 6d., it calculated, women workers were left, after paying for their lunch at the factory canteen, with little or nothing for other incidental expenses.[57] In fact, most women were earning more than the minimum rate thanks to overtime and bonuses, but for those who were not, hostels were indeed expensive.[58]

Employers who built hostels to house their women workers did so out of necessity: there was no other housing available and hostels seemed the most expedient way to provide accommodation. However, when they were compelled to subsidize the hostels in order to keep the charges comparable to the rates of local lodgings, they came to regard hostels as a subsidy in kind to the wages the women received. Partly for this reason, unions, for whom it was a cardinal principle that workers should never be paid in kind but only in cash, were opposed to hostels. The secretary of the Coventry branch of the National Federation of Women Workers wrote to the Ministry of Munitions, protesting that she was "opposed to the whole idea of feeding and housing girls under the nose of the employer." "Some agitators," the ministry noted, "have gone so far as to say that a hostel run by a private firm resembles [a] compound for black labour."[59] While unions were definitely opposed to hostels run by private

55. Agnes K. Foxwell, *Munition Lasses: Six Months as Principal Overlooker in Danger Buildings* (London: Hodder and Stoughton, 1917), 131–32.

56. *History of the Ministry of Munitions*, pt. 5, ch. 8, 77.

57. "Overworked Women," *The Englishwoman* 36 (October 1917): 5–6.

58. "Housing of Women Munition Workers," *The Pioneer*, 24 March 1916, 7.

59. "First Report on Hostels, May 1917: 10. Views and Policy of Trade Union and Labour Leaders on Hostels and Hostel Charges," PRO, MUN 5/93/346/131.

companies for their employees, they did not object to hostels run by local public bodies. Government-run hostels, they felt, were acceptable, but suffered from centralized administration and needed more local control. It is not clear how pervasive this resentment of being housed by the employer was among workers in general; it was union leaders who spoke out against the system.

It was, however, clear that hostels were viewed differently by workers in different parts of the country. It soon became a matter of common observation that hostels were less popular in Scotland and the north of England than they were in other regions. In southern England, it was reported, "many workers like Hostel life and speak highly of the comforts obtainable in Hostels."[60] The fact that Glaswegian munitions workers would take any kind of lodgings rather than live in a hostel was explained as follows: hostels in Scotland were reputed to be like reformatories. The overly strict tone of Scottish hostels was not helped by the fact that the Church of Scotland Women's Hostels were managed by committees consisting only of ministers of religion.[61] At least to some ministry observers, the explanation for the poor rating of hostels in Scotland lay in the fact that most of the munitions workers there were of the "rougher type," rather than the "refined type," of working women.[62]

Despite the fact that a good proportion of the women's hostels built for the war emergency were operated by such agencies as the YWCA, the Girls' Friendly Society, the Church Army, and the Salvation Army, the ministry's observers noted that the hostels were less rigid in style than their prewar counterparts had been. The change had occurred, they thought, because whereas prewar hostels had been founded on the basis of a spiritual mission, the wartime hostels were built for the practical purpose of housing working women. In particular, the women workers who lived in such hostels before the war earned very meager wages and were therefore considered in need of moral guidance to be kept away from prostitution. In contrast, women munitions workers were

for the first time in their lives in an independent position earning good wages. They were mixing in their daily work and recreation with large numbers of young men and women of their own age and class and were housed in areas where soldiers were quartered for training.

60. "Hostels from the Point of View of 2. The Employee," no. 13, ibid.
61. *Report of the Intelligence and Record Section,* 9 June 1917, 23, and 14 July 1917, PRO, MUN 2.28, 19.
62. "First Report on Hostels, May 1917: 14. The Future of Hostels," PRO, MUN 5/93/346/131.

> The net result of the war as regards womens [*sic*] hostels has been to
> develop the old protective hostel and to create a new type of hostel for the
> new independent type of working girl. The old fashioned hostels are slowly
> adapting themselves to the new conditions.[63]

The overwhelming practicality of their mission to house women munitions workers caused unforeseen consequences internally for the YWCA.[64]
Under pressure to allow a convivial atmosphere in which workers could
relax and restore themselves away from the factory, YWCA wartime
hostels permitted dancing, smoking, and card playing among other
recreational activities on their premises. While this permission was considered a reasonable compromise in the circumstances by pragmatic,
career social workers of the YWCA, the older, conservative members and
those who believed that religious piety meant sober behavior were
scandalized by it.[65]

At munitions factories in both remote rural areas and urban centers,
hostels tried to be the core of social organization for their residents.[66]
Sporting, literary, and dramatic clubs formed, libraries were organized,
and evening classes were offered, sometimes with the advice of residents'
committees. The YWCA developed a lecture syllabus, the most popular
subject of which turned out to be descriptions of the battlefronts, illustrated by lantern slides. Whereas before the war classes in YWCA and
Girls' Friendly Society hostels had focused on sewing, singing, and Bible
classes, during the war dancing and literature classes became the most
popular. Hostel residents clamored for libraries with "modern books,"
and the Welfare Department gave small grants to facilitate the establishment of such libraries.[67]

For some hostels, halls were built where lectures were given and dances
held, and in some cases cinemas were built. At Woolwich, for example,
when in mid-1916 hostels and bungalows were being planned to accom-

63. "Effect of the War in the Pre-war Hostels," no. 6, ibid.

64. "First World War: 1914–18 and Onwards," Modern Records Centre, University
of Warwick (hereafter MRC), YWCA Papers, MSS. 243/62.

65. Lady Constance Coote, President of the Tunbridge Wells branch of the YWCA,
wrote to one of the central directors to protest this behavior in YWCA hostels. MRC,
YWCA Papers, MSS. 243/14/23/4, Letter to Miss Campbell, May 1918. It was this
controversy, concerning the operation of both hostels and clubs for munitions workers,
which provoked a later split between the progressive, reform-minded wing and the religious,
conservative wing of the YWCA right after the war.

66. "Woolwich Girls' Hostel," *The Pioneer*, 9 June 1916.

67. "Second Report on Hostels, January 1918: 8. Recreation for Hostels," PRO, MUN
5/93/346/131.

modate thousands of women workers, one hostel for 750 was to include "several public rooms and a quite imposing theatre with a big stage, where the girls can have private theatricals. This theatre can be converted into a dancing hall or a restaurant, as the kitchen and buffet counter are close by." These facilities, along with such amenities as club rooms, lawn tennis courts, and pink geraniums underneath windows, prompted the writer to the rhetorical question: "In spite of the twelve hours' day, who would not be a woman worker at Woolwich?"[68]

It was evident, from the fact that hostels were rarely full until the housing situation reached its maximum constriction in late 1917 and 1918, that women workers preferred lodgings, on the whole, to hostels. Hostels became more popular because of the acute shortage of other housing; also, the attractiveness and availability of private lodgings diminished as food rationing became more stringent and people became less willing to share their homes and rations with lodgers. The occupancy level of women munitions workers' hostels increased from about half the available capacity in May 1917 to two-thirds in January 1918.[69] Although hostels for men workers were marginally fuller than the women's, there were far fewer of them, and it was commonly observed that men workers, like women, preferred lodgings.[70] This preference, it was frequently stated, was due to the complete independence lodgings offered, whatever their drawbacks might be.[71] In hostels, in contrast, there were curfews: at the "Hand-in-Hand" Hostel in Little Portland Street, London, for example, curfew was 10 P.M. six nights a week, with one late night a week decided on by the majority of the residents.[72]

To become munitions workers, women in Britain in the Great War moved around the country farther, more quickly, and in larger numbers than ever before. Frequently they moved away from home and family to an unfamiliar area and had to find accommodation in a hostel provided by the ministry or factory, or in private lodgings. Away from home, many

68. "Girls' Welfare at Woolwich: Hostels and Bungalows to Be Built," *Daily News*, 1 July 1916.

69. "Second Report on Hostels, January 1918: 9. Popularity of Hostels," PRO, MUN 5/93/346/131.

70. "Memoranda on Housing Scheme at Barrow, Lancs. 1917 Oct. 12; Nov. 17; Nov. 26," PRO, MUN 5/96/346.2/4.

71. For example, "Girls' Objection to Hostels," 26 May 1917, PRO, MUN 2.28, 18.

72. "New Women's Hostel: Government Workers at the 'Hand-in-Hand,'" *Our Own Gazette* (YWCA) 34 (February 1917): 60.

had to develop a greater degree of self-reliance than had been necessary before the war.

Women workers' experience of living in hostels paralleled some aspects of army life for men: not only were the hostels often like barracks, but women mixed with others of different backgrounds more than in any prewar occupation or circumstance. It seems probable that women's experience living and working closely with a mass of other women created a sense of group identity and at the same time an awareness of their own diversity. The results of this mixing were occasionally hostile. More often, though, women overcame the strangeness of each other's accents and idiomatic speech and were enriched by what amounted to cultural exchange. The rubbing of shoulders between classes created some friction: working-class women often felt that their social superiors were being arrogant or patronizing, while upper- and middle-class women in turn found the workers at times unfriendly or too rough. Occasionally, extended contact resulted in a friendly rapport being established, at least at work if not after hours.[73]

Perhaps what is most important about the heterogeneity of women munitions workers, for my purposes, is the fallibility of generalizing about their experience. The wages earned by an unskilled worker of fourteen or fifty were quite different from those earned by a skilled worker of twenty-five or thirty. The attitude toward her work of an upper- or middle-class woman "doing her bit" for the war was essentially different from that of a working-class woman who had always worked and would probably always have to. The after-work occupations of an energetic, single sixteen-year-old living in a hostel were different from those of one who lived at home and had to help mind her younger siblings, and different again for both of them than for a married, thirty-five-year-old woman with two or more children to care and cook for. The whole experience was different for a munitions worker living in a suburb of London and working at Woolwich Arsenal than it was for a South Wales woman working in a small or medium-sized factory twenty miles from her village. While as a cohort women munitions workers shared many of the same circumstances and features of daily life, the factors of difference among them constantly modified their commonalities.

73. Sherna Berger Gluck found, among the women who worked in the defense industries of the U.S. in World War II, that cross-race mixing was limited and not unproblematic, yet it was enough to break down barriers in an important and lasting way. *Rosie the Riveter Revisited: Women, the War and Social Change* (New York: Meridian, 1987), 264.

CHAPTER THREE

"Industrial Work Is Good for Women"

Health, Welfare, Deaths, and Injuries

One of the most remarkable things about this war is . . . the impetus given to movements for social amelioration which existed before the war and will continue after it—movements which are essentially domestic and concerned with normal conditions. . . . So far from having interrupted efforts for the promotion of these . . . the war has stimulated them in an extraordinary degree.

Edinburgh Review, *October 1916*

The night shift had just started operations on 4.5 inch shells, when a shell, which had been placed in position on the machine for the purpose of having the fuse firmly screwed in, burst with a loud report, and other projectiles close at hand followed suit with disastrous results. . . . [W]ithin a few hours, when repairs had been completed, girls were found readily volunteering to work in the very room where the accident happened. Meanwhile the injured were conveyed to the Leeds General Infirmary.

Description of an explosion at the Barnbow
National Factory, 5 December 1916,
in which thirty-five people were killed

HEALTH

In March 1919, the London Association of Medical Women met to discuss "the effect of industrial employment upon women." Dr. Rhoda Adamson, one of the leading innovators in programs for keeping pregnant women at work during the war, asserted that "on the whole . . . industrial work was good for women, and . . . some who had never gone out to work before brightened up mentally, developed hobbies, and improved in health." Dr. Janet Campbell, of the Health of Munition Workers Committee and author of a memorandum on the "Health of Women in

Industry," contended that "industrial occupations were less injurious to
women than to men, and . . . they were less liable to accident." Further,
she stated that "the high sickness rate among working women must be
attributed to poverty, lack of fresh air, long standing and improper food.
In munitions work the results upon health were found to be good, owing
to good wages, healthy conditions, and welfare supervision."[1] The consensus of the meeting was that, despite the physically demanding nature
of the work, women munitions workers had benefited from it because
their higher wages had improved their standard of living and the welfare
programs of the Ministry of Munitions had dramatically improved working conditions.

Given not only the long hours and continual strain of munitions work
but also the frequent involvement with explosives, toxic chemicals, and
heavy machinery, it seems at first paradoxical that it could have improved
women's health. The resolution to the paradox lies in the fact that poor
women had always worked hard, and that prior to the war their diet and
living standards had been, to say the least, inimical to their health. Further,
those who were injured, poisoned, or killed by their work were in the
minority, particularly after measures were taken to monitor workers'
health. J. M. Winter, in his study of the health and fitness of the British
populace in World War I, shows that the mortality rates of both women
and infants dropped during the war. He argues that this improvement
was due to better nutrition, as increased incomes in working-class households, coupled with rationing, brought about a more equitable distribution of food throughout society.[2] Linda Bryder has challenged some of
Winter's statistics and reasoning, but her main point, that lack of nutrition
was a cause of tuberculosis, only reinforces the conclusion that women
workers earning steady and higher wages were likely to be healthier.[3]

Contemporaries widely commented on the improvement in the health
of women workers during the war. Adelaide Anderson, Principal Lady
Inspector of Factories, pointed "to the unquestionable fact that before
the War far larger numbers of our working women were under-fed,
because under-paid, than is now the case during the greatest War the

1. "Industrial Employment of Women," *British Medical Journal* 1 (29 March 1919):
380. Dr. Janet Campbell's memorandum was published as part of the *Report of the War
Cabinet Committee on Women in Industry.*

2. Winter, *Great War,* 117–53 passim, and ch. 7 passim.

3. Linda Bryder, "The First World War: Healthy or Hungry?" *History Workshop Journal*
24 (Autumn 1987): 141–57.

world has ever seen."[4] One scholar has recently doubted that, given
rationing and the persistence of bad eating habits, women munitions
workers' nutritional intake could have been better during the war.[5] But
the improvement in women workers' health despite these obstacles is
testimony to how little even the respectable working class had lived on
prior to the war, and in particular how abysmally inadequate the diet of
women workers had been.[6] The daily factory diet, despite rationing, long
queues, and a short, aggregate food supply, was a vast improvement on
prewar eating for many women workers, not only because food was now
affordable and available to them but also because it had been standard
practice in the working class to give priority in food consumption to the
male breadwinner. Mothers customarily gave food first to their husbands
and then to their children before they ate. Now that women munitions
workers were relatively high wage-earners, they could consider themselves
deserving of the more substantial diet that welfare personnel and others
. exhorted them to have and that was available to them in canteens.[7]

FOOD ECONOMY AND RATIONS

What most makes the improved dietary standard of women workers
remarkable is the fact that it was obtained despite food shortages and
rationing. Through the first two years of the war, concern about the food
supply and protests over the inflated prices of staple items were widespread, yet little governmental action was taken to control the situation
for the civilian population. By late 1916, however, it was clear that state
intervention was called for. One of the last acts of the Asquith government
was to establish the office of the food controller in November 1916.[8]

In April 1917, then Minister of Munitions Dr. Addison appointed a
committee to inquire into the problem of the adequate feeding of munitions workers. In its May 7 report, the committee linked the problem

4. A. M. Anderson, *Women Workers and the Health of the Nation* (London: John Bale,
Sons & Danielson, 1918), 22.

5. L. Margaret Barnett, "Upgrading the Diet of Working Women: Canteens and Hostels
in Munitions Factories in Britain During World War One" (Paper delivered at the North
American Conference on British Studies, October 1990).

6. See, for example, Maud Pember Reeves, *Round About a Pound a Week* (1913; reprint,
London: Virago, 1979), chs. 7–10.

7. Related to this see Roberts, *A Woman's Place,* 40–41.

8. G. E. Underhill, "The Food Problem 1914–1916," *Quarterly Review* 230 (July
1918): 145, 164–65.

of feeding munitions workers to the nationwide problem of food supply and distribution. Besides urging the government to take positive steps in this regard, it emphasized the importance of canteens to the healthy diet of munitions workers and advocated that factory canteens be widely established.[9]

Actual food rationing began at the end of 1917. The items rationed were sugar, meat, butter, margarine, and lard; bread and tea stayed in sufficient supply to escape rationing. The administrative procedure used developed from a partial centralized system to a larger regional one with food districts and local committees, and then finally reversed itself into a full-fledged centralized scheme. By the inclusion of workers' representatives in the administration of the rationing scheme, popular protest was transformed into acceptance, so that "on the introduction of national rationing many Trade Unions sent votes of thanks to the Food Controller."[10] Although people suffered under food shortages in latter 1917 and early 1918, by mid-1918 rationing and distribution had been smoothed out sufficiently that queues were much reduced.

In early 1918, when meat was in short supply and bread rationing seemed imminent, the food controller decided on a scheme of supplementary meat rations for manual workers. Workers were divided into three categories: very heavy industrial workers; heavy agricultural workers; and heavy industrial workers, including all women (over eighteen) and boys in industry. This scheme provoked a barrage of protests over the discrimination between workers at all, and over the classifying of women, some of whom were doing the same work as men in the first class, into the third class, as well as the complete exclusion of young women workers less than eighteen years old.[11] Elsie McIntyre, who worked at the Barnbow National Factory outside Leeds and lived at home with her mother and siblings, remembered the shortages vividly:

> The most awful thing was food. It was very scarce. And as we were coming off shift someone would say "There is a bit of steak at the butchers." And I would get off the train and then go on a tram. And I can get off at Burley Road and run to the shop only to find a long queue. And by [the time] it got to my turn there would be no more meat only half a pound of sausage, you

9. "Report of the Munitions (Food) Committee," PRO, MUN 5/95/346.1/12, 7 May 1917, 1, 6.

10. G. E. Underhill, "British Rationing During The War," *Quarterly Review* 234 (October 1920): 299.

11. Ibid., 294, 296.

see. And that's coming off the night shifts. You went straight into a queue before you could go to bed.[12]

In the spring of 1917 the Ministry of Food, under the pressure of the German submarine attacks on shipping, sought to maximize food economy by starting a system of national or communal kitchens. This short-lived phenomenon made it possible for the working woman to obtain basic meals for herself and her family easily and affordably.[13]

Another nationwide measure toward efficient food supply and production was the provision of allotments: individually worked gardening plots for vegetables. The belief that these were a real help to the national food supply was such that, at least in the Coventry district, factories organized allotment systems for their workers. At the White and Poppe factory, the allotment scheme, sometimes called "the girls' garden scheme," ran to the extent of annual shows to exhibit their produce, a "Champion Challenge Cup," and competition between women's hostels.[14] Factory and hostel allotments must have contributed to the improved diets of women workers.

CANTEENS

Ironically, although factory canteens were one of the most successful parts of the welfare platform introduced during the war and were one of the few parts retained after the war, they were not initiated by the Welfare Department of the Ministry of Munitions. The move to introduce factory canteens, rather, came early in 1915 as part of Lloyd George's "prohibition" campaign. Traditionally, factory workers in Britain took their lunch in nearby pubs; the idea to provide canteens in factories began with the motive to keep workers out of pubs. Lloyd George, whose Welsh chapel upbringing predisposed him against alcohol, although in fact he was not a teetotaler, believed that industrial productivity suffered from the drinking habits of workers. In the interest of maximizing munitions production, he contended, workers needed to be kept sober.

As soon as it was established in 1915, the Central Control Board

12. IWM, DSR, 000673/09, reel 02:13.

13. For a description of these kitchens see C. S. Peel, *How We Lived Then, 1914–1918: A Sketch of Social and Domestic Life in England During the War* (London: John Lane The Bodley Head Ltd., 1929), 83–85.

14. *The Limit* (magazine of the White and Poppe factory, Coventry) 2 (August 1918): 16, 22. See also "Allotment News," *Georgetown Gazette* 2, no. 12 (September 1918): 390.

(Liquor Traffic) appointed a canteen committee, under the chairmanship of Sir George Newman, to oversee the introduction of canteens for workers. The committee particularly recommended that canteens be provided in munitions factories. Although the ministry believed canteens were very important, it was reluctant to undertake the responsibility of opening and running them. In fact, most wartime canteens were initiated by voluntary organizations. By 1917 the committee had approved munitions factories' canteens run by the YMCA (England), the YWCA (in both England and Scotland), the YM&WCA (Scotland), the National People's Palaces Association, the Salvation Army, the Church of England Temperance Society, the Church Army, the British Women's Temperance Association (Scotland), the Glasgow Union of Women Workers, the Women's Volunteer Reserve, and the Women's Legion.[15] Other voluntary organizations formed specifically to organize wartime canteens. Lady Lawrence established the Munition Makers' Canteens Committee, which ran canteens in Woolwich Arsenal and surrounding factories, at the royal aircraft factory at Farnborough, at Sheffield, Birmingham, Portsmouth, and elsewhere.

By 1917 there were thirty-one dining halls and fourteen coffee stalls throughout Woolwich Arsenal; by early 1918, the canteens supplied eighty to ninety thousand meals a day, took in a thousand pounds a day, employed a thousand workers, and processed between twenty and twenty-five tons of food per day.[16] Apart from the arsenal, the largest-scale undertakings in catering occurred at the national factories built by the government in league with businessmen during the war, particularly the factories in remote places. The royal factory at Gretna had to provide more than just factory meals: because of Gretna's isolation, it had to become a self-sufficient township. Central kitchens were built in the middle of the nine-mile-wide development providing twenty thousand meals a day, with a bakery that supplied the canteens and hostels with five to six thousand two-pound loaves of bread a day, as well as cakes, scones, and pies.[17]

The *Engineer* reported in September 1917 that nearly a million workers were being provided with complete meals daily in the national factories and controlled establishments alone. "The results obtained," it editorialized, "have firmly established the 'industrial canteen' as a sound business

15. H. M. Usborne, *Women's Work in War Time: A Handbook of Employments* (London: T. Werner Laurie, 1917), 21.

16. Hogg, *Royal Arsenal,* 986–87.

17. "H. M. Factory, Gretna," IWM, Women's Work Collection, Mun. 14/8.

method of increasing the efficiency and productivity of the worker, and, therefore, of the factories of the country."[18] Thus sanctioned, the industrial canteen had proved its economic value to employers and would last as other welfare innovations would not.

Canteens in factories were organized hierarchically and were segregated. At the Cardonald National Projectile Factory, for example, there were the "manager's dining room," two "staff rooms," a modest room for chargehands (who oversaw small groups of women workers), and then separate, large dining halls for the "girls" and the "men."[19] The single most obvious mark of distinction between these ranks of canteens, apart from the size, was that in the rooms for managers and staff the tables were adorned with tablecloths, whereas the workers had to be satisfied with bare board or perhaps oilcloth. If workers were dissatisfied with the food or conditions in canteens, there was usually little they could do: as Mr. Blake, a worker at Woolwich Arsenal, testified to the Women's Service Committee, the fact that women workers used a canteen heavily did not mean they were happy with it, because, especially in the so-called "Danger Buildings," they simply had nowhere else to go.[20]

Yet, the factory canteen was clearly a beneficial innovation for workers, a facility that made life at work significantly easier and less unpleasant.[21] The canteen was probably the single most important factor in improving the diet of workers. With adequate wages and plain but nutritious food available, during the war women workers were able to eat better than they ever had. The result showed in their improved health, despite the strain of the war and their long hours of work.

WORKING HOURS

The improved health of women workers during the war occurred in spite of the exhaustion they suffered from their long, often arduous shifts at work. From the late nineteenth century to the outbreak of war, there had been a general movement in which employers, workers, and union leaders had participated to shorten women's working hours and to ameliorate their working conditions. Amendments to the factory acts improved working hours and conditions somewhat. Because of the war, the gov-

18. "Canteens at Munitions Works," *The Engineer,* 28 September 1917, 269.
19. "Souvenir of Cardonald National Projectile Factory 1915–1919," IWM, Women's Work Collection, Mun. 12/6, 8.
20. IWM, Women's Work Collection, Mun. 18.3, 28 November 1916.
21. "Munition Workers' Canteens," *Common Cause* 7 (13 August 1915): 243.

ernment decided to waive the factory acts when necessary. Thus during the war the Home Office allowed night work, longer hours, long overtime, Sunday work, shorter breaks, and hazardous working conditions for women, all of which had been prohibited or controlled before the war. What it allowed, in effect, was an anarchic situation in which workers in different factories around the country experienced widely different regimens.

At Georgetown, which was a model factory in terms of working hours and in other ways, women worked a forty-eight-hour week in shifts of either five-and-a-half days or five nights.[22] It was common practice to work a half-day on Saturday unless workers were on a full six- or seven-day schedule. In the Manchester area the normal working week for an engineering shop was fifty-three hours, but most women were working more than this due to overtime.[23] At Woolwich Arsenal twelve-hour shifts were the rule for both day and night workers, from 7 A.M. to 7 P.M. and vice versa. Excesses beyond such shifts were not uncommon: for example, in 1917 Fairey Aviation Company of Southampton employed one woman for 74.5 hours in one week excluding meal breaks, and over the Easter weekend employed eighteen women on a continuous shift of twenty-three to twenty-four hours.[24]

Some workers felt a certain bravado about doing hard work in this time of national emergency, as Joan Williams (who did either a ten-and-a-half- or a thirteen-hour day, depending on overtime) reported: "It was tiring but you got used to it and in those days would have despised to even lean against a bench and run the risk of being thought soft by the others."[25] But even for those so spurred by patriotism, continuous, long working days took their toll on health and fitness. Night shifts were implemented in the majority of factories in the drive to keep machinery actively producing. Night work was especially draining: observers commonly noticed women sleeping next to their machines during breaks rather than going to the canteen. Monica Cosens commented of her coworkers before the night shift began that "more than half of them were sitting round the tables, their heads buried in their hands, trying to snatch a few last winks of sleep."[26]

Concern about the health of workers and industrial efficiency grew in

22. Ministry of Munitions, *Scottish Filling Factory,* 4:150.

23. Manchester, Salford and District Women's War Interests Committee, *Women in the Labour Market (Manchester & District) during the War* (Manchester: William Morris Press, 1917), 11–12.

24. PRO, MUN 2/28, 9 June 1917, 13.

25. Williams, "Munition Workers' [sic] Career," IWM, DPB, 13–14.

26. Cosens, *Lloyd George's Munition Girls,* 73.

reaction to both the lack of uniformity of hours and the horrific excesses occurring in some factories. The war provided a laboratory situation for health experts and social scientists to run studies on health, fatigue, and industrial output, studies enthusiastically undertaken by those interested in the newly popular ideas of efficient or scientific management. The Ministry of Munitions established the Health of Munition Workers Committee in 1915, briefing it to study these questions and report on their findings.

One member of the committee, Dr. H. M. Vernon, conducted an experiment with women workers turning aluminum fuse bodies on capstan lathes. He found that whereas in a 74.5-hour week (which was not uncommon) their average output was 108 fuse bodies, when their week was reduced to 55.5 hours their average output increased to 169 fuse bodies.[27] The committee, on the basis of such experiments, recommended the abolition of Sunday work, overtime only as strictly necessary, and shorter working weeks. These findings were circulated by the ministry, and some employers chose to follow them, especially when their own empirical findings confirmed them.[28] As the war continued there was a movement toward three eight-hour shifts in place of two twelve-hour ones.

Running directly against the findings of efficiency experts were the demands of the armed forces for supplies. When there was a "push" on at the front, all caution was thrown to the winds. In the buildup before the launching of the Battle of the Somme, the *Woman Worker* complained that, despite union protests and questions in the House of Commons, the Ministry of Munitions had allowed the Vickers factory at Erith and a national factory at Huddersfield both to change from eight-hour shifts to twelve-hour ones, and Vickers at Barrow seemed about to do the same.[29] Factory holidays were often postponed or canceled due to the exigencies of war as decided by the Ministry of Munitions, so that the working year of the munitions worker was at times long and unrelieved, although in some factories at least workers were allowed a week or ten days of holidays per year, usually unpaid. When forced to work on public holidays, the worker did at least receive special rates of pay.[30]

27. H. M. Vernon, *The Health and Efficiency of Munition Workers* (London: Oxford University Press, 1940), 17–18. In this volume Dr. Vernon was recapitulating his World War I work for the benefit of World War II production.

28. For example, "An Extemporised Munition Factory," *The Engineer* 125 (12 April 1918): 314–15.

29. *Woman Worker* 5 (May 1916): 12.

30. PRO, LAB 2/57/MT.123/6/1917.

Clearly the main operating principle of the Ministry of Munitions was the supply of the armed forces in the quantities they demanded, and the health and efficiency of the work force was a lower priority. Having raised several questions on the matter in the House of Commons without satisfaction, Lord Henry Bentinck wrote to the editor of the *Times* in September 1917 to draw public attention to the fact that the Ministry of Munitions continued to employ women on ten-and-a-half-hour days despite the system having been "doubly and trebly damned by the Ministry's own committees."[31]

Employers and others often complained during the war that women workers kept "bad time" at work, both through absenteeism and unpunctuality. Most factories had a system by which those late to work were docked a quarter- or half-hour's pay to encourage punctuality. The national factory at Gretna began overstaffing by 5 percent to counteract absenteeism but found that they had to raise that amount to 10 percent.[32] One reason for absenteeism was the burden of domestic duties and childcare often borne by women workers; it was because of this that many factories built or provided nurseries for workers' children. Another major reason for absenteeism was the fatigue produced by the excessive hours and heavy work women were doing: most munitions workers' jobs involved standing all day, and one of the common side effects of this was varicose veins, especially in older women who had had children.

WELFARE

WOMEN FACTORY INSPECTORS

Although factory inspectors had been created in 1833, it was not until 1893 that women factory inspectors were appointed to deal solely with conditions for women workers.[33] Women factory inspectors dealt with a range of issues including excessive overtime, overtime for young women, outwork done at home, changes in wage rates, fines and deductions from wages, and other questions about the well-being of women workers. The advent of women factory inspectors gave working women a channel for complaints, something they had never had before. Although a male

31. "Overworked Women," *The Times,* 12 September 1917.

32. "Women and Their Work During the War at H. M. Factory, Gretna," IWM, Women's Work Collection, Mun. 14/8, 31–32.

33. On women factory inspectors see Mary Drake McFeely, *Lady Inspectors: The Campaign for a Better Workplace 1893–1921* (New York & Oxford: Basil Blackwell, 1988).

factory inspector asserted in 1892 that women workers "rarely complained," once women inspectors were appointed, women workers began to lodge complaints in a volume that rose from three hundred eighty in 1896 to more than a thousand per year by 1904.[34]

While legislation such as the 1901 Consolidation Act, which laid down standards for ventilation and sanitary accommodation, continued to improve the work environment in factories, working conditions at the start of the war were often very poor. Long hours, a stuffy and overcrowded atmosphere, and a lack of canteen, toilet, washing, and first aid facilities obtained in the majority of factories, especially smaller ones. As the *Woman's Dreadnought* frequently pointed out, many women workers continued to work under conditions of "sweating." Isolated or remote factories were sufficiently invisible that they could evade regulation: even in April 1917 Miss West recorded the horrific conditions in the explosive factory at Pembrey, South Wales, a place she dubbed "the back of beyond":

> This factory is very badly equipped as regards the welfare of the girls. The change rooms are fearfully crowded, long troughs are provided instead of wash basins, & there is always a scarcity of soap & towels. The girls [*sic*] danger clothes are often horribly dirty & in rags, many of the outdoor workers, who should have top boots, oilskins & s.westers [*sic*], haven't them. Although the fumes often mean 16 or 18 "casualties" a night, there are only 4 beds in the surgery for men & women & they are all in the same room. . . . There are no drains owing to the ground being below sea level. . . . The result is horrible & smelly swamps. There were until recently no lights in the lavatories, & as these same lavatories are generally full of rats & often very dirty the girls are afraid to go in.[35]

In contrast to this revolting state of affairs, some of the national factories built during the war were exemplary about providing lavatory, washing, changing, first aid, canteen, and other facilities.

Nevertheless, the majority of complaints lodged by women workers during the war were about facilities and conditions. Adelaide Anderson noted that, when hours rose substantially after the outbreak of war, women worked them without complaining. On matters of "sanitation and safety," in contrast, complaints rose from being 47.3 percent of all complaints lodged in 1913 to 63.1 percent in 1917.[36]

34. Adelaide M. Anderson, "Factory and Workshop Law," ch. 6 in *Woman in Industry: From Seven Points of View,* ed. Getrude M. Tuckwell et al. (London: Duckworth & Co., 1908), 151, 152, 164, 165.

35. Diary of Miss G. M. West, 10 April 1917, IWM, DD, 77/156/1.

36. Adelaide M. Anderson, *Women in the Factory: An Administrative Adventure 1893 to 1921* (London: John Murray, 1922), 239–40.

Concern about conditions and facilities in factories during World War I was part of a broader interest in the health, welfare, and efficiency of workers. Awareness of the poor health of the working class in general had been growing since the turn of the century. Medical and eugenist discourses blended with others. Organizations concerned with women workers, such as the Women's Trade Union League and the National Federation of Women Workers, called for an increase in the number of women factory inspectors.[37] The *Woman's Dreadnought*, while criticizing women factory inspectors for not being sufficiently aggressive, continued to call for more of them during the war, suggesting that as male factory inspectors left for military duties women should be taken on to replace them.[38] Those who were aware of industrial conditions realized that the need for women factory inspectors was greater than ever because of the wartime relaxation of the industrial code and the longer hours and increased pressure most workers were enduring. Even the politically docile YWCA social workers believed that, although the number of women factory inspectors had been increased, it was still inadequate to the task.[39] The number of women factory inspectors increased to a total of thirty during the war, but this was far from sufficient for the enormously expanded volume of work they had to do.[40]

Women factory inspectors were professionally concerned with women workers' health and safety, their status in the work force, and their psychological well-being. They became closely associated with the welfare movement in which welfare supervisors were employed in factories to supervise numerous aspects of women workers' lives. Welfare supervisors, however, in no way made factory inspectors redundant. Inspectors were an essential part of the central administration of factory and workshop laws, empowered to charge employers who failed to comply with standards laid down by law. Their importance as guardians was reflected in workers' attitudes toward them. While women workers frequently expressed hostility toward welfare supervisors, they felt that factory inspectors were on their side.

37. For example, *Manchester Guardian*, 4 August 1913.

38. "Factory Inspector's Report," *Woman's Dreadnought*, 8 July 1916, 505; "Why Not More Women Factory Inspectors?" *Woman's Dreadnought*, 24 February 1917, 601.

39. Mary E. Phillips, "The Effect of the War on Women in Factories and Workshops," *Our Outlook* (YWCA) 9, no. 96 (April 1916): 75.

40. Anderson, *Women in the Factory*, 237.

THE WELFARE DEPARTMENT OF THE
MINISTRY OF MUNITIONS

During the nineteenth century a few manufacturers had experimented with schemes for making their work force contented and thus productive. Toward the end of the century, a group of Quaker employers became renowned for their enlightened methods of labor management, including the provision of women secretaries or supervisors to see to the welfare of their women workers.[41] As the idea of welfare and its resultant efficiency spread, even small firms began to experiment with it, often with the wife of the employer or manager concerned with the lives of employees in a manner reminiscent of the pre-industrial workshop.[42] By the eve of the war, an organized movement had developed to introduce welfare supervisors into factories. As soon as munitions factories began to take on women workers in significant numbers, employers and government both decided that women welfare supervisors would make more efficient the administration of a large female work force. The large-scale introduction of welfare supervisors was one dimension of the enormous wartime growth of state bureaucracy under the stewardship of businessmen.[43]

The Welfare Department of the Ministry of Munitions was established in late December 1915 with Seebohm Rowntree at its head. Even before Lloyd George appointed Rowntree to introduce welfare work and welfare supervisors into munitions factories around the nation, he had set in motion a body that would apply the methods of scientific management, albeit not pure Taylorism, to munitions factories. In September 1915 he appointed the Health of Munition Workers Committee, with Sir George Newman as chair, "to consider and advise on questions of industrial fatigue, hours of labour, and other matters affecting the personal health and physical efficiency of workers in munition factories and workshops."[44]

41. Charles Dellheim, "The Creation of a Company Culture: Cadburys, 1861–1931," *American Historical Review* 92, no. 1 (February 1987): 13–44.

42. Anderson, *Women in the Factory*, 260; E. Dorothea Proud, *Welfare Work: Employers' Experiments for Improving Working Conditions in Factories* (London: G. Bell & Sons, 1916), 66.

43. In Harold Perkin's view, this was the culmination of the Edwardian concern with "national efficiency," a drive toward total efficiency to meet the demands of total war. *The Rise of Professional Society: England Since 1880* (London and New York: Routledge, 1989), 158, 189.

44. "Report of the Welfare and Health Section for the Year Ending 1917," PRO, MUN 5/94/346/39.

Dr. H. M. Vernon, committee member and lecturer in physiology at Oxford University, used the methods of scientific management to measure output in relation to hours of work, as mentioned earlier. Similarly, he worked out the optimum working time for certain factory processes and trained junior staff to carry out experiments in various regions.

Captain M. Greenwood, reader in medical statistics at the University of London, was coopted by the Welfare Department to use "calculating machines" and to establish a "medico-statistical laboratory" to work on "physiological problems." Greenwood surveyed exactly what munitions workers were eating, evaluated the nutritional content of their diet, and then instructed factory and hostel canteens on how to give munitions workers diets appropriate to their daily work. The welfare officers who visited factories helped carry out this process, thus effecting a useful bridge between scientific management techniques and welfare work.[45] The Health of Munition Workers Committee published several memoranda on fatigue, hours, and other health matters. Other related reports were published by bodies such as the Industrial Fatigue Board.[46]

While the Ministry of Munitions employed an amalgam of the techniques of welfare work and scientific management, it did so with the primary aim of maximizing efficiency and the subsidiary one of maintaining control of labor in a turbulent time. Whatever the aims of individual welfare workers and charitable organizations that undertook work in factories, the ministry's sight was fixed on producing sufficient munitions.[47]

WOMEN WELFARE SUPERVISORS DURING THE WAR

In 1917 there were an estimated six hundred welfare supervisors throughout the United Kingdom, and by the end of the war there were as many as a thousand. The welfare movement had indisputably taken off. Wartime welfare work helped middle-class women stake out an area of professional employment; what it did for women workers is another matter.

The ratio of welfare supervisors to women workers varied greatly from factory to factory, which affected the nature and amount of work that any one supervisor could carry out. The ministry's approximate rule of thumb was that a factory with three hundred or fewer employees required

45. "Research Work," ibid.
46. For example, Industrial Fatigue Board, report no. 13, *A Statistical Study of Labour Turnover in Munition and Other Factories* (1921).
47. *History of the Ministry of Munitions*, pt. 5, no. 3, ch. 1, "The Establishment of a Welfare Policy," 1.

only one welfare supervisor.[48] At Woolwich Arsenal the staff of welfare supervisors went up to twenty. In some factories, the duties they were given by management were limited to, for example, overseeing the canteen and the ambulance room, whereas in others duties were much more wide-ranging.[49] It was extremely common for the welfare supervisor to make arrangements with the local labor exchange, to interview all women applicants for work, and to decide whom to hire. In some factories, the supervisor would then assign the woman to a particular job or area, but in others this was left to the foreman or forewoman or a manager.

Workers could go to the welfare supervisor with any complaints about conditions or other work-related problems, and supervisors were supposed to check that wages paid were in accordance with rates laid down by the ministry. Complaining to the supervisor was encouraged because it was believed to avert more serious unrest: supervisors were conscious of their role "to dispel any gathering cloud of discontent."[50]

Ambulance rooms, first aid facilities, and rest rooms, widely introduced into factories during the war, came under the control of the welfare supervisor. She conducted rudimentary health checks of workers and prospective workers and ensured proper examinations by "medical officers," some of them full-time factory staff (often women) and others local doctors employed by the factory to visit regularly. In some factories dental care was provided as well as regular medical inspection; septic teeth were found to be a problem for those working with poisonous substances. In TNT or other factories where workers were given milk daily as a prophylactic against poisoning, and factories where workers were supposed to take baths to wash off dangerous substances at the end of the shift, the supervisor administered these arrangements. The cloak rooms, locker and changing areas, lavatories, and washing amenities that became widespread during the war were also under her supervision. She monitored the supply of towels and organized the cleaning of these areas.

Welfare supervisors monitored the timekeeping and absenteeism of women workers, checked doctors' certificates when necessary, and in other ways exercised discipline over women workers. The welfare supervisor was also considered the moral guardian of women workers. She

48. "Intramural Work in National Factories 1916 to 1917," IWM, Women's Work Collection, Mun. 18.9/4:2.

49. The munitions section of the Women's Work Collection at the IWM includes numerous manuscript and typed reports by welfare supervisors describing their work.

50. "Humanising Industry: Notable Experiments in Bradford," *Yorkshire Observer*, 30 August 1917.

could decide that a woman was "undesirable" and dismiss her in consequence. Stealing was a constant problem in most factories, both the theft
of other workers' possessions or money and pilfering from factory canteens. The welfare supervisor was charged with controlling this as far as
possible and exercising discipline over cases not deemed to require police
involvement. Under her supervision also were the uniforms the women
workers wore: she attended to their supply, mending, washing, and
correct usage at all times.

She organized benevolent funds in some factories, taking up collections
from workers to distribute to other workers who suffered particular
hardship, or to donate to causes such as helping wounded soldiers. A
welfare supervisor also ran war savings schemes, including the sale of war
bonds and war loans in the factory; more generally, she encouraged thrift
among the workers.

In a similar way, she encouraged proper eating and other healthy habits
among workers. Whatever the kind of canteen facility the factory offered,
whether a simple mess room supplying hot water or a full-scale canteen,
these facilities and the provision of drinking water were under the welfare
supervisor. Experiments with new facilities, such as the provision of seats
while working, were overseen by the welfare supervisor. In the spirit of
efficient management, supervisors also investigated the causes of accidents
at work and sometimes made recommendations for ways in which machinery or processes might be made safer. Welfare supervisors commonly
worked long hours and came back at night to check on the night-shift
workers.

In some factories, a separate welfare supervisor provided what was
called extramural work, and in factories with more than one supervisor
the responsibilities were shared. This work included the supervision of
the arrival of new workers and lodgings lists as described above. Where
hostels were provided for women workers, welfare supervisors kept in
contact with hostel matrons and sometimes inspected the hostels.

If a woman was sick at home or in the hospital, a supervisor might
visit her; if a woman was charged with an offense that involved the police,
the supervisor might either give testimony to the police or the court or
help the woman in some practical way. Before factory nurseries were
established, and in factories that never had one, the extramural welfare
supervisor occasionally visited the homes of workers who had children,
to check on how they were being looked after in their mother's absence.
In other cases in which it seemed there might be a problem at home,
such as when a woman regularly was absent or unpunctual, the supervisor

visited the woman's home; although the point of such visits was to "make friendly inquiries," workers could easily consider them an intrusion. While welfare supervisors provided numerous tangible benefits, their maternal attitudes toward workers were a benevolent gloss on what was fundamentally a position of managerial authority.

PREGNANT WORKERS AND NURSERIES

With the enormous influx of women into industrial work, the issue of pregnant workers drew unprecedented attention in regard to both married and unmarried women. The steady decline of the birthrate over the forty years preceding the war had raised alarm about the future and health of the race, which was spurred by a more general concern about the health of the population sparked by the Boer War. Wartime concern about the wastage of men and the birthrate in conjunction with the welfare movement led to unprecedented efforts to help pregnant workers and working mothers.[51]

The Health of Munition Workers Committee formed a subcommittee to enquire into "maternity questions": they received reports of destitution among unmarried mothers in Lancaster and Chatham and investigated maternity care in Woolwich and Hayes initially and other centers later.[52] Because factory practice had always been to fire women who were pregnant, some women had kept their condition a secret and therefore had not been spared strenuous work. For those fired, destitution was a common fate.

Throughout the war, individual pregnant workers were helped by welfare supervisors. When "J. B.," unmarried and aged twenty, was reported by the welfare supervisor at her factory in Coventry to a welfare officer as being in trouble, the officer took her to a "girls' night shelter" and found her a daytime job as a domestic. When she was no longer strong enough for that, the welfare officer found her piecework from a baby-linen shop, visited her regularly, and then finally persuaded her to inform her married sister of her condition and saw that she and the baby were taken in by that sister. In the report on "individual cases" attended

51. See Deborah Dwork, *War Is Good for Babies and Other Young Children: A History of the Infant and Child Welfare Movement in England 1898–1918* (London and New York: Tavistock Publications, 1987).
52. "Extra-Mural Welfare," 26 May 1917, PRO, MUN 2.28, 18.

to by welfare officers in Birmingham, Manchester, the southwest, and North and South Wales, 147 such cases were recorded.[53]

A maternity subsection of the Welfare Department of the Ministry of Munitions was formed to see which kinds of munitions work could safely be done by pregnant women, thus enabling women to keep earning necessary wages without endangering themselves or their babies. Welfare supervisors and medical officers in munitions factories began to experiment with providing special arrangements for pregnant workers in the hope of encouraging them to admit their pregnancy at an early stage and thereby receive special consideration. M. A. S. Deacon, M.B., instituted a scheme at the national amatol factory in Aintree outside Liverpool in which the work at the factory was all classified as heavy, medium, or light, and pregnant workers could be transferred from heavy to lighter operations. She argued that the system of keeping pregnant women on and encouraging them to report their condition was both efficient for management and beneficial to workers. "All the women whom I have seen since their confinements report that they have had easy confinements, very healthy children, and that they never felt better while carrying. One woman who worked until 10 days before had the 1st healthy baby that she had ever had out of eight."[54]

These schemes received attention and publicity because they were novel: instituted late in the war, they became casualties of the peace. What they signified was not a lasting change but the radical interest in industrial welfare produced by the war. The clear results of the experimental schemes permeated other munitions factories. Later in the war, pregnant women were usually kept on unless the factory was an explosives or TNT one. Some factories adopted steps of expediency to permit mothers to fill industrial jobs: at the rolling mills in Southampton, for example, when Dorothy Haigh was recruited for work she had a baby a few months old, but her mother volunteered to look after it and the factory allowed her a half-hour's work time in the middle of the day or night to go home and breast-feed.[55]

Corollary to the concern with pregnancy in the factory was a concern

53. "Individual Cases," IWM, Women's Work Collection, Mun. 18.9/10.
54. M. A. S. Deacon, "National Amatol Factory, Aintree," 12 July 1918, IWM, Women's Work Collection, Mun. 26/4, 13. See also "A Report of Work Done for Expectant Mothers," IWM, Women's Work Collection, Mun. 18.9/17; R. Adamson and H. Palmer-Jones, "The Work of a Department for Employing Expectant Mothers in a Munition Factory," *British Medical Journal* 2 (21 September 1918): 309–10; "Mothers in Factories," *The Englishwoman* 41 (January 1919): 9–11.
55. IWM, DSR, 000734/07, 13–14.

with circumstances during and after childbirth. In August 1918, the Welfare Advisory Committee reported to Winston Churchill, then Minister of Munitions, that there was a drastic shortage of midwives in munitions districts. The committee recommended that in districts where there had been a large influx of women because of munitions factories, the ministry ought to take action to provide fully trained midwives at a proper guaranteed salary.[56] The ministry approached the Local Government Board in order to undertake concerted action, but this initiative too was ended by the war before anything much was done. In the last year of the war, the Welfare Department undertook the provision of maternity homes in munitions areas. In July 1917 it began arranging to take over a YWCA hostel as a maternity hospital at Barrow; in early 1918 a hostel was opened at Ealing for munitions workers with babies; and just as the war ended it was in the process of opening a maternity home at Foleshill, Coventry.[57]

Another radical wartime innovation was the factory crèche or nursery, deemed eminently practical for wartime exigencies but dropped as an outrageous luxury when the war ended. Working women had their own well-worn methods of childcare. If there were older children or female relatives available, they would be given responsibility for the baby while the mother was at work. If there were no relatives nearby or available, neighbors filled the same role, often as one part of an intricate web of neighborhood support in which goods and services were exchanged and small amounts of money changed hands.[58] Some women made something of a career out of taking in neighborhood children while their mothers were at work.

By October 1916 the Welfare Department of the Ministry of Munitions had decided that it must begin to provide nurseries for women workers. It proposed that if other agencies opened temporary crèches for war purposes only in munitions areas, it would provide 75 percent of the cost of the nursery as well as 7d. per child per day or night; the rest of the costs would be made up partly by contributions of the mothers themselves and partly from the agency that started the nursery. The nurseries thus

56. "Shortage of Midwives in Munitions Areas," PRO, MUN 5/93/346/140.
57. "Welfare," 21 July 1917, PRO, MUN 2/28, 19; "Welfare," 15 December 1917, ibid., 20; "Women's Welfare: Work of New Coventry Home," *Midland Daily Telegraph,* 8 February 1919.
58. See Ellen Ross, "Labour and Love: Rediscovering London's Working-Class Mothers, 1870–1918," in *Labour and Love: Women's Experience of Home and Family 1850–1940,* ed. Jane Lewis (Oxford: Basil Blackwell, 1986), 73–98.

established were staffed by a matron and several trained nurses, preferably with experience with children. They fed and washed the infants, changed them into nursery clothes with a view to preventing the spread of any infections, and provided cots for them to sleep in. With the schedules of munitions workers, it was immediately clear that they needed to be open nights as well as days. Night-shift workers could also leave their children in the nursery during the day so as to get proper sleep. Later, women were able to leave their children in the nursery from Monday to Friday if they wished.

By early 1917 there were fourteen to sixteen nurseries operating for munitions workers in England and Wales.[59] By August 1917 arrangements were made with the Scottish office of the Welfare Department of the Ministry of Munitions for the establishment of nurseries in Scotland.[60] Various voluntary societies opened nurseries under their own auspices and were then eligible for grants-in-aid from the Board of Education or the Ministry of Munitions.[61] By 1917 the National Society of Day Nurseries was formed as an umbrella organization for all nurseries.[62]

While voluntary organizations took the initiative in urban areas, remote factories faced a tougher problem. By the later stages of the war several had become convinced of the utility of nurseries, and several factory nurseries were on the drawing boards when the Armistice removed all support for them. By August 1918, the Board of Education administered 130 nurseries, providing for about seven thousand children, and the Ministry of Munitions had separately established 31.

Dr. Scurfield, the medical officer for Sheffield, contended at the end of the war that the system of crèches had been wrongheaded all along and that instead the government should have endorsed and improved the system of "minders" that working-class women had always used. In Sheffield during the war, the city had opted to supervise this system, had encouraged the minders to attend the welfare center for expert advice on childcare, and had found the system more economical than nurseries.[63] The abolition of nurseries for workers' children after the war added

59. E. W. Hope, *Report on the Physical Welfare of Mothers and Children* (Carnegie United Kingdom Trust, 1917), 1:94, 2 (England and Wales): 123–25.

60. "Extra-Mural Welfare: Day Nurseries in Scotland," 4 August 1917, PRO, MUN 2.28, 17.

61. For example, E. Sylvia Pankhurst, *The Home Front: A Mirror to Life in England during the First World War* (London: Hutchinson & Co., 1932), ch. 22.

62. "Creche Matrons," in Usborne, *Women's Work In War Time*, 29.

63. "Welfare Advisory Committee: Notes and Report on the Advantages and Disadvantages of Creches in Industrial Areas," PRO, MUN 5/93/346/140.

weight to Scurfield's argument. But programs for pregnant workers and nurseries for munitions workers' children showed that, even though the maternalist emphasis on women's familial roles (i.e., the contemporary social ideology that stressed women's supposed maternal nature) had not lessened, employers and government could remove these normal restrictions on women's industrial work when they wanted.

SCENES OF THE WAR:
DEATHS, POISONING, AND INJURIES

FIRST AID, ACCIDENTS, AND INJURIES

In conjunction with the triumph of welfare work, the numbers of workers in metal trades, engineering works, and explosives factories pointed up the need for proper first aid facilities in factories. Before the war, facilities had often only had rudimentary first aid supplies, usually applied by a foreman. During 1915, there were 159,413 reported cases of industrial accidents, the majority of which occurred to teenagers between thirteen and eighteen years old, more often boys than girls.[64] Awareness of these accidents spurred the Welfare Department of the Ministry of Munitions to encourage private employers to provide better first aid facilities, and to insist that government factories do so. As they could other expenditures on welfare, employers could deduct the cost of building or converting an "ambulance room" or first aid facility from their excess profits. The Welfare Department employed medical officers in government factories and required them in controlled establishments (privately owned factories brought under government control for the duration of the war) where TNT, lethal gas, or other poisonous substances were handled. It also appointed health inspectors specifically to report on the first aid and medical facilities in factories, beginning in May 1917.[65]

Another result of wartime pressure was the provision of convalescent hospitals for workers. The Barnbow National Factory, for example, found it necessary to provide for recuperating workers after the serious explosion in December 1916: it established its convalescent home at Weetwood Grange, which then stayed in operation, sometimes taking in women workers who simply needed several weeks' rest.[66] Either separately or as

---

64. "Mistaken Economy," *Woman's Dreadnought*, 15 July 1916, 511.
65. PRO, MUN 2/28, 29 December 1917, 24.
66. W. Herbert Scott, *The Story of Barnbow: Embodying a Complete Record of War Work and Service at the No. 1 Filling Factory, Leeds* (Leeds: Jns. D. Hunter & Sons, 1919), 45. See

part of the factory benevolent fund, workers commonly donated to their own convalescent hospital to help those who were there and thus not earning wages; they similarly donated to hospitals and homes for other workers and wounded soldiers.[67] By mid-1918, there were fifty-six rest homes or convalescent homes for munitions workers registered with the Welfare Department of the Ministry of Munitions.[68]

Most women who took jobs in munitions factories probably did not give a great deal of prior thought to the dangers inherent in the work. All industrial work had its attendant hazards, and workers with any factory experience were accustomed to accidents or injuries. For machine-tool workers such as lathe operators, eye injuries were a constant problem.[69] Another constant danger was that of getting one's hair caught in machinery, especially when workers disregarded the regulations for covering up their hair. Some women lost part or all of their hair and scalps. Hands were very susceptible to injury because of their necessary proximity to the moving parts of machinery. Women commonly lost fingers or parts of them, or cut their hands.[70] Adelaide Anderson later noted that some women drivers of overhead cranes "met with fatal accidents."[71] Although the Liberal government had passed the Workmen's Compensation Act in 1906, the principle of compensation for injury and disability was not yet properly in place and compensation was haphazard and token when given.

TNT AND OTHER POISONING

Working with the poisonous chemicals that formed the substantial ingredients of shells and other explosive devices was inherently dangerous. Poisoning was commonly suffered by workers in shell-filling factories and although the suffering occurred to varying degrees, it was frequently both insidious and lethal. Some people were more susceptible than others, and different explosives were more poisonous than others. One powder

also "The New Convalescent Home," *The Pioneer,* 12 January 1917, 3; *Georgetown Gazette* 2, no. 11 (August 1918): 341.

67. "Gift to Calibae Rest Home, Killearn," *Georgetown Gazette* 2, no. 12 (September 1918): 379.

68. PRO, MUN 5/93/346/131, mid-1918 addendum to January 1918 report of the Welfare and Health Dept.

69. Williams, "A Munition Workers' [*sic*] Career," IWM, DPB, 22.

70. "Lily and the Law: A True Story," *Woman Worker* 14 (February 1917): 4.

71. Anderson, *Women in the Factory,* 234.

used in shells, "CE" (compound explosive), was not lethal but caused sickness, discoloration of the skin, and dermatitis. Because it was not considered poisonous, women workers could be compelled to work with it under penalty of being discharged without a leaving certificate. Cases of recalcitrant workers were brought before munitions tribunals, taken up by women's unions, and reported in the press.[72]

Lyddite had been the preferred explosive before the World War I promotion of TNT, and it had long been known to have toxic effects including jaundice. Cordite produced toxic fumes; it also caused sickness if eaten, which, unlikely though it would seem, some workers did a little because they found it tempting. Lily Truphet recalled: "It was ever so nice to eat, we used to suck a bit, it was very sweet, but they used to say you shouldn't do that, because it would affect your heart. . . . It was the soldiers used to do that, it'd affect their heart, to get out of the army."[73] Factories commonly paid a higher rate to workers in the poisonous explosive area to offset any reservations they might have.

As mentioned in chapter 1, the "dope" that was used to varnish, tighten, and waterproof the wings of aircraft, a job performed by women during the war, was poisonous. At least two women, and probably more, died from this work, and many experienced fainting, nausea, and headaches.[74]

More prevalent, however, and responsible for more deaths of women workers, was poisoning from the TNT with which women workers filled shells. The most visible effect of TNT poisoning was jaundice, and the bright yellow coloration of TNT workers' faces and hands, and their bright ginger hair, became their emblems. Tetryl, lyddite, and CE also had the same effect, so that women who worked with these poisonous explosives became publicly known as "canary girls." Mrs. Dean, who worked in Woolwich Arsenal on sewing in the Danger Buildings, was very grateful not to have been made a TNT worker because of their awful yellow coloration and the illness they suffered. She remembered that the TNT workers had their own separate canteen because "everything they touched went yellow, chairs, tables, everything."[75] Lilian Miles, who worked with tetryl, remembered how she was yellow and her black hair

72. Such cases included those reported in *The Pioneer,* 16 February 1917; *Woman's Dreadnought,* 24 February 1917; *Woman Worker,* 15 (March 1917): 1–2.

73. IWM, DSR, 000693/07.

74. "Dope Poisoning: Dangers to Women Aircraft Workers," *Woman's Dreadnought,* 15 July 1916, 511.

75. IWM, DSR, 9381/01.

had gone "practically green": "you'd wash and wash and it didn't make no difference. It didn't come off. Your whole body was yellow."[76]

Some enterprising manufacturers decided that there was a potential market here for preparations promising to restore women workers' skin to its normal color, and advertisements began to appear in the papers and magazines that women workers read (see figure 5). "Ven-Yusa, The Oxygen Face Cream," admonished women workers to "remember, that while it is patriotic for girls to help their country with war-work, it is also patriotic for them to preserve the natural beauty of their skins and complexions with the help of Ven-Yusa."[77]

For the women workers affected, their outward yellowness often meant miserable suffering, if not death. A canteen worker in a munitions factory wrote to *Common Cause* to express her admiration for the tenacity of the women in the Danger Buildings: "the girls turn yellow, and then many of them get horrible rashes, and their faces swell up so that they are for a day or two quite blind, and most repulsive objects. Nevertheless, when they are cured, they go back, and run the risk of getting ill again."[78]

By the middle of 1916 the fact that women and men workers were dying from TNT poisoning gained some publicity.[79] When twenty-year-old Florence Gleave died in May 1917, the *Chronicle* headlined her dying remark to her father: "If I die, they can only say I have done my bit."[80]

An August 1916 report by the Ministry of Munitions noted that, to date in 1916 alone, they were aware of twenty cases of toxic jaundice among men munitions workers and forty-two among women, and that of these, six men and twelve women had died, in addition to two TNT workers who had died of anemia. These figures came from only fifteen munitions factories so they significantly underrepresented the situation.[81] A later report stated that throughout 1916 there had been one hundred

76. IWM, DSR, 000854/04.

77. *Woman's Life,* 7 October 1916, 25; *Woman Worker* 22 (October 1917): 15.

78. *Common Cause,* 29 September 1916, 305.

79. "T.N.T. Poisoning At Woolwich Arsenal," *The Pioneer,* 23 June 1916, 1.

80. "Rudheath Girl Dies For Her Country: 'If I Die, I've Done My Bit,'" *Chronicle,* 19 May 1917. See also "Woman Munition Examiner's Death," *The Times,* 14 October 1916; "Dangers of T.N.T.," *Daily Telegraph,* 14 October 1916. According to Antonia Ineson and Deborah Thom, "T.N.T. Poisoning and the Employment of Women Workers in the First World War," in *The Social History of Occupational Health,* ed. Paul Weindling (London: Croom Helm, 1985), 91–92, from 1916 onward reports on TNT poisoning were censored in both the public newspapers and the medical press in order to keep the public and workers ignorant of the problem.

81. PRO, MUN 5/92/346/38.

eighty-one cases of "toxic jaundice" and fifty-two deaths.[82] By August 1916, due to a leap in the figures in early summer coincident with the buildup for the Battle of the Somme, the Ministry of Munitions was under pressure to take action to prevent further deaths of TNT workers.

On 12 August, the medical journal *The Lancet* published the findings of Drs. Agnes Livingstone-Learmonth and Barbara Martin Cunningham, both medical officers in munitions factories, who had studied women TNT workers for five months.[83] They divided the symptoms of TNT poisoning into irritative ones, including nasal and throat problems, headaches, chest pains, abdominal pain, nausea, vomiting, constipation, diarrhea, and skin rashes; and toxic ones, including continuous "bilious attacks," fainting, swollen hands and feet, drowsiness, depression, and blurred vision. They recommended ventilation of factories because the TNT dust was much of the cause, but pointed out that respirators and masks were problematic because irritation was exacerbated by warmth and moisture. Further, they emphasized the need for good plain food and bland drinks; a protective powder to coat the face; the use and frequent washing of veils, gloves, and overalls; and good "personal cleanliness." They recommended that managers not employ workers under the age of twenty-one or over forty on TNT and that they shift the workers elsewhere after twelve weeks, put them on eight-hour daytime shifts, and provide good washing facilities and a weekly medical examination of each worker.

In May 1916 TNT work had been scheduled as a "dangerous trade," which allowed the home secretary to stipulate conditions for the protection of workers. However, no coherent set of regulations was established until a meeting on 15 August 1916, at which the managers of the national filling factories met with representatives of the Ministry of Munitions and the Health of Munition Workers Committee, and a new section of the ministry was created to administer new regulations dealing with TNT.[84] Prior to this the ministry had appointed medical superintendents to all the larger filling factories. It soon appointed full-time doctors to all the large factories and local doctors on a part-time basis to the smaller ones. With the employment of doctors in the explosives factories and the

82. PRO, MUN 5/94/346/39. Report in 1919.
83. Agnes Livingstone-Learmonth and Barbara Martin Cunningham, "Observations on the Effects of Tri-Nitro-Toluene on Women Workers," *The Lancet* 2 (12 August 1916): 261–64; "Annotations on the Effects of Tri-Nitro-Toluene on Women Workers," *The Lancet* 2 (12 August 1916): 286–87.
84. PRO, MUN 5/92/346/38.

implementation of preventive measures, in 1917 the situation in TNT factories was marginally better than in 1916. While there were more cases of toxic jaundice (189 to 181), there were fewer deaths (44 to 52).[85] By 1918 the efforts at prevention were taking effect: incidences of toxic jaundice dropped to 34 and deaths to 10.[86]

EXPLOSIONS

While there was a concerted effort to reduce the poisoning in explosives factories, the greater danger, that of explosions, was viewed fatalistically. It seems that explosions were thought to be in the hands of a higher power than the ministry or factory managers. The only positive steps taken toward controlling explosions were inspection of workers to remove matches and metal objects, the supply of firefighting equipment, the organization of firefighting personnel at every factory, and the provision of some kind of first aid facility (see figure 6).

Explosions in munitions factories occurred far more often and with worse consequences than the British public ever imagined. At the No. 6 National Shell Filling Factory at Chilwell, near Nottingham, on 1 July 1918 an explosion in the mixing house killed 134 people, including 109 men and 25 women, and injured a few workers seriously and many slightly.[87] Lottie Barker, who worked as a crane driver in the factory, escaped the explosion because she was on the day shift and the accident happened soon after the night shift began. But she vividly recalled hearing and feeling the blast of the explosion from her home, seeing the "huge mushroom spiral of smoke and debris rising to the sky," and rushing toward the factory along with everyone in the neighborhood:

> [W]hat a scene of horror met us. Every available vehicle had been comman-deered to take the casualties to the hospitals. Men, women and young people burnt, practically all their clothing burnt, torn and dishevelled, their faces black and charred, some bleeding with limbs torn off, eyes and hair literally gone. It was rumoured that it was possible the whole mixing house and mills would go up and dad decided it would be best if we made our way to the fields, which we did, still hearing the carts, lorries and ambulances making

85. "Toxic Jaundice," PRO, MUN 5/94/346/39. Page 2 of this memorandum outlines measures in 1917 to compensate affected TNT workers and to regulate conditions in TNT factories.

86. Ibid., later page.

87. PRO, HO 45/10896, report on the explosion, 7 August 1918, 3–7.

their way with their gruesome loads to the hospitals. We came back home after mid-night, but still the conveyances were making their way to Nottingham. The High Road, Beeston had never before seen a cavalcade such as this and I hope please almighty God it never will again.[88]

Explosions in munitions factories were scenes of the war as surely as were battles at the front.

One of the worst explosions of the war was, ironically, one that the government could not successfully cover up because it happened in the East End of London and nearly all of the city either saw the light from it or heard the explosion or both. The explosion occurred on 19 January 1917 at the chemical factory of Brunner, Mond & Co. in Silvertown. The official figures, which were widely held to be lower than the real figures, reported that sixty-nine people were killed and four hundred injured. One of the frightening aspects of the explosion was that the site was directly across the Thames from Woolwich Arsenal, and the flames at one point extended across the river far enough to set alight a gasometer near the arsenal.[89] Buildings in and around Woolwich Arsenal had the glass blown out of their windows, and many arsenal workers panicked, thinking the arsenal itself was going up.

The injury and damage in Silvertown extended beyond the chemical factory and its workers to adjacent factories and blocks of surrounding houses in the densely populated, lower working-class neighborhood.[90] One reporter described the aftermath: "There were whole streets containing just shells of houses, the windows broken, the doors gone, and the ceilings and floors fallen in. . . . The nearer we came to the actual scene the more terrible did the ruins become. Men and women with their heads bandaged, their arms in slings, stood aimlessly about as though on view. Motor-cars filled with well-dressed sight-seers slipped along."[91] Compelled by the horror of the explosion and the widespread knowledge of it through people's own observations and those of the press, the Ministry of Munitions publicly announced that it would "without ad-

---

88. Barker, "My Life as I Remember It," 58–61. For other examples, see Arthur Percival, "The Faversham Gunpowder Industry," *Faversham Papers* no. 4 (The Faversham Society, 1967): 24; Miss O. M. Taylor, "Recollections of the Great War, 1914–1918," IWM, DD, 83/17/1; *Georgetown Gazette* 2, no. 7 (April 1918): 198; *Georgetown Gazette* 2, no. 8 (May 1918): 237.

89. Michael MacDonagh, *In London During The Great War: The Diary of a Journalist* (London: Eyre and Spottiswoode, 1935), 171.

90. "The Great Explosion," *The Pioneer,* 26 January 1917, 3.

91. "The Explosion," *Woman's Dreadnought,* 27 January 1917, 655.

mitting any liability . . . pay reasonable claims for damage to property and personal injuries caused by the explosion."[92]

Most of the explosions in munitions factories during the war occurred on the outskirts of industrial cities or in remote country areas, and so could be kept from wide public knowledge.[93] Quite rightly, the government believed that general knowledge of these tragedies would undermine a public morale already fully challenged by the battlefronts of the war and would jeopardize the labor force necessary for munitions production.

The effect of this blanket of silence on the munitions workers themselves was to build mystery and uncertainty into any doubt or fear they already felt about the dangerous work they were doing. They knew that explosions could and did occur, but they also knew that they were not told the extent of them, even when they happened at the factory in which they worked. In the absence of official reports of explosions at their own factories, the workers' grapevine rapidly supplied an account of each disaster.[94] Caroline Rennles remembered vividly that she and the other workers in her cartridge-filling factory at the arsenal had a particular vantage point from which they could tell when an explosion had occurred: the hospital was right opposite them. One night they saw six ambulances arrive at the hospital, and they knew they were from the arsenal even though management had made no announcement for fear of workers leaving.[95] Although their managers tried to keep them in ignorance, women workers became well aware of the dangers they faced and commonly exhibited great bravery.[96]

A danger of a quite different origin, although with potentially the same effect, was that of the recurrent enemy air raids, either by bomb-carrying zeppelins or airplanes. The raids were frequent enough to become a marked feature of wartime life in London and southeastern England.[97] For those who lived to experience the Blitz on London in World War II,

92. "The Great Explosion," *The Pioneer,* 9 February 1917, 3.

93. There were some newspaper reports of explosions, however. For example, an explosion at a factory in Ashton-under-Lyne on 13 June 1917 that killed forty-one men, women, and children was reported in at least three newspapers. "A TNT Disaster," Beckman Center for the History of Chemistry, *NEWS* 8, no. 2 (Fall 1991): O–4. I am grateful to Alan Rocke for this note.

94. George Truphet, IWM, DSR, 000693/07.

95. IWM, DSR, 000566/07, 18.

96. One manager of a munitions works was quoted as saying, "Bravery is a commonplace with them." *The War-Worker* 2, no. 2 (July 1918): 29.

97. Trevor Wilson, *The Myriad Faces of War: Britain and the Great War 1914–1918* (Cambridge: Polity Press, 1986), 156–57.

the air raids of World War I came to pale by comparison. They were never much more than an exciting tremor on the surface of daily life.

Workers in explosives factories, however, knew that they themselves were the probable targets of these raids and that a well-directed bomb could wreak exponentially greater damage. Rennles recalled an airplane raid one day when she was working in a shell-filling factory at Slades Green in Kent: "Our manager came flying in one day, he said 'Run for your lives, girls' . . . they said there was ninety ton of T.N.T. there. . . . [The men workers] were all soldiers that had come back from the war, you know, so one or two of them grabbed us kids and they run as far . . . as they could and they tore our aprons off us . . . and they made us lie flat on our faces and they covered over these white aprons at the back so that we looked like cows."[98]

Zeppelin raids were a more common experience for night-shift workers than day-shift. Nighttime blacking out of windows was a standard factory regulation, and all workers were supposed to know the procedure to follow in the event of a raid.[99] Workers not uncommonly spent hours sitting in a darkened canteen or other area waiting for the "all clear" to go back to work. During the war Woolwich Arsenal factories, for example, closed down sixty-six times on account of air raids: twenty-nine times because of zeppelins and thirty-seven times because of airplanes. Despite this high incidence of raids, only six bombs were dropped on the arsenal, one of which killed one man and injured nine others.[100]

Zeppelin raids did, quite rationally, engender fear among women workers and some women experienced panic at work, on the way to and from work, and even at home. But they were also good for a joke. YWCA canteen workers became used to being asked for "two Zepps and a cloud," the standard fare of two sausages and mashed potatoes.[101]

Munitions workers were expected to keep a stiff upper lip, to remain calm in the event of an explosion, and to help clean up afterward. Unless the factory was destroyed beyond viability, they were required to present themselves at the start of the next shift as though nothing had happened. For acts of bravery performed under such circumstances, a few workers received public recognition in the form of medals of honor. In October 1917, for example, the Order of the British Empire was bestowed on Jennie Algar "for presence of mind and good example on the occasion of

98. IWM, DSR, 000566/07.
99. Reminiscences of Mrs. Kaye, IWM, DD, P. 371 T.
100. Hogg, *Royal Arsenal,* 959–60.
101. Emily Kinnaird, *Reminiscences* (London: John Murray, 1925), 161.

an explosion at a shell-filling factory," and on Isabella Dixon "for courage in entering a burning room in an explosive factory."[102] More tragically, in January 1918 Agnes Peters of Brighton received the British Empire medal "'for work of an exceptionally dangerous nature' resulting in an accident by which she was 'totally blinded and otherwise injured.'"[103]

The effects of munitions work on the health of women workers in World War I were wildly variant. For the unlucky minority, work in a munitions factory cost them their lives, limbs, hands, fingers, sight, or well-being, sacrifices comparable to those of soldiers. For the majority, fortunate enough to survive the war without being the victim of an explosion, an accident, or poisoning, their improved diet and standard of living were clearly beneficial to their health. On balance, their war experience provided direct evidence to workers of how their well-being was correlated to wages and conditions. They learned what was possible in the way of industrial innovations such as canteens, programs for pregnant workers, and nurseries for their children. Women workers saw that, when they were desperately needed, normal gender restrictions were set aside and the state adopted far-reaching measures to ensure their health and productivity in industry.

102. *Our Own Gazette* (YWCA), 34 (October 1917): 145.
103. "Munition Girl's Heroism," *Daily Sketch,* 12 January 1918.

Status and Experience as Workers

But that 'afterwards'—how the mind begins to tremble at the thought of the difficulties and dangers of peace.

Not the least of its problems will be the demobilization of the factory girls. Will they, indeed, return to the healthier and duller paths of life, with attendant trammels and absence of clean, crinkling Treasury notes every Friday? At present many say they will, but there are troublous days ahead for each and all. Meanwhile, they are learning much, barriers are breaking down, *esprit de corps* is growing up, there is great pride in the turning out of good work, for it is rare indeed to find a girl who sets quantity above quality.

The Englishwoman, *January 1919*

Munitions jobs for women were created by the male state and male industrial employers, because of the (male) war, and were permitted by the powerful, dominant male trade unions. Thus women workers' status and experience as workers was overlaid with their status as women in a patriarchal society. While working-class women were divided from middle-class women in the factory by the tension and alienation of class difference, they were at least united in their knowledge that the sources of power and authority were male. Although women welfare supervisors were part of factory management, for example, they too had to negotiate their position within a male-defined and -controlled environment, under the direction of men. As Sonya Rose shows for industry in nineteenth-century England, class and gender are not separate systems or structures; rather, "the content of class relations is gendered and the content of gender distinctions and gender relations is 'classed.'"[1]

"Tommy's sister" was lured, cajoled, and welcomed into the munitions factories by a barrage of government propaganda, jingoistic journalism, and the public atmosphere of frenzied enthusiasm for any work or effort

---

1. Sonya Rose, *Limited Livelihoods: Gender and Class in Nineteenth-Century England* (Berkeley: University of California Press, 1992), 193.

that would help "our boys" or hasten the progress of the war. Once on the job, the basic facts of her life were determined by the needs of the state and employers. On the factory floor, she was constantly reminded of the patriotic nature and military importance of her work by employers and supervisors anxious to keep up production and minimize absenteeism. Women in munitions factories were allowed some male privileges for the duration of the war, while the nation needed to draw on a fuller range of their capabilities than usual.

It is difficult to disentangle the ways in which women munitions workers were oppressed as workers per se from the ways they were oppressed as women. Under the authority of the state and employers, both of whom continued to subordinate women as workers even though they allowed their wartime jobs and wages, they were also oppressed by the male aristocrats of labor, the skilled workers who feared and fought against the entry of women into their privileged trades. In relation to all others in the world of the factory, working-class women occupied the position of least power, on the underside of all of the three interconnected divisions of gender, class, and managerial authority.

THE MINISTRY OF MUNITIONS: ROLE AND POLICIES

The Ministry of Munitions was created by an act of Parliament in June 1915 to take overall responsibility for the production of munitions of war to meet the needs of the armed forces.[2] Under the Munitions of War Act in July 1915 it was empowered to declare any private munitions works a "controlled establishment" and thereby bring it under the ministry's control. The act further empowered the ministry to introduce a system of leaving certificates to make it almost impossible for workers to leave jobs in munitions. It also established a system of munitions tribunals to deal with offenses committed under the terms of the act. The coercion that the ministry exercised over munitions workers through leaving certificates and munitions tribunals was well beyond that tolerated during peacetime. Under this coercion, munitions workers experienced a system that was military-like in its restrictions and enforcement.

The ministry was authorized to regulate the wages of munitions workers; an amendment act in January 1916 specifically enunciated the power of the minister to control the wages, hours, and conditions of

2. For a history of the Ministry of Munitions in its first two years see Adams, *Arms and the Wizard*.

women workers in munitions factories. Pay rates for women were set down in schedules and appendices to the Munitions of War (Amendment) Act of 1916 and the Munitions of War Act of 1917. By the end of the war, the ministry's orders covered the wage rates of "certainly far in excess" of one million women.[3]

In the first years of the war, one of the ministry's main tasks was to introduce the process known to the ministry, to employers, and to male unionists as "dilution," meaning the employment of unskilled and women workers.[4] In the view of the ministry, women were essential to the production of a sufficient quantity of munitions. Its internal reports disclose a real enthusiasm for the work performed by women and the women's attitudes toward it. One report in January 1916 noted: "Striking instances of the efficiency, trustworthiness, and enthusiasm of woman [*sic*] workers have made their appearance in numerous reports. These newcomers have won their way to the confidence of foremen and works managers, and are proving their usefulness in many new departments."[5]

Beneath the enthusiasm was the need to persuade reluctant employers to "dilute" their work force. The government and other agencies of war propaganda were largely responsible for inducting women into munitions factories, although the government had to obtain the agreement of skilled men's unions to do so. As in other areas, the overarching effect of the war on labor patterns was to accelerate trends that had been occurring for some time. For decades, unions had been concerned about the incursion of unskilled laborers into the preserve of the skilled workers, the "aristocracy of labour." Their fears about women workers in particular were based on, besides patriarchal interests, the fact that women received lower wages than men, making them threatening as a pool from which employers might draw. Likewise, workers in the mechanical trades had been aware of the shift before the war toward machinery that was less esoteric in operation. With both these threats strengthened by the war, the metal and engineering crafts' unions were spurred by insecurity to take a strong stance. The war years, therefore, witnessed a period of

3. Wolfe, *Labour Supply and Regulation,* 295.

4. The word "dilution," used by all governmental and official sources to refer to the entry of women into skilled trades during the war, connotes both the image of women as of weaker, more watery substance than men and the vision of their entry into engineering factories as a threatening flood. For an interpretation of the pervasive cultural and historical equation of the female body with water, floods, and streams, see Klaus Theweleit, *Male Fantasies* 1 (Minneapolis: University of Minnesota Press, 1987), 272–88.

5. Ministry of Munitions, "Report of Intelligence and Record Section," 15 January 1916, PRO, MUN 2/27:3.

increased rank and file militancy and the rise of the shop stewards' movement.[6]

Workers in the Clydeside engineering and munitions works were particularly militant during the war, beginning by staging an important strike in February 1915. This strike was a significant backdrop for the Treasury Conferences of March 1915, the meeting between government and unions at which most unions agreed to suspend union prerogatives for the duration of the war in order that dilution could occur. The Amalgamated Society of Engineers (ASE), the union most nervous about the intrusion of women workers, signed a separate agreement with the government, implicit in which was the promise that all women "dilutees" would be forced out at the end of the war as part of the return to the status quo. The substance of the Treasury Agreements acquired the force of law by being incorporated into the Munitions of War Act in 1915, and the compact between government and male unionists was sealed: the workers would submit to unusual forms of compulsion in order to enhance the war effort, and the government would see to it that they received all their privileges back at the end of the war.[7] In 1919 the ASE pushed the government into passing the Restoration of Pre-War Practices Act to give a procedural form to their promise of a return to the prewar status quo and a deadline after which an employer could be penalized for noncompliance.

The Ministry of Munitions included a "dilution section" whose role in relation to employers was "to help the willing, to convert the unbelieving, and to push the unwilling" to take on unskilled men and women workers.[8] By September 1917 the training section of the Ministry of Munitions had established instructional workshops to train women in the diverse trade skills needed for munitions work "in London, Birmingham, Bristol, Luton, and Manchester . . . in twelve Metropolitan areas and in twenty-four provincial districts, as well as in four centres in Scotland."[9] These courses were for both men and women at first, but the demand for women increased as the war dragged on.

One training course advertised in May 1916 aimed to turn out "shell-makers in six weeks" by giving would-be workers "the chance to learn

6. See James S. Hinton, *The First Shop Stewards' Movement* (London: George Allen & Unwin, 1973).

7. G. D. H. Cole, *A Short History of the British Working Class Movement 1789–1947* (London: George Allen & Unwin, 1948), 354.

8. "Women in Industry," *The Engineer* 123 (1 June 1917): 502.

9. "Ministry Orders: Women Engineers," *The Engineer* 124 (28 September 1917): 279.

something of shell-making before they present themselves as patriots eager to make the munitions which are to help us win the war." Run by the London County Council Education Offices, this course was offered in various areas to make it accessible. Other training courses specialized in teaching welding, electrical repair work, and woodwork, particularly as needed in aircraft construction. Because the airplane industry was new and the demand for planes grew dramatically, women were allowed more opportunities and met with less prejudice in learning skilled work in that industry.[10]

By January 1918 the training centers run by the ministry were paying a weekly maintenance allowance of between 15s. and 25s.[11] Even so, the allowances were not as much as working-class women could make in the factory (particularly with overtime and bonuses), and often they would not opt to earn less for six weeks or so to acquire training that they were not sure they could keep using. T. F. Hirst, who studied the training schools in the engineering trades in South London from 1915 to 1918, has concluded that the women who took advantage of them were either educated and middle-class, or working-class women who had been domestic servants or unemployed before the war. The women who did not enter these schools, according to Hirst, were those who had worked in food factories or other such unskilled manufacturing and for whom immediate earnings were the strongest incentive.[12]

On 23 May 1918 Frederick George Kellaway, Secretary to the Minister of Munitions, was able to announce with satisfaction at the London Exhibition of Women's Work in Munition Production that women were being sent from training schools into munitions factories at the steady rate of five hundred a week, and that "since the Ministry of Munitions had started the schools between 40,000 and 50,000 trained women had been placed in munitions industries."[13] That thousands of working-class women had received the benefit of this job training, besides the more privileged women "doing their bit," should have been a significant factor of change in the profile of the female work force after the war. But in fact, neither the ministry, the unions, nor most employers saw this process as permanently entitling women workers to a greater share in skilled jobs

10. "Technical Training for Women," *Common Cause,* 11 February 1916, 582.
11. "Home and Empire Club," *Our Own Gazette* (YWCA) 36 (January 1918): 25.
12. T. F. Hirst, "An Investigation of the Incorporation of Women Into the Engineering Trades in South London Between 1914–1918," (M.Ed. thesis, University of Reading, 1976), 49–50.
13. "Women Help More In War," *New York Times,* 24 May 1918, 3.

and higher rates of pay. Rather, they were trained to do specific tasks for the duration, and the schools were not set up to attract the bulk of women workers, those who needed most to earn what they could.

EMPLOYERS' ATTITUDES

For dilution to succeed, and for production to be what it needed to be, it was critical that employers accept women as workers. This was, however, not entirely straightforward. Women workers cost less than men to employ and were regarded as more docile, but employers often shared with male unionists a patriarchal resistance to the presence of women. This was complicated for employers by the need to provide extra facilities for women in the factory: at first, this meant a separate toilet facility, but as the war went on and the welfare movement gained impetus under the Ministry of Munitions, it came to mean washing, changing, canteen, and first aid facilities also (although these benefited men workers too).

Ultimately, employers had no choice. They wanted munitions contracts and needed workers; if men were not available, they had to turn to boys, women, and girls. Faced with the fact that "employers themselves have been and still are the greatest obstacle to dilution," the ministry girded itself with determination and propaganda.[14] Revealing its tactics, a January 1916 report noted: "Employers are showing great interest in experiments in the employment of female labour. These are having the result of increasing very rapidly the sphere of women's usefulness in the factory. When visiting firms inspectors constantly find women employed on new work, and spread the news to other firms of how such work can be arranged."[15]

The ministry was aware that some of the reasons for the success of dilution with women workers did not relate to women's aptitude for the work. *The Englishwoman* reported the view of the manager of one large factory that women workers "are just splendid, eager and quick to learn, punctual and regular in attendance, obedient and tractable, and they don't 'raise trouble.'"[16] Moreover, women's wages were less than men's.

Yet most owners and managers of munitions firms remained at least ambivalent about employing women in areas in which they had tradi-

14. "Women In Industry," *The Engineer,* 1 June 1917, 502.
15. PRO, MUN 2/27, 15 January 1916.
16. Mrs. Ellis Chadwick, "The Women Munitioners: Their Bit," *The Englishwoman,* September 1916. See also PRO, MUN 2/28, sec. 12, 24 February 1917.

tionally employed only men. One cause of their apprehension was the underlying reason why it was possible to train unskilled men and women so quickly: changes in machinery facilitated the process of dilution and signaled that fully skilled workers would not be as necessary after the war. There was clear incentive for the employers in this prospect, as unskilled and semiskilled workers drew lower wages. However, their resistance to change is apparent in the reports and discussions of dilution in their journal *The Engineer*.

The exhibition of skilled work by women staged by the ministry in March 1917 created anxiety of a different order among employers. To this point, many had regarded women workers as semiskilled at best, performing skilled work only when it was broken down into component parts. A report on the work shown at the exhibition, however, admitted that women were now fully operating mechanics' machines and tools, taking over from skilled men workers. "The design of the machines has in no respect been simplified to suit the limitations which women might be thought to possess. . . . Whatever the machine, the women, once trained, can do with it all that its design permits."[17] Provoked by the ministry's display of women's work, *The Engineer* called on employers to face up to the significance of the existence of trained women mechanics:

> What attitude should the manufacturing engineer adopt towards this devel-
> opment? Women labour, introduced tentatively into munitions factories solely
> for war emergency purposes, has within two years become something more
> than a passing phenomenon. The woman engineer is not yet, but the skilled
> woman mechanic is with us to-day and may remain with us for the future.
> . . . Whatever time can now be spared should be spent in considering the
> matter in all its bearings.[18]

Although employers recognized that this new development held potential benefit to themselves, they worried rightly about the conflict with male workers and trade unions that the new situation heralded.

On 15 March 1918, the Institution of Mechanical Engineers took an unprecedented step: they allowed themselves to be addressed by a woman. Miss O. E. Monkhouse, on the staff of the Ministry of Munitions, addressed the engineers on the topic of "The Employment of Women in Munition Factories." The discussion following her paper was so animated that it went overtime and then had to be continued at the next meeting

17. "Skilled Women Mechanics," *The Engineer,* 30 March 1917, 296.
18. "Women Mechanics," *The Engineer,* 30 March 1917, 293.

on 3 May. Despite the intensity of debate, no consensus among the engineers and employers was apparent; in fact, the opinions expressed ranged over a wide spectrum. Mr. Charles Wicksteed, who owned a small works employing "a hundred girls" in a town of thirty thousand inhabitants, complained of the bad timekeeping of his women workers and asserted that the "girls were not so truthful, or so honest, or so reliable as the men, and now and then they seemed to lose themselves." He concluded that "men need not be afraid of the competition of women as engineers, and that he was convinced that the girls would all be dispensed with after the War." This view was not by any means representative. He was taken to task by, for one, Mr. William H. Allen, vice-president of the institution, who, with his son, ran an engineering firm in Bedford that employed "nine hundred girls." Mr. Allen's view was that

> there had been no trouble with the girls in any way; provided they were left alone, they did their work. . . . They had come literally out of the streets and had not been away from their homes before. He suggested that girls should be properly apprenticed; why should they not be? It might be a great change in the status of England to do such a thing, but it would be to our enormous industrial advantage to have those one and a half million women helping in the engineering industry after the war. He hoped the trades unions would not be offended with him for making such a suggestion. There would be work enough for everybody.[19]

But the trade unions refused to countenance allowing women to stay on in skilled engineering work after the war.[20]

JOB MOBILITY AND MUNITIONS TRIBUNALS

Some women workers left one munitions job for another, enticed by higher wages, bonus schemes, or the promise of a better job. Mrs. P. L. Stephens's story was an exceptional case of mobility, in part because early on in the war she bought a secondhand Triumph motorcycle and thus gained her freedom. Her first munitions job was as a fuse examiner in Bradford, Yorkshire, in late 1915. From there she went to Birmingham and learned to work a capstan lathe, cutting fins on airplane cylinders, and thence to Southampton where she worked first as a cordite examiner

19. "Employment of Women in Munition Factories," *Excerpt Minutes of Proceedings of the Meetings of the Institution of Mechanical Engineers* (London: Institution of Mechanical Engineers, 1918), 223–25, 231–33.

20. For a longer discussion of employers' and male trade unionists' attitudes toward women workers, see Braybon, *Women Workers,* ch. 3.

and later at Pemberton Billings's on a cutting machine. After her last munitions job in Lincoln, again on a capstan lathe, bored her, she found her ideal wartime job: she became a motorcycle chauffeur and courier at the R. A. F. Scampton Aerodrome.[21]

Mrs. Stephens's story is unusual, partly because of her restlessness and her resourceful independence, but also because the Ministry of Munitions had established a system in which workers could not simply decide to leave a job. Anxious to keep the vital munitions industry work force in place, a system of "leaving certificates" was instituted. Any worker who lost a job in a munitions factory, either through being sacked or laid off, was required to have a certificate to that effect from the employer. If a worker left a munitions job without such a certificate, any employer hiring her within the next six weeks was liable to punishment, and she herself was not allowed any unemployment benefit in the interval. This system was introduced under Section 7 of the Munitions of War Act of 1915.

The Munitions of War Act established a system of special courts to try any offenses committed under its provisions. There were two kinds of munitions tribunals, the general tribunals that had jurisdiction over the more important offenses, such as trade disputes, and local tribunals that covered "domestic" offenses. In both cases the tribunal was to consist of a chair appointed by the Minister of Munitions and an even number of assessors drawn equally, on a rotating basis, from separate panels representing employers and workers. Complaints could be lodged before either class of tribunal by any aggrieved worker or employer, by the Ministry of Munitions, or by a trade union representative of a worker if the complaint occurred under Section 7. The act listed twelve kinds of offenses that could be committed by an employer, such as failing to comply with the terms of a dispute settlement or changing the rates of pay without the ministry's approval, and seven kinds of offenses that could be committed by a worker, such as taking part in a strike or breaking the rules about wearing badges for war work. For each offense the act listed the maximum fine to be imposed (ranging from three to fifty pounds).[22]

Statistics gathered in July 1916 indicate the significance of munitions tribunals. Up to 24 June 1916 there had been 20,625 cases heard, 346 before the general tribunals and 20,279 before the local ones. These cases had involved 31,790 defendants, about half of whom were employers

21. Mrs. P. L. Stephens, "My War Service during World War I—1914–1918," IWM, DD, "P"348 W/W/1 T.
22. "Munitions of War Act, 1915: Munitions Tribunals," PRO, HO 45/10785.

and half workers. Prosecutions had involved 16,177 defendants, with 11,223 convictions, and the total amount of fines paid by that date was £11,413 0s. 8d. Only 3,850 leaving certificates had been granted, out of 14,596 applications. The number of workers claiming compensation for dismissal or refusal of certificates was 1,013, but only 419 had been awarded compensation and they had shared merely £873 7s. 5d.[23] The rate of munitions tribunals cases escalated from a weekly average of 0.5 in July 1915 to 314 in December 1915, and to 772 in June 1916.[24]

Women workers resorted to munitions tribunals for leaving certificates for a variety of reasons. In December 1915 an eighteen-year-old woman asked the Birmingham tribunal to grant her a certificate because she was earning only 10s. 6d. per week; the tribunal held that this rate was less than that agreed on by the Midland Employers' Federation and the Workers' Union and granted her the certificate.[25] A few months later a woman was granted a certificate by the Coventry tribunal because she could not do night work as she needed to look after her young children, and refused to do the day work of the firm because it was dangerous work.[26] In May 1916 six women employed by Messrs. Buchanan & Sons applied to the Liverpool tribunal for leaving certificates because the firm had no work to give them and therefore was not paying them but had refused them certificates because work might start again soon: the certificates were granted.[27]

One of the problems generated by the leaving certificate system was a widespread confusion about which jobs were munitions within the definition of the act and therefore required leaving certificates. Evie May, aged sixteen, asked the London tribunal for a leaving certificate from her job with a firm that manufactured "micamite" insulation for dynamos for the admiralty: the tribunal decided that the firm was in manufacturing rather than engineering and therefore did not fall under the definition.[28] Several women shirtmakers were turned away by the Woolwich Labour Exchange wrongly, on the grounds that they did not have leaving certificates, when in fact they did not need them.[29] This kind of confusion was

---

23. PRO, MUN 5/97/349/5.
24. "Return of Cases Heard before Munitions Tribunals," PRO, MUN 5/98:3.
25. "Report of Intelligence and Record Section," 1 January 1916, PRO, MUN 2/27:3.
26. Ibid., 4 March 1916, 8.
27. "Liverpool Munitions Court," *Woman Worker* 5 (May 1916), 4.
28. "News and Notes," *Woman Worker* 4 (April 1916).
29. *Woman's Dreadnought*, 29 January 1916, 413.

one cause of a profound resentment of the control that the Ministry of Munitions exercised over workers.

The National Federation of Women Workers (NFWW) constantly protested against the system and represented women workers at munitions tribunals as often as it could. When moves were afoot in the middle of 1917 to amend the acts that had established leaving certificates, the federation earnestly pressed its views on the relevant parliamentarians and officials of the Ministry of Munitions.[30] When Winston Churchill, Minister of Munitions, announced in late September 1917 that leaving certificates would be abolished as of 15 October, there was great relief among workers, and *The Pioneer* even ran the news as a front-page banner headline.[31] A woman munitions tribunal assessor hailed the abolition as an important restitution of freedom: "For nearly two years the leaving certificate system was an intolerably irksome burden both to men and women. The very withholding of liberty which it involved tended, I believe, to make the workers less willing to put up with the rubs and disagreeables that came in their way, and the very feeling that change was impossible, made change seem desirable for its own sake."[32]

The NFWW could also claim at least part of the credit for the section in the 1916 Amendment Act that stipulated the presence of at least one woman at tribunals where women's cases were heard. There were several ways in which it helped women workers to have a woman present as a tribunal assessor. One reason was exemplified by a case in November 1915 when a group of young women asked for leaving certificates because of the sexual harassment they were suffering from a foreman. Because "the girls were too shy to state plainly to a tribunal exclusively masculine what the foreman had done," the presiding lawyer made light of the case and was about to dismiss their application until someone "quietly intimated" to him just what was the nature of their complaint.[33] A related reason was the moral support that a sympathetic woman could give young women otherwise very intimidated by their surroundings. One woman assessor described their nervousness: "Young girls, some of them almost

30. "The New Munitions Bill: How the Federation Fought and Won," *Woman Worker* 21 (September 1917): 3.

31. "Winston Churchill Abolishes Leaving Certificates," *The Pioneer,* 28 September 1917.

32. "The Amended Munitions Court," *The Englishwoman* 37 (March 1918): 218–19.

33. "Women Assessors Wanted for Munitions Courts," *Common Cause,* 26 November 1915, 434.

children, [appear] before the court; they are tongue-tied with terror of the ordeal which they will have to go through; they are unable to distinguish between the tribunal and a police-court, especially as it is generally held in the same place, only without the policemen."[34]

Lilian Bineham stood in front of a munitions tribunal at Caxton Hall, Westminster, in the middle of her time at Woolwich Arsenal. She and her best friend had had their uniforms stolen or misplaced from their shift-inghouse and were therefore compelled to go to the office to get new ones when a manager, with whom they had once before had a trivial run-in, saw them, accused them of "skiving off" from work, and laid a charge against them. They were clearly overawed by the atmosphere at Caxton Hall, so much so that on their way out they had to ask the door porter how much they had been fined because they had been too nervous to listen. They were also upset at the size of their 5s. fine, which represented a lot of money to them, but overall Bineham remembered the whole incident as "a great joke."[35] The prospect of attending a munitions tribunal was not a joke, however, for one unfortunate fourteen-year-old Birmingham girl who, a day or two before she was to appear in front of the tribunal, threw herself into a canal. She was rescued but was still unconscious in the hospital when her case was called, so the tribunal dismissed it.[36]

Women assessors played a critical role in tribunal cases of women workers because many men failed to perceive the reality of women's lives.[37] One common charge laid against women workers by their employers was that they were bad timekeepers. An irate letter to the editor of the *Midland Daily Telegraph* fumed that the "way women are prosecuted for losing time, mainly due to indisposition or domestic trouble, is nothing short of refined cruelty."[38]

Munitions tribunals were used by munitions firms to punish workers for a whole gamut of offenses—an institutionalized form of control that invoked the authority of the government. A Teesside munitions firm took a woman worker to the tribunal over her refusal to carry cast-iron frames weighing about a hundred pounds when men doing the same work were

34. "Women in the Munitions Court," *The Englishwoman* 33 (March 1917): 213.

35. IWM, DSR, 8778/02.

36. "Girl's Dread of Tribunal: A Leap into the Canal," *Woman Worker* 13 (January 1917): 4.

37. "Some Impressions of a Woman Assessor," *Woman Worker* 10 (October 1916): 5.

38. "Women Munition Workers," *Midland Daily Telegraph*, 1 November 1916. See also "Women in Works: Not all Slackers in Sheffield," *Sheffield Independent*, 28 August 1916; "Women in the Munition Courts," *The Englishwoman* 33 (March 1917).

allowed assistance.[39] Conversely, some women workers, at least, identified in munitions tribunals a way in which they could fight for their rights. Large numbers of women workers joined the NFWW and the National Union of General Workers and cooperated with them in fighting tribunal cases on their behalf to secure the payment of just wage rates. Gerry Rubin, who studied the munitions tribunals in Glasgow from 1915 to 1921, found that women workers' participation in munitions tribunals revealed an assertiveness and a confidence that belied the usual conception of women workers at this time as passive and docile.[40]

A last sting in the tail of the munitions tribunal system was, ironically, the way it was used against both women workers and employers by men workers and their unions after the war to enforce the implementation of the Restoration of Pre-War Practices Act of 1919. Thus when, for example, the firm of Smith Barker and Willson continued after the war to employ women on fitting, turning, slotting, and general machine work, they were brought before the Halifax Local Munitions Tribunal by one Arthur Taylor on 26 January 1920. The firm argued that they were not committing an offense under the act because both the machinery and the work processes were different from those used before the war, but they lost their case and were fined fifty pounds.[41]

TRADE UNIONISM AND WOMEN'S INDUSTRIAL ASSERTIVENESS

Wartime growth in union organization was an acceleration of a prewar trend rather than a new phenomenon. In 1896 the female membership of all unions affiliated with the Trades Union Congress in Britain was 118,000. In 1906, this figure rose to 167,000, of which 85 percent were women textile workers.[42] During the war, women joined trade unions at a much greater rate. Whereas at the end of 1914 there were 360,936

39. "Assistance Provided for Men Denied to Women," *Woman's Dreadnought*, 10 February 1917, 671. See also "A Day in a Munitions Court," *Woman Worker* 17 (May 1917): 11.

40. Gerry R. Rubin, "The Enforcement of the Munitions of War Acts, 1915–1917, with particular reference to Proceedings before the Munitions Tribunal in Glasgow, 1915–1921" (Ph.D. thesis, University of Warwick, 1984).

41. Arthur Taylor v. Smith Barker & Willson, Halifax Local Munitions Tribunal, 26 January 1920, PRO, LAB 2/58/M.T.133/6/1916 PTII.

42. Margaret G. Bondfield, "Women's Trade Unions," in Gates, ed., *The Woman's Year Book 1923–1924*, 336.

women in trade unions, this had jumped to 773,663 by the end of 1917, and to 1,086,000 by the end of the war.[43]

The 200 percent increase in women trade unionists during the war reflected a new enthusiasm for unionism among women.[44] This altered attitude was forged by being in factories where they mingled with many others like themselves instead of being isolated as domestic servants or in small laundries or workshops, by being in continuous employment, and by higher wages that meant they could afford union dues. Moreover, women witnessed the effectiveness of union representations to the Ministry of Munitions, thanks to which, to some degree, their wages rose steadily during the war. Joan Williams, a middle-class "war worker" who did not join a union and was offended by the examples of women's labor militancy around her, stated that she had actually intended to join the "Women's Union" (presumably the NFWW) because "I believe they got us the Government rises which I was very glad to benefit by."[45] Women's wider belief in union organization was furthered by the self-esteem they acquired through doing men's jobs, earning more money, living at a higher standard, and enjoying more autonomy over their income.

Women munitions workers mostly joined the large general unions that enrolled the mass of unskilled workers in a range of trades. The general unions that welcomed women workers and actively recruited them during the war were the Workers' Union, the National Union of General Workers, and the NFWW.[46] The most prominent woman union organizer was Mary R. Macarthur, secretary of the NFWW, who had served on the executive committee of the Women's Trade Union League since 1903, but a whole league of women union organizers worked hard at recruiting during the war.

The NFWW had been formed in 1906 to recruit women in isolated

43. Ministry of Reconstruction, *Report of the Women's Employment Committee,* 94; Barbara Drake, *Women in Trade Unions* (London: Labour Research Department and George Allen & Unwin, 1920; reprint, London: Virago, 1984), 97; Norbert C. Soldon, *Women in British Trade Unions 1874–1976* (Dublin: Gill and Macmillan, 1978), 98; Sarah Boston, *Women Workers and the Trade Union Movement* (London: Davis-Poynter, 1980), 126.

44. Norbert Soldon and Sarah Boston have extremely different calculations of the percentage increase of female trade union membership but agree on the 45 percent increase for men. Soldon, *Women in British Trade Unions,* 98; Boston, *Women Workers,* 126.

45. "A Munition Workers' [*sic*] Career," IWM, DPB, 42.

46. Clear evidence of the craft unions' attitude toward women workers is the fact that they did not try to recruit the eligible newcomers. The skilled men's unions did, however, actively push for equal rates of pay for women doing the same work as their members, for it was vital to their interests to maintain pay rates and avoid being undercut. G. D. H. Cole, *Workshop Organization* (Oxford: Clarendon Press, 1923), 41.

trades not yet organized. By 1912 it had seventy-one branches and over twelve thousand members.[47] During the war the NFWW set out to recruit members among women workers in munitions factories around the country. By the time of the Armistice, the NFWW's membership was around eighty thousand, which was about the same as the female membership of the Workers' Union but greater than that of the National Union of General Workers, which boasted sixty thousand. Although the three general unions were competing among women munitions workers for members, their total female membership jumped from about 24,000 in 1914 to about 216,000 in 1918.[48]

Needless to say, munitions employers did not always welcome union organization. At Creed's Munition Factory in Croydon, workers were receiving only 8s. a week. When a worker held a meeting at her lodgings in order to start a branch of the NFWW, she was dismissed the next day.[49]

Despite the majority of women munitions workers having access only to the general labor unions, some slight breakthroughs were made during the war in establishing skilled unions for women. The Society for Women Welders was formed in 1916 as a union for women who had acquired training and become oxyacetylene welders.[50] By 1918 its membership had grown to 630, by which time also it had achieved equal pay for its workers at firms in Bristol, Cheltenham, Manchester, and London.[51] Toward the end of the war a few craft unions, other than the ASE, agreed to accept skilled women munitions workers as members, and the NFWW arranged for transfers of their eligible members.[52] The ASE, which had been formed in 1851, did not admit women members until 1943, the longest exclusion of women by any British craft union in the modern period.[53]

The opinions of commentators varied with respect to the general interest shown by women workers in union activity. Some observers thought women workers docile and apolitical, in keeping with the stereotypical image that had long been held of them. A welfare supervisor at the royal factory at Gretna, for example, commented at the end of the war that "they are generally contented and not prone to agitation over

47. "Women Workers: Trade Union League's Report on a Busy Year," *Daily Herald*, 22 May 1912.
48. Drake, *Women in Trade Unions*, 97.
49. "8s. a Week for Munition Work!" *Woman's Dreadnought*, 5 February 1916, 418.
50. "The Society of Women Welders," *Common Cause*, 27 April 1917, 27–28.
51. Women's Trade Union League, *Forty-third Annual Report* (1918), 5.
52. Ibid., 2.
53. Walby, *Patriarchy at Work*, app. 1:250.

unimportant working conditions. They have great faith in the integrity of their employers and so long as there is no injustice done they remain satisfied."[54] It is probably relevant here, however, that the factory at Gretna was brand new, excellent facilities were built as part of the township, and there was much provision made for the well-being of the workers.

In contrast, other commentators believed that women workers evinced decided interest in their rights as workers and in union organization during the war. A girls' club leader asserted at the end of the war: "I have been startled by the growth and strength of the trade union movement among my own club members. I overhear them discussing work and wage conditions, and their language is free and forcible. Just how far their opinions have been solidified into action I do not know, but employers of female labour in years to come will find the women workers a difficult lot to handle. To gain their point they will 'rise as one man.'"[55] Similarly, Adelaide Anderson, Principal Lady Inspector of Factories, recorded her observations:

> In addition to the gain of a higher standard in women's own expectation as regards their conditions, there is a new atmosphere in the factories, traceable to the women's increased self-reliance engendered by the appreciation that has been expressed for their work and capacity. No one can realise this more thoroughly than Women Factory Inspectors, meeting it as they do on the spot, and there comparing past and present. In a factory where formerly a woman worker would not have disclosed the fact that she belonged to a trade union, there is a woman shop steward ready to come forward and show the Inspector round, the manager expecting her to do so.[56]

Not only is Anderson's testimony authoritative, it is also borne out by the statistics.

Women's level of strike activity, however, seems to have been far below that of men. The following figures are from my survey of the internal reports of the Intelligence and Record Section of the Ministry of Munitions, which were printed weekly and always incorporated a section on trade disputes, for the period from 1 January to 30 June 1917. Out of 201 trade disputes, 129 were started by men, 16 were started by women, 15 were started by women and men together, and in 41 cases the sex of

54. "Report: Women and Their Work during the War at H. M. Factory, Gretna," 1919, IWM, Women's Work Collection, Mun. 14/8, 33.

55. "War Girls 'Pack Up,'" *Daily Mail,* 9 November 1918, 2.

56. Anderson, *Women in the Factory,* 247. See also Beryl Stanley, "Women in Unrest, 1914–1918," *Labour Monthly* 22 (August 1940): 458.

the instigators was not reported.[57] One of the disputes begun by women, for example, was a strike staged by about three thousand women workers employed by Messrs. Greenwood and Batley Ltd. of Leeds on 31 January 1917. The women's protest was over wages, specifically a demand for a war bonus of 4s. a week, because their piecework rates had recently been altered. Six hundred men were idled by the strike because their work was dependent on that of the women. Surprisingly, the women were not members of a union.[58]

Policewoman G. M. West's experience was that, indeed, women workers, at least in some factories, were prone to striking. She recorded several strikes in which she and other policewomen played the role of strikebreakers. At the cordite factory in Pembrey, South Wales, to which she was assigned early in the war, she commented on one segment of the women workers: "Then there are the relatives of the miners from the Rhondda & other coal pits near. They are full of socialistic theories & very great on getting up strikes. But they are very easily influenced by a little oratory, & go back to work like lambs if you spout at them long enough."[59]

DEMOBILIZATION

In late 1917 women munitions workers began to be laid off, then wider demobilization began when Russian armaments orders were canceled, the effect of which was felt early in 1918. When one thousand women were dismissed from a Leeds munitions firm in February 1918, the district secretary of the NFWW (to which a number of them belonged) stated that most of them had been in the wholesale clothing trade before the war, some of them did not want to go back to that trade after the wages they had enjoyed on munitions work, and even the ones who were prepared to go back could not find jobs.[60] These and other women dismissed soon afterward in the same district met with a hostile reaction to their demand for unemployment benefits of 30s. a week, which was probably less than they were earning on munitions, but certainly more than they had earned before the war. Some of the dismissed women reported being "subjected to some unpleasantness, both in the streets and in the tramcars" in the form of jeering comments from people who

57. PRO, MUN 2.28, reports of the Intelligence and Record Section of the Ministry of Munitions for the first half of 1917.

58. Ibid., 3 February 1917, 14.

59. Diary of Miss G. M. West, 10 March 1917, IWM, DD, 77/156/1.

60. *Yorkshire Post,* 21 February 1918.

thought that they should have saved money while they were working instead of asking for unemployment benefits.[61]

In March 1918 the problem intensified as more women were dismissed, such as the eight hundred let go from Kynoch's munitions works at Stanford-le-hope in Essex.[62] At the end of the month, the Ministry of Munitions received a deputation from the National Federation of Discharged and Demobilised Soldiers, which protested that its members were "not being fairly treated in regard to the influx of woman labour, and that men who had fought and been wounded were being released and their places filled by women and girls" in munitions factories.[63] Thus, eight months before the end of the war, the issues surrounding demobilization had already been laid out.

For women munitions workers, as for the rest of the nation and the empire, the Armistice on 11 November 1918 was a day for immoderate rejoicing, even though for many the shadow of personal loss hung over all celebration. One witness to the Armistice celebrations on the Strand in London observed: "It was the women that I noticed most: they were wilder than the men, making more noise, cheering, shouting and singing themselves hoarse, dancing and romping themselves tired. Quite undisguisedly the soldiers were led by them. It was Woman's Carnival as well as Victory Night."[64]

Joy was shortlived for most women workers, except perhaps for those whose men survived and returned home safely to them. The peace was quickly soured by the angry protests of workers displaced and desperate for employment and financial security. At the time of the Armistice, the government promised an "out-of-work pay" to women workers who had been or were about to be dismissed. The pay was to be 20s. a week (compared to 24s. a week for men), but the government did not say when it was to start; in the meantime, discharged women were receiving 7s. a week.[65] Girls under eighteen years old were only entitled to 3s. 6d. a week.[66]

On 19 November, "Whitehall was considerably astonished" when about six thousand women munitions workers, coming chiefly from

61. Ibid., 26 February 1918.
62. Munson, ed., *Echoes of the Great War,* 4 March 1918, 228.
63. *The Pioneer,* 29 March 1918, 1.
64. C. G. Hartley, *Women's Wild Oats: Essays on the Re-fixing of Moral Standards* (London: T. Werner Laurie Ltd., 1919), 9.
65. "Munition Girls' Out-of-Work Pay: Unfulfilled Promise of the Government," *Daily News and Leader,* 16 November 1918.
66. "Unemployment Insurance," *Woman's Dreadnought,* 7 October 1916, 561.

Woolwich Arsenal but complemented by others from munitions factories all over London, marched on Parliament to convey to the prime minister and the Ministry of Munitions their demand for "immediate guarantees for the future." The women marched in a procession with "many large and small banners, and each one of them wearing her munitions badge." When they reached Whitehall they were "in excellent order and loudly cheered by soldiers and others, marched past the Horse Guards, accompanied their deputation to the Ministry, and then proceeded to Kingsway Hall to await the result."[67] The *Woman Worker's* account of this demonstration was highly excited, noting the banner that read "Shall Peace Mean Starvation?" and "Rise like lions out of slumber, In inconquerable number."[68] On 3 December, another group of women munitions workers, this time five or six hundred women all from the same firm that was about to lose its government contract, marched to Downing Street and demanded to see Lloyd George. Rebuffed by the prime minister, a deputation from the protesters was met by some officials at the Ministry of Munitions, but the women refused to be placated, "demanded the immediate withdrawal of their discharges, and their attitude, it was said at the Ministry of Munitions, was uncompromising." Even after this interview, the "women continued to parade through the streets for hours."[69] Such spontaneous protest by munitions workers is evidence of a sense of group identity and of their value as workers that had not been widespread among women workers before the war.

The complete out-of-work benefit offered to women at first was 20s. a week, or 3s. 4d. a day, for thirteen weeks; widows and women with dependent children were entitled to claim an extra weekly benefit of 6s. a week for the first child and 3s. a week for any other.[70] Within a couple of months, the benefit for women was raised to 25s. a week.[71] In Birmingham, by 11 December there were estimated to be ten times more women unemployed than men.[72] In Newcastle, by 20 December there were fifteen thousand women unemployed, most of whom were dismissed

67. "6,000 Women March to Whitehall: Munition Workers' Demands," *The Times,* 20 November 1918.

68. "March of the Woolwich Women," *Woman Worker* 36 (December 1918): 11.

69. "London Women Protest: Discharged War Workers Besiege Downing St. and Munitions Ministry," *New York Times,* 4 December 1918, 3.

70. "Woolwich Girls Return Home: Satisfactory Plan to Secure Work: Labour Exchanges & the Problem," *Daily News and Leader,* 27 November 1918.

71. *Our Own Gazette* (YWCA) 37 (January 1919): 9; Letter to editor from "Mother of Six," *Manchester,* 14 February 1919.

72. *The Times,* 11 December 1918.

munitions workers, and it was expected that more would be unemployed by Christmas. Of these unemployed women, "scores have daily to be turned away disappointed from the Women's Employment Exchange at the Old Infirmary" due to the lack of available work.[73]

Months into 1919, the gloomy prospects for many dismissed women workers were still unalleviated. On 7 February 427,734 women and 26,770 girls (under eighteen) were receiving the out-of-work benefit; at the beginning of April these figures had actually increased to 486,945 women and 31,070 girls.[74] The government, however, on the basis that most dismissed women had now enjoyed their thirteen weeks of "out-of-work pay," reduced the unemployment benefit women could receive to 15s. a week.[75]

The administration of unemployment benefits was bitterly criticized throughout these months by the labor movement. Women who turned down any job, no matter how low the wage or unattractive the work, were cut off from receiving the benefit. In March 1919 the *Labour Woman* reported that in one district where seven hundred women had recently been discharged, the highest wages offered were 15s. a week, and one woman had been struck off from the benefit for refusing a job paying 3s. a week. In Manchester, in one week a thousand women lost their appeals against being refused unemployment benefits.[76] In April 1919 the NFWW reported numerous cases of refusal of the benefit, such as that of one woman who refused a domestic service job paying 8s. 6d. a week, and another who turned down a live-in domestic service position because her husband was expected home soon.[77]

Few women had any luck at the employment exchanges where they registered. The advice they commonly received was to look for work in domestic service. A minority of women workers were fortunate to find that their employers had continuing need of them even though peace had been restored. Beatrice Lee, who had worked for most of the war as an electric crane driver at the Yorkshire Copper Works in Leeds, was one of only two women crane drivers kept on when they let the other women drivers go. When her husband returned from the war he was ill and

73. "Dismissal of Munition Workers: 15,000 Girls Idle in Newcastle," *Newcastle Daily Journal*, 20 December 1918.

74. "Demobilised Women Workers," *Labour Woman* 7 (March 1919): 30; "News of the Month," *Our Own Gazette* (YWCA) 37, no. 5 (May 1919).

75. "The Unemployed Woman," *Labour Woman* 7 (April 1919): 39.

76. *Labour Woman* 7 (March 1919): 30.

77. Ibid., 7 (April 1919): 39.

unable to work, so it was lucky that she was kept on as a crane driver and later as an inspector; she gave up the job sometime later when she was pregnant.[78]

The demobilization of women munitions workers ran into a thicket of issues surrounding the status of women in the labor force. Some women tried to salvage professional or craft status out of their wartime work, particularly members of the Women's Engineering Society and the Society of Women Welders.[79] Their hopes ran up against unionists like the Burnley and District Allied Engineering Trades, which declared that as of 24 May 1919 no local engineering shops were to employ *any* female labor.[80] As the unions for skilled and semiskilled trades had insisted in 1915, and as they were now prepared to enforce under the Restoration of Pre-War Practices Act of 1919, all "dilutees" were to give up their jobs. This act sought to reintroduce prewar trade practices, union rules, and the privileges of skilled workers by compelling all munitions industries to return to the old practices within two months of the passing of the act and to maintain such practices for a year following the act. Any employer not complying with prewar practices (particularly by continuing to employ workers considered unskilled, mostly women) was liable to be called before the munitions tribunals, which were sustained for this purpose, and was further liable to fines that the tribunals were empowered to levy.[81] Male unionists were determined to exclude women in order to ensure that men should be employed and the prewar hierarchy of labor reinstated.

On the whole, women workers acquiesced in this attempt to restore the prewar status quo. Most women accepted that they ought to vacate jobs that would be needed by returning servicemen, but they protested dismissal where it was not clear that their job was one that a serviceman would want.

The reality of women's lives dictated having to make a choice from severely limited options. Two days before the Armistice, a journalist printed the results of an "informal plebiscite" she or he had taken among the more than a thousand members of a particular girls' club, on the

78. IWM, DSR, 000724/06.
79. "The Women Welders," *Common Cause*, 7 March 1919, 566; Carroll Pursell, "'Am I A Lady or An Engineer?': The Origins of the Women's Engineering Society in Britain 1918–1927," *Technology and Culture* 34 (January 1993): 78–97.
80. *Daily News*, 13 May 1919.
81. Restoration of Pre-War Practices Act, 9 & 10 Geo. 5, ch. 42, 15 August 1919, 1–3.

question of their plans for when peacetime resumed. Not all the young women polled were munitions workers; 70 percent of them were shop, office, and warehouse workers. The results of the poll, nonetheless, are valuable. Ten percent of the young women answered that they planned "peace weddings" and were anticipating having homes of their own, while 5 percent were already married and looking forward to returning to domesticity.

The 30 percent who were munitions workers reportedly expressed a marked degree of self-confidence. Planning to return to their former occupations (significantly, they had to keep earning money), they held the attitude, summarized by the reporter, that "we have discovered that our services have a value to our country. They should be worth at least as much to a private employer." Domestic service was considered by many of these women a good possibility, but only on certain conditions. "What we ask is a good home, a reasonable mistress, more liberty, and higher wages!" one woman stated, apparently voicing the opinions of others.

Fifteen percent of those polled were keen to emigrate, having heard from American or dominion soldiers glowing accounts of life in the New World; notable among these were women who had lost their sweethearts during the war or were worried about the sex ratio at home because of the numbers of men killed.[82] Other newspaper reports noted this same phenomenon of demobilized women workers expressing a desire to emigrate. On 2 December 1918 the *Daily Chronicle* quoted a lady superintendent of the training section of the Ministry of Munitions as observing that "many of the girls leaving munitions want to go abroad."[83]

That women munitions workers should think of emigrating after the war testifies to the fact that many women had been uprooted by the war, leaving their homes for the first time and sometimes moving to another part of the country. Having made the break, no doubt it was easier for them to contemplate emigrating. Moreover, various agencies had been at pains to put this idea into their heads. The British Women's Emigration Association (BWEA), for example, had distributed circulars advertising its services to women munitions workers through both factories and clubs.[84] At least a few women who had worked as emigration matrons or conductresses before the war, for the BWEA, the YWCA, and other organizations, had become welfare supervisors in munitions factories.[85]

82. D. G., "War Girls 'Pack Up'," *Daily Mail*, 9 November 1918, 2.

83. See also *Empire News*, 15 December 1918.

84. For example, "Sweethearts' Passports," *Daily Mail*, 23 October 1918.

85. Una Monk, *New Horizons: A Hundred Years of Women's Migration* (London: HMSO,

Presumably, as welfare supervisors they used their contact with thousands of women workers to extol the advantages of emigration. Despite this propaganda, however, and no matter how genuine their desire to emigrate, there were several factors working against women workers' emigration after the war, such as restrictions on passports and the shortage of available ships.

What most ex-munitions workers needed were employment openings. In some areas of Britain, other industries were poised to accept women workers as soon as they were discharged from munitions. In Manchester, for example, the clothing trade was said to be taking on women munitions workers in late November 1918, while in Sheffield the silver and electroplating trades were hoping to take on many women workers, depending on the supply of their materials.[86] In early December a large Yorkshire munitions factory reported that of the women who had been dismissed, more than 30 percent had gone into the textile trade, 10 percent into tailoring, 4 percent into domestic service, and 2 percent into hospitals, shops, and laundries.[87]

Despite the return of many women munitions workers to domestic service, the employment situation for women workers, particularly unskilled ones, remained grim in the new era of peace. Even if the government had been disposed toward dealing with the plight of women workers, which it in fact considered a lower priority than helping returned servicemen and unemployed men find work, the problems lay deep in an economy greatly overstretched by war expenditures and foreign debts and in the vagaries of international trade.

One of the great problems faced by women workers in need of employment was the pervasive social prejudice against women working, a prejudice based on the belief that the returned servicemen needed, or deserved, jobs more than anyone else. While the gratitude widely felt toward returned men was natural, the failure to perceive the equally real need of women workers who were widowed or who supported themselves, dependent children, or other family members was the product of the long-held patriarchal desire to minimize women in the work force. The *Common Cause* reported in November 1919 on the pervasiveness of

1963), 52–53; "Correspondence between Ada S. Perry, Welfare Supervisor at Faversham Munitions Factory, Kent, and Miss Cox and Mrs. Smith-Carington of the YWCA, re the Work of the YWCA's Emigration Dept., March and April 1917," MRC, YWCA Papers, MSS. 243/131/8/5.i & 6.i.

86. "Idle Shell Girls," *Daily Sketch*, 23 November 1918.

87. *Daily Mail*, 9 December 1918.

this anti-women prejudice. "Sweeping assertions are made without instancing any particular cases of women actually taking the positions of demobilised soldiers," it reported. "Educated women who have done excellent work in Government offices are termed 'flappers,' and are jeered at and boycotted. . . . It is extraordinary that at a time like the present the services of every experienced man and woman should not be considered of value to the country." In the same issue it quoted from a report of the Women's Industrial League on the status of women in engineering and other trades. Based on information received from 1,422 firms, of 245,300 women employed during the war, only 79,700 were still employed in May 1919. The report noted that many of these firms explicitly stated that they would have preferred to retain more of their women workers, but their hand was forced by the Amalgamated Society of Engineers.[88]

Because of massive state intervention in industry with the compliance of employers, women workers could and did avail themselves of well-paid jobs and new skills during the war. Women's wartime work challenged some of the premises on which the gendered system of labor rested, such as their ability to do skilled work previously closed to them. The strength of the challenge was reflected in the determination of the male craft unions, particularly the ASE, to eject women from engineering after the war. This dramatic upheaval in industry came at a juncture when the relationship between skilled and unskilled work was changing and increasing automation of machinery heralded new forms of manufacturing.[89]

During the war women's status and value as workers improved because their labor was needed; they received support from the Ministry of Munitions and its tribunal system. Their improved status occurred in the face of employers' skepticism, the restrictions of the leaving certificate system, the intimidating judicial process of the munitions tribunals, and the hostility of the male craft unions. Women workers' wartime independence was reflected by their interest, during demobilization, in the possibility of emigrating. Their sense of self-worth was shown in the dramatic leap in their union membership; its material foundation lay in their munitions wages and the very real autonomy their wages allowed them.

88. "Turning Out the Women," and "Women in Engineering Trades," *Common Cause*, 7 November 1919, 374.

89. Women became an increasingly important component of the new industries in the interwar period. See Miriam Glucksmann, *Women Assemble: Women Workers and the New Industries in Inter-war Britain* (London and New York: Routledge, 1990).

1. The emblematic parity of these two figures, representing wartime service to the nation, reflects public acknowledgment of the patriotic role of the woman munitions worker. (Cover of *The War-Worker* 1, no. 1 [June 1917])

2. Women operating cranes in a shell-filling factory, Chilwell, Nottingham.
(Trustees of the Imperial War Museum, London)

3. World War I poster by Septimus Scott used to recruit women into munitions work. The formal balance of the two "salutes" represents an equation between women's work on munitions and men's work in the armed forces. (Trustees of the Imperial War Museum, London)

4. Women workers on the steps of an airplane factory in Birmingham, September 1918. This photograph reveals the extreme youth of some female workers, while also suggesting their camaraderie and the physical proximity to which they were accustomed. (Trustees of the Imperial War Museum, London)

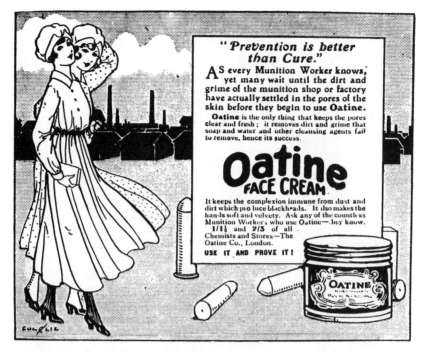

5. Advertisement for Oatine Face Cream. In depicting women munitions workers' skin problems as cosmetic, such advertising both invoked the very real effects of toxic jaundice and trivialized them. (*The War-Worker* 2, no. 6 [November 1918])

6. A firewoman bringing out a woman worker apparently overcome by smoke fumes. This photograph may have been taken during a drill rather than an actual fire or explosion. (Trustees of the Imperial War Museum, London)

7. Palmers Munitionettes, a football team from Palmers Shipbuilding Co. Ltd., Hepburn-on-Tyne. The presence of the nurse suggests the close association between welfare work and sport for women. (Trustees of the Imperial War Museum, London)

8. Performance by the Purple Poms, members of the King's Norton Club for Women Munition Workers, at Abbey Wood, ca. 1917. The costumes suggest a style usually associated with the 1920s. The term "flapper," also associated with that decade, was applied to women munitions workers. (Trustees of the Imperial War Museum, London)

9. Scene at a girls' club. The caption reads, "Visitor (at Girls' Club): 'Of course, you know, dear girls, ladies never talk to gentlemen unless they have been properly introduced?' Head Girl: 'We knows it, Mum, and we feels sorry for yer.'" (*Punch* 154 [23 January 1918]: 59)

10. Canteen superintendent demobilized. The text of the caption is, "Late superintendent of Munition Canteen (in dairy where she has dealt for over three years): 'And you won't forget the cream as usual.' Dairy Girl: 'Sorry, Madam. I regret you cannot have any more cream, as you have ceased to be of national importance.'" (*Punch* 156 [5 February 1919]: 99)

11. Lady Maud and the taxi driver. The caption is, "Taxi-driver (who has received bare legal fare, to Lady Maud, on munitions): ''Ere, wot's this? Calls yerself a gentleman, do yer?'" The fact that women munitions workers' uniforms often included trousers or leggings provoked some contemporary anxiety about gender transgression, although in this case the joke is about Maud's failure to behave like a man. (*Punch* 155 [2 October 1918]: 213)

FOOD FOR THE GUNS.

12. Postcard issued for the war bond campaign by the National War Savings Committee. The caption casts women's production of shells as feminine and domestic, while the male figure in the center of the shed stands for authority. Invoking traditional gender roles in this way cut against the gender inversion of women doing "men's work."

CHAPTER FIVE

"High Wages and Premature Liberty"

Wages, Autonomy, and Public Censure

Reconstruction after the war will be extraordinarily difficult,
hundreds and thousands of girls will be released from
munition factories and other works in which they have
replaced men. They will have had high wages and premature
liberty, which may in some instances have become licence.

National Union of Women Workers, March 1918

Grace Wright, daughter of Jesse Samuel Wright, often earns
two pounds 10s. a week at munitions work, and (says her
cousin, Lily Wright) spends it all.

Diary of the Reverend Andrew Clark,
22 September 1917

WAGES

Women workers' wages in most industries before the war were insufficient
for a woman to support herself adequately, let alone to support dependents. Despite this common characteristic, until 1909 there had been no
uniformity of wages within any one industry: they varied from place to
place and employer to employer. The Trade Boards Act of 1909, which
applied particularly to women in trades considered "sweating," laid down
a (still low) minimum wage.[1] Therefore the uniformity imposed on the
wages of women in munitions industries during the war, under the aegis
of the Ministry of Munitions, was a positive advance in itself that helped
toward the postwar extension of trade boards to include many industries
in which women worked.

For the first year or so of the war, women's wages did not rise. Initially
women workers were struggling with unemployment, and it was not
until late 1915 that a sense that there was a shortage of women's labor

1. Drake, *Women in Trade Unions,* 57–58.

gave employers an incentive to raise wages. There is evidence that in the early stages of the war women were doing long shifts in unpleasant, ill-equipped factories, with few facilities, for about the same wage rates as sweated labor.[2] As women's wages were increased in munitions factories under the orders of the ministry, there was a spill-over effect so that women workers in other areas of industry also benefited.

The question of women's wages had been raised in the discussions leading to the Treasury Agreement of 19 March 1915, in the context that men's wages must be protected by women being paid at the same rate for the same job.[3] The Ministry of Munitions, when it took control of women's wages under the Munitions of War Act of July 1915, decided that only piece rates needed to be exactly equal. In October 1915 the ministry issued the famous Circular L2, which stated that women employed at "men's work" should be paid at the rate of one pound a week for a normal working week, and those doing skilled "men's work" or piecework should receive the men's rate. At first this circular was issued as an instruction to the national or government-owned factories but only as a recommendation to the controlled establishments, which were privately owned. Under pressure from the Amalgamated Society of Engineers, however, the ministry extended its powers through the Munitions of War (Amendment) Act of January 1916 and issued the same circular to the controlled establishments as a statutory order in February.

Although Lloyd George, the first Minister of Munitions, stated, and Circular L2 laid down, that women doing the same work as fully skilled men should receive the same pay, there were various ways in which employers obviated this regulation. A few men workers were sometimes kept on to set up machines, so that although women did all the operating of the machines, they were not doing exactly the same work as the men they replaced. Alternatively, the job of a skilled man was broken down into component parts so that no one woman was doing the whole job the man had been doing. The weekly time-rate wage of 20s. was laid down in 1915 as a minimum, but employers chose to interpret it as a standard. However, this "minimum" was raised several times. Few women on skilled work were allowed piece-rate wages, which in most cases would have garnered them more money for the work they did, especially as their production frequently outstripped that of the men they replaced.

    2. See, for example, Taylor, "Recollections," IWM, DD, 83/17/1; *Woman's Dreadnought,* 5 February 1916; *Reynold's Newspaper,* 30 October 1915; *Daily Sketch,* 9 November 1915.
    3. The next several paragraphs are distilled from "Women's Wages During the War," in *Report of the War Cabinet Committee on Women in Industry,* ch. 4, 109–21.

In March 1916, the ministry constituted a special arbitration tribunal to settle disputes arising under the Munitions of War Act and to advise on women's wages. Women working on jobs that had always been "women's work" first came under regulation with the issuance of Statutory Order No. 447 in July 1916. This order, which greatly improved the wages in traditional "women's work," laid down that such women eighteen and over working on time rates were to receive 4 1/2d. per hour, and those on piece rates to receive 4d. per hour, with a downward scale of 1/2d. an hour less for each year of age under eighteen. Piece rates in unskilled "women's work" had been very low, and the provision of an hourly rate for such workers in addition to their piece rate was an unprecedented innovation not welcomed by employers. Order No. 447, which applied to about fourteen hundred establishments, also laid down that women working in danger zones should receive an additional 1/2d. per hour. Further orders were issued to cover special cases of work, and from March 1917 onward orders for special "war advances" were designed to help wages keep up with inflation.

By April 1918, under the statutory orders issued by the Ministry of Munitions, men in the national shell factories were earning an average of £4 6s. 6d. a week and women were earning £2 2s. 4d. a week. At the same time in the national projectile factories men were making an average of £4 14s. 8d. a week and women an average of £2 16s. 8d. a week.[4] Average earnings were higher than the stated weekly rates for these jobs because of overtime and bonus rates for work done beyond a certain amount.[5] These averages make clear that although women doing "men's work" were paid at the men's rate in theory, in the great majority of munitions occupations men were still earning much more than women.

Throughout the war, women trade unionists and others campaigned vociferously for "equal pay for equal work." As Harold Smith has demonstrated, however, "while the war aroused great expectations of reform in the problem of women's wages, what seems most striking about the effect of the war is the very limited degree of change which occurred."[6] Neither the government nor employers wanted to raise women's wages to parity with men's, and the men's unions turned a blind eye as long as men's wage rates were not threatened, so equal pay continued to be a major issue for feminists in the 1920s.

4. Ibid., 121.
5. IWM, Women's Work Collection, Mun. 14/8, 36.
6. Harold Smith, "The Issue of 'Equal Pay for Equal Work' in Great Britain, 1914–19," *Societas* 8 (Winter 1978): 49.

Although the NFWW and the Women's Trade Union League (WTUL) were not surprised that women did not get equal pay, they were insistent that women should receive the wages promised by the ministry. The controlled establishments frequently resisted paying women workers the rates the ministry laid down. Julie E. Tomlinson, chair of the Manchester, Salford, and District Women's War Interests Committee, wrote to the editor of the *Manchester Guardian* in November 1915 complaining that Circular L2 "seems clear enough, but the fact remains that the local munition factories, with one or two notable exceptions, are not paying these wages to women."[7] She suggested that there ought to be an arbitrator, and indeed that was the ministry's solution. As well as the Special Arbitration Tribunal for Women's Wages established in March 1916, munitions tribunals were empowered by the ministry to try cases in which either workers or employers were not complying with orders and regulations. The NFWW used these tribunals regularly to put forward cases in which employers were not paying workers according to the level of skill the federation believed they were using, and it often won.[8] On a more general level, the federation was responsible for the extension of the statutory wage orders to Ireland, where women had been working in munitions factories at miserable wages.[9]

Before the war, women who worked in factories, where the pay was better than domestic service or sweated labor, earned on average between 10s. and 14s. a week. By the end of the war, women in munitions industries were earning, on average, between 30s. and 35s. a week, often with overtime and bonuses on top—roughly a threefold increase.[10] This jump is the single clearest sign that employers and the Ministry of Munitions desperately needed female labor during the war. The urgent necessity for the tools of war dictated government policy, which allowed women workers an unprecedented income. Yet this was granted neither quickly nor cleanly. A distinction was drawn between women doing jobs previously done by women and those who were "dilutees" doing "men's jobs." The gap between these two classes was such that at the end of the war women doing skilled "men's work" in engineering were earning as

7. "Women's Wages in Munition Factories," *Manchester Guardian,* 16 November 1915.

8. The federation's magazine the *Woman Worker* regularly had a column of reports on cases under arbitration; for example, "More Arbitration Cases," *Woman Worker* 24 (December 1917): 14.

9. Woman's Trade Union League, *Forty-second Annual Report,* September 1917, 6.

10. Wolfe, *Labour Supply and Regulation,* 295.

much as 60s. a week before overtime and bonuses.[11] The main reason for this gap was the militant resistance of male trade unionists to dilution, fearing the loss of their hard-won hierarchy of labor, which elevated skilled labor to a class of its own above unskilled. Thus the gap between men's and women's wages persisted; although women's wages rose, the men who stayed in the factories earned more than ever.

Despite this continuing inequality, for most women workers the wages they earned in wartime munitions factories were an unheralded bonanza. For Elsie Bell, who before the war had worked as a daily domestic servant seven days a week from 7 A.M. to 6 or 7 P.M. for 2s. 6d. a week, her job during the war at Pirelli's wire-cable factory in Southampton, which earned her about £3 (60s.) a week, was evidence enough that "you was better off in a factory."[12] For workers on piece rates and bonus rates, weekly earnings could be extraordinarily high. Beatrice Lee worked in two different munitions factories during the war: at the Yorkshire Copper Works as a crane driver she earned £2 10s. a week, but in the bag factory at Scarborough, where she sewed munitions bags for guns, she recalled that some weeks, with overtime, her earnings could be as much as £5.[13]

COST OF LIVING, STANDARD OF LIVING

Despite the ministry's refusal to grant really equal pay for equal work and the tricks of recalcitrant employers, most women munitions workers' wages rose steadily to dramatic levels. Because of wartime inflation, however, it did not necessarily follow that higher wages translated directly into a better standard of living.

In 1918 a committee was appointed to investigate wartime changes in the cost of living for the working classes. Limiting its scope to food, rent, clothing, fuel, insurance, household sundries, and transport fares, the committee collected 1,306 household budgets and other documentation. It measured the increase in the cost of these basic items to workers between 1914 and 1918 and found that for the standard working-class family the total weekly expenditure on food had increased from 24s. 11d.

11. A. L. Bowley, *Prices and Wages in the United Kingdom 1914–1920* (London, 1921), 189.

12. IWM, DSR, 7435/01. Interview by Southampton Oral History Project.

13. IWM, DSR, 000724/06.

in June 1914 to 47s. 3d. in June 1918, a rise of 90 percent.[14] When considering also expenditures on rent, fuel and light, fares, insurance, and clothing, they arrived at the figure that the average rise in weekly household expenditures for the working classes had been 74 percent.[15] Further, they pointed out that these increases hit the unskilled, as opposed to the skilled or semiskilled, workers hardest. Most women workers were unskilled.

The effect of rising prices was felt soon after the start of the war. The at first abrupt and then steady rise in prices is shown by the official index of the average change of retail food prices, which, beginning in July 1914 at an arbitrary base figure of 100, rose to 132.5 in July 1915, 161 in July 1916, 204 in July 1917, and 210 in July 1918.[16] For women munitions workers, who only began entering the factories in large numbers in May 1915 and whose numbers grew substantially after the introduction of military conscription in 1916, wages did not catch up with inflation in the first year or so of the war.

Workers and their representatives protested the escalating cost of their food and other necessities but felt powerless to halt it. Many blamed the government for negligent disregard, while others, alert to the trading disorder caused by the war, pointed to the huge profits being made by merchant shipowners and wholesalers. On 28 February 1915, unions and socialist organizations joined together in a demonstration in Trafalgar Square to protest rising prices. Sylvia Pankhurst noted that the "feeling of the meeting was one of strong indignation against the Government for its cowardly inaction."[17]

The fact that women workers' wages were not rising at the same rate or proportion as the cost of living provoked W. C. Anderson, always the ally of the workers, to confront the representative of the Ministry of Munitions in the House of Commons. Pointing out that women in controlled establishments were bound by the system of leaving certificates and could not therefore change jobs to earn better wages, Anderson charged that "if you tie her up and say that she is essential for national work there is a moral duty resting on the Ministry to see that proper

14. Working Classes Cost of Living Committee. *Report of the Committee Appointed to Enquire into and Report upon (i) the Actual Increase since June, 1914, in the Cost of Living to the Working Classes and (ii) Any Counterbalancing Factors (Apart from Increase of Wages) Which May Have Arisen under War Conditions.* Cd. 8980, 1918, vol. 7, 825: 18, table 5; 6, para. 29.

15. Ibid., 7, para. 34.

16. Bowley, *Prices and Wages*, 35, table 13.

17. "Towards Cheaper Food," *Woman's Dreadnought*, 6 March 1915, 205.

wages are paid in the establishment in which she works. . . . I do wish that the Ministry would take full account of the great increase in prices and the worsening of conditions, and see that the women who are doing work of a valuable national character are properly paid for that work."[18]

A significant financial benefit to many women was the institution of separation allowances for soldiers' and sailors' wives. A separation allowance was part of the husband's salary but was paid directly to the wife for the support of herself and any children. This allowance was sometimes as much as the husband had earned in prewar times and was often in addition to the woman's own earnings (and perhaps went further, now that the husband was away).[19] Thus, despite a surveillance system that meant some women were denied separation allowances for purportedly immoral behavior, other women had incomes of which they had previously only dreamed. Yet for most women workers, even for many receiving separation allowances, working was not merely an option but an absolute necessity, especially with the rising cost of living.

This need was pointed out by a "lady superintendent" at a national ordnance factory in Leeds, when she justified establishing a special work program for pregnant women and nursing mothers on the basis that these women had to be able to stay at work to have the incomes to support their families.[20] Similarly, a writer concerned with the welfare of mothers and children justified the necessity of providing nurseries for workers' children: "Women who had just enough to live on in normal times, for example, soldiers' wives or widows, and many women with families whose husbands' wages have not increased in proportion to the cost of living, are being driven into the labour market, partly through patriotism, but also through sheer necessity."[21]

BREADWINNERS: FAMILY AND DOMESTIC RESPONSIBILITIES

Even taking into account wartime inflation, the truism that nothing is so good for an economy as war was borne out in Britain during the Great

18. *Parliamentary Debates, Commons,* 5th ser., 90 (19 February 1917): 1582.
19. On the separation allowance system see Susan Pedersen, "Gender, Welfare and Citizenship in Britain during the Great War," *American Historical Review* 95, 4 (October 1990): 983–1006.
20. H. Palmer-Jones, "A Report of Work Done for Expectant Mothers," IWM, Women's Work Collection, Mun. 18.9/17:1.
21. Hope, "Day Nurseries or Creches: Nurseries for Children of Munition Workers," in *Physical Welfare* 2 (England and Wales): 123.

War by evidence of the improved standard of living in working-class families. One American commentator, writing in the later stages of the war, exclaimed that "60,000 fewer persons in London were in receipt of poor relief in September, 1915, than in 1903, the previous most prosperous year known to the Board of Trade." Moreover, while upper- and middle-class families were patriotically counting their "meatless" days, "in the East End, families are celebrating meat days that were never known before the war."[22] Likewise, the Working Classes Cost of Living Committee, in its discursive comments at the end of its report, noted that not only had wages enabled working-class families to purchase food of the same nutritive value at the end of the war as at the beginning but that the unskilled workers, those whose expenditure increased the most, were slightly better fed at the end of the war than at the beginning.[23]

Although there are no statistics giving an exact proportion, many of the women who worked in munitions industries during the war were married and many had children. While the location of munitions factories meant that women in great numbers had to move away from their homes, it was much easier for single and childless women to move than for those with family responsibilities. Some women with children did move, nevertheless, and had to find accommodation for them all. More often, however, women with children worked only where they could commute on a daily basis and found female relatives, nurseries, or neighborhood women to look after their children while they were at work. The *Evening News,* addressing the difficulty of munitions factories finding enough women workers, said that "most women have some kind of home responsibility. When a woman has made up her own mind to be a martyr she has to persuade someone else to be one also."[24]

The rationale for women being paid less than men (the so-called family wage) before, during, and after the war was specious, based on patriarchal constructions of women's role that were belied by the realities of working women's lives. This rationale consisted of the notions that women ate less than men, they did not indulge in expensive habits like drinking and smoking, and, primarily, they were not supporting families or dependents.

Several surveys were carried out just before the war on the question

22. Mabel Potter Daggett, *Women Wanted: The Story Written in Blood Red Letters on the Horizon of the Great World War* (New York: George H. Doran Co., 1918), 151.
23. Report of the Working Classes Cost of Living Committee, 9, para. 51.
24. "A Call to the Women: Your Country Needs You Now," *Evening News,* 6 February 1917.

of what proportion of women workers were self-supporting or supporting dependents. In 1915 the Fabian Women's Group collated the results of their own survey with those of six others, with a total number of 5,325 women providing the sample between the seven different surveys. The women surveyed included professional women; only a minority were industrial workers (despite their efforts to include more such women). The result they obtained was that 15 percent of working women were not quite self-supporting; more than 33 percent supported themselves but no one else; and 51 percent were supporting themselves and maintaining dependents (on average, 1.75 persons).[25]

A study conducted by Seebohm Rowntree and Frank D. Stuart soon after the war differed significantly with that of the Fabian Women's Group. According to their survey, only 12.06 percent of women workers at any time were supporting anyone besides themselves.[26] But their basis of measurement was ideologically defined: they measured whether a male breadwinner's wage was above or below their estimated poverty line. Women's earnings were only considered if the male breadwinner's wage was below the line; otherwise all dependent household members were deemed dependent on him.[27] By this standard many women whose wages were critical to the family income were simply considered to be without dependents. While Rowntree and Stuart's conclusion on this issue is thus dubious, another finding of their survey is illuminating. They had included in their survey the reasons why women workers had dependents and found that 65.83 percent of cases were due to the death of the father or husband and 12.6 percent were due to the illness of the father or husband. Other causes, in descending order, were having been deserted, having aged parents or other relatives, inadequate old age pensions, low wages and large families, unemployment of the male family members, being an unmarried mother, and having dependent sisters.[28]

Women munitions workers who supported dependents were most commonly mothers. Daisey Miller, for example, was charged in Woolwich Police Court in April 1917 with having stolen another worker's handbag, purse, and money from a canteen at the arsenal. A detective-sergeant

25. Ellen Smith, *Wage-Earning Women and Their Dependants* (London: The Fabian Society, 1915), 34. See also Barbara Drake, "The Tea-Shop Girl," *Women's Industrial News* 17, no. 61 (April 1913): 124.

26. B. Seebohm Rowntree and Frank D. Stuart, *The Responsibility of Women Workers for Dependants* (Oxford: Clarendon Press, 1921), 36.

27. Susan Pedersen, "The Failure of Feminism in the Making of the British Welfare State," *Radical History Review* 43 (1989): 92–93.

28. Rowntree and Stuart, *Responsibility of Women Workers,* 32–33.

informed the court that she had an invalid husband and three children to support; she was remanded on bail.[29] Others had dependent parents. When a ministry official investigated housing at Barrow for the Vickers' workers, he met a retired postman and his wife who had moved to Barrow before the war to be near their daughter. The daughter had held a good job in an umbrella factory in Barrow, but the factory failed and "in the summer of 1914 the old people were in despair, when 'luckily for us the war broke out. Our daughter is making better money than ever.'"[30]

A woman lathe operator who worked on shells wrote to Mary Macarthur in 1916, complaining bitterly about the lack of equal pay. She was earning 3 1/2d. per hour at a job for which a man had received 7d. per hour, even though she was turning out more shells. The foreman, she said, had explained it to her thus: "A man, he said, has got a wife and children. He needs more money than a girl, and women are cheaper than men because their wants are fewer. For instance, they don't require tobacco; and tea and toast is cheaper than beer and beefsteaks." In fact, "Miriam" complained, she was supporting her aging parents, and her brother had been killed at Gallipoli.[31]

Most women workers simply had to keep working to keep themselves and their dependents alive. Munitions work, at least, offered relatively well-paid, full-time, year-round work for the duration of the war. While munitions wages were attractive to all kinds of women workers, it was young single women with no children, husband, or parents dependent on them who most experienced these wages as offering unprecedented spending choices or entertainment opportunities. Even women in this group, however, commonly took their wages home to their mothers or sent part of their wages home to help support siblings. For women workers who had financial dependents, being the breadwinner often also entailed being the household manager, cook, and cleaner. Domestic duties, after an eight- or twelve-hour day in a munitions factory, meant that little else in life was possible.

AUTONOMY AND SPENDING

It was normal in English working-class households at this time that the wife should control the household income provided by her husband,

29. *The Pioneer,* 20 April 1917, 3.

30. G. H. Duckworth, memorandum, "Barrow Housing Scheme," 17 November 1917, PRO, MUN 5/96/346.2/4:15–16.

31. Mary Macarthur, "Women Workers' Fellowship," *Woman's Life* 217 (1 April 1916): 1.

herself, and any wage-earning children living at home. This system thrust a great deal of responsibility onto the wife, who had to stretch a small income, often already reduced by the husband's spending at the pub, to maintain the whole family. But within this, the wife exercised control.[32] Wives dealt with the local tradespeople, paid the rent, oversaw the distribution and pooling of income within the family, and engaged in complicated financial arrangements with neighbors, contributing toward assistance for neighbors in distress, or paying for small services.[33]

Some working-class wives experienced World War I, at least in part, as a liberation from the grind of eking out an inadequate weekly income. A writer who interviewed women on this point quotes one as saying, "I'd never known what it was to be a free woman before," and another, more pointedly, "For a woman who has a bad husband, being dependent is hell."[34] Wives had exercised control over the household budget before, but now those who were sole heads of households exercised autonomy. That autonomy, however, was only translated into exercising choices when the women had sufficient income, through separation allowances or their own earnings, to enable options.

Particularly from 1916 onward, women munitions workers had wages beyond what they had known before, and many had real options for spending them. Especially for young women who had left home to go to the munitions areas, and for wives whose husbands were away at war or dead and who now had their own pay packets at their disposal, this was a time when they could make real choices about spending any amounts of money left over after the essentials were covered.

One choice that women were making in household budgets is pointed out in the Working Classes Cost of Living Committee Report: the increased expenditure during the war on coal and gas was greater than the rise in prices of these fuels, showing a greater consumption rate per consumer.[35] This report also shows that larger proportions of the household budget were being spent on food and clothes in 1918 than in 1914. The committee was informed by a major boot firm that in 1918 it was

32. On wives balancing the family budget see Roberts, *A Woman's Place,* 148–51.

33. For discussion of these financial arrangements, see Ellen Ross, "Survival Networks: Women's Neighbourhood Sharing in London Before World War I," *History Workshop* 15 (Spring 1983): 5, 11, 16; Ellen Ross, "Labour and Love," 86–88; Jane Lewis, "The Working-Class Wife and Mother and State Intervention, 1870–1918," in *Labour and Love: Women's Experiences of Home and Family 1850–1940,* ed. Jane Lewis (Oxford: Basil Blackwell, 1986), 106–8; Gareth Stedman Jones, *Languages of Class: Studies in English Working Class History* (Cambridge: Cambridge University Press, 1983), 219, 227.

34. Peel, *How We Lived Then,* 171–72. See also Daggett, *Women Wanted,* 152.

35. Report of the Working Classes Cost of Living Committee, 25, para. 11.

unable to keep up with the demand for high-quality boots in poor neighborhoods, where before the war only the cheapest boots were sold.[36] Increased wages meant that there was something in the purse after essentials were bought, and the greater expenditures on fuel, food, and clothing, as well as on entertainment, reflected women's choices.

Women workers also saved money and made gifts of it. From all sides, they were urged to put some of their hard-earned wages back into the national war effort.[37] Women and men workers frequently bought war savings certificates, and they also donated to charities for wounded soldiers, other charities, and their own benevolent funds to help out their less fortunate workmates.

PUBLIC CENSURE: DRINKING AND EXTRAVAGANCE

The knowledge that working-class women were exercising control over some little extra income made some of the more fortunate classes, and various authorities, quite uncomfortable. Some actually believed that the freedom workers thus acquired resulted in their depravity. Policewoman Mary Allen, writing with Julie Heyneman about the war from the vantage point of the 1930s, asserted that

> the generous separation allowances to wives of the absent fighting forces, and their pay, in addition, as servants, caretakers, charwomen, munition workers, or in other fields, gave great masses of women more money than they had ever before dreamed of handling. It drove them to feverish excitements or extravagances, and, coupled with their anxiety and loneliness, often to drink; so that some of them sank, during the four years of their freedom from all supervision, to a terrible and often scarcely human condition.[38]

Apart from the hyperbole of the last descriptive phrase, it seems particularly ironic that, having been second in command of the Women Police Service during the war, Allen would describe wartime women workers as "free from all supervision."

For the middle and upper classes, the entry of so many women workers into munitions factories meant that domestic help was hard to come by. Complaints about "the servant problem" were a perennial feature of bourgeois life in Britain, but the war actually depleted the ranks of

36. "Quality," ibid., 22, esp. para. 9.
37. For example *Woman's Life* 337 (20 July 1918): 71.
38. Mary S. Allen and Julie Helen Heyneman, *Women at the Crossroads* (London: Unicorn Press, 1934), 77.

servants as many left to take jobs in munitions factories. The inconvenience and grumbling that this situation produced was perhaps one cause of the outrage at working-class comfort that percolated throughout the upper social echelons, including stories about women workers buying fur coats, silk dresses, elaborate jewelry, and gramophones; drinking excessively; and eating delicacies.[39]

In 1917 Madeline Ida Bedford parodied a munitions worker's high living, purportedly in the worker's voice:

Munition Wages

Earning high wages? Yus,
   Five quid a week.
A woman, too, mind you,
   I calls it dim sweet.

Ye're asking some questions—
   But bless yer, here goes:
I spends the whole racket
   On good times and clothes.

. . . .

We're all here today, mate,
   Tomorrow—perhaps dead,
If Fate tumbles on us
   And blows up our shed.

Afraid! Are yer kidding?
   With money to spend!
Years back I wore tatters,
   Now—silk stockings, mi friend!

I've bracelets and jewellery,
   Rings envied by friends;
A sergeant to swank with,
   And something to lend.

I drive out in taxis,
   Do theatres in style.
And this is mi verdict—
   It is jolly worth while.

Worth while, for tomorrow
   If I'm blown to the sky,
I'll have repaid mi wages
   In death—and pass by.[40]

39. "War Time Extravagance," *The Vote* (29 August 1919), 308.

40. Madeline Ida Bedford, "Munition Wages," in *Scars Upon My Heart: Women's Poetry and Verse of the First World War,* ed. Catherine Reilly (London: Virago, 1981), 7–8. This poem was first published in Madeline Ida Bedford, *The Young Captain* (Erskine Macdonald Ltd., 1917).

A proportion of the scandalized stories about munitions workers' high wages dealt equally with men and women workers. One genre of complaint was about the new shopping habits of the wives of men munitions workers.[41] Another complaint was specifically about the recreational habits of men munitions workers. Criticism of the number of new motorcycles to be seen in Woolwich was aired, and according to one writer who purported to apologize for working-class "extravagance," it was said "that working-men from the Black Country hire motor-cars and drive into Birmingham to book dress-seats in the theatres for the pantomime!"[42]

But while such complaints were class-based and indicted what was seen as high living among both sexes of the lower orders, there was a body of criticism that applied to women munitions workers in gender-specific ways. In particular, middle- and upper-class critics condemned what they claimed were an increase in drinking among women workers and an indulgence in clothing and accessories above their station. Underneath both accusations lurked the fear that women workers, in a state of greater freedom and autonomy, would become sexually promiscuous and thus threaten the moral order and spread venereal disease. While conspicuous spending in men workers signified a threat to the established hierarchy of social privilege, in women workers it was also considered portentous of uncontrolled sexuality. Further, men could participate in criticism of women's behavior as symptomatic of the social problems arising from high levels of women's employment, with its relative independence for women.

DRINKING

Allegations that working-class women were drinking excessively because of the removal of the controlling presence of their husbands, and especially because of their extra income, began almost as soon as the first shot of the war was fired. In November 1914, the Home Office issued orders that the wives and dependents of soldiers and sailors were to be subject to police surveillance so that any woman who was reported to be drinking excessively or behaving "loosely" would have her separation allowance

41. "Waste of Wages: Big Pay and Big Spending at Woolwich: Extravagance in Food," *Daily Graphic*, 29 November 1915.

42. Carol Ring, "Working Class Extravagance: An Apology," *Common Cause*, 28 January 1916, 564.

cut off. This surveillance work and the great fear of "loose" women infecting the troops with venereal disease were prime reasons for the instigation of women patrols in late 1914.[43]

In October 1915, the Liquor Control Board appointed a women's advisory committee to inquire into the allegations of excessive drinking among women. The committee reported that the war had not changed women's drinking patterns, nor had the receipt of separation allowances. There was no evidence that women and girls who did not drink before the war were drinking now. In fact, they reported evidence of improvement in homes, the better condition of children, and wise spending on the part of the majority.[44] In the last year of the war, the chairman of the Liquor Control Board, Lord D'Abernon, announced that drunkenness among women had decreased by 73 percent since before the war and that "evidence and figures show that occupation, steady wages, and an independent, self-supporting career have developed the best qualities in women, have increased their self-respect and self-control, and have been in all respects—particularly from the health aspect—profoundly beneficial to the community."[45] Similarly, in November 1918 the British Information Bureau in San Francisco issued a report on a survey of women workers in Liverpool. Refuting stories that women were wasting their higher income (from both separation allowances and their higher wages) on "dissipation and amusements," the report gave evidence that drunkenness was in fact decreasing and cited the testimony of observers that the health of children was improving (particularly because their footwear was better) and that the "convenience and beauty of the home" were being enhanced.[46]

From 4 April to 1 May 1918, under directions from their central organizing committee, two women patrols conducted a systematic survey of women's drinking behavior in the Woolwich district. They found that most women drinkers ranged in age from thirty-five to fifty. The most important conclusion they came to about women's drinking, they felt, was that although in "the present diluted state [of beer] they seem little the worse for wear for this form of amusement . . . it is a habit they have

43. Lucy Bland, "In the Name of Protection: The Policing of Women in the First World War," in *Women in Law: Explorations in Law, Family & Sexuality*, ed. J. Brophy and C. Smart (London: Routledge & Kegan Paul, 1985), 26–30.

44. Second Report of the Central Control Board (Liquor Traffic) 1915, Cd. 8243, vol. 12 (1916): 493, 8.

45. "Sobriety among Women," *The War-Worker* 1, no. 8 (January 1918): 118.

46. "British Women Earn Big Salaries in Wartime Work," *Santa Maria Times* (California), 9 November 1918, 2.

acquired, the danger of which will be all too evident should liquor after the war return to its old strength."[47] For some women, they considered, drinking was attractive because they were "anxious and lonely." For others, frequenting pubs was a form of social activity, such as the "great many smartly dressed Woolwich girls [who] throng the Beresford Square houses after 8 o'clock, drifting from house to house, and consuming port and spirits."[48]

As for munitions workers, they seemed to drink less than other women: "We have watched several shifts of munition girls coming in and out at noon, and early evening, and very few of these call at any of the public houses, and then only get a glass of stout."[49] Most women munitions workers fell below the age group the women patrols reported as containing most women drinkers. The fact that women workers were accused of widespread drunkenness in the face of evidence to the contrary reveals the challenge that their increased autonomy posed to the dominant social order.

CLOTHES AND CULTURAL MEANING

The challenge that women workers' relatively high income posed to the social and cultural order, and the responses to it, were even more tellingly encoded in the public discourse about women workers' wartime purchasing of clothes. The abundant evidence that working women were spending more on clothes, and wearing finer clothes than they had before, excited a mixture of approval and criticism from the press and social commentators.

One observer noticed at a London general hospital in November 1918 that among the crowd who rushed up the stairs before him there were only to be seen smart rather than shabby shoes, and neat stockings, many of which were silk.[50] (Shoes and stockings had acquired new importance as skirts shortened during the war.) Another writer, referring to the munitions workers in the Newcastle area, noted approvingly that besides spending a considerable amount of money on food, which they needed, these women "spent lavishly on their clothes, and very well dressed many of them were, in smartly-cut tailor-mades of carefully chosen colour, with

47. "Report on Drinking Conditions Among Women and Girls in Woolwich and District," May 1918, PRO, MEPOL 2/1710:2, 3.
48. Ibid.
49. Ibid., 4.
50. Peel, *How We Lived Then*, 8.

hat and blouse, gloves and stockings all to match, and particularly neat boots or shoes, and not only did they spend on their outer clothes, but their underclothes were in the best of taste."[51]

In contrast to these approving comments, other commentators were stridently critical of what they saw as working-class women's extravagance and aspirations to dress as though of a superior class. In January 1916, for example, the *Sheffield Weekly Independent* reported as though newsworthy two instances of "the thriftless manner in which some working-class women are squandering money." In one instance, in a "high-class draper's establishment in a great Northern town," a woman munitions worker "with the characteristic shawl over her head" entered and demanded to be shown the fur department. "Here she selects a fur coat and cap to match—price, 32 gs. [guineas]. She pays cash and departs with her new glories." In a separate instance, another woman worker entered a jewelry store, "asks for a diamond ring, selects one, and asks the price— 13 gs. 'Here's brass,' she says, and off she goes."[52]

Peggy Hamilton, a middle-class munitions worker, was outraged by such accusations against her coworkers. She later recalled an incident in which she became embroiled in a public argument, in the usually decorous dining room of the boarding house in which she stayed in Birmingham. When a newcomer announced during dinner, "'I think it's disgraceful all these munition makers and their fur coats; they're getting too much money,' I told her I was a munition worker, that no one I knew owned a fur coat, that we worked from 7 to 7, six days a week, for £1 a week and what sort of fur coat did she think she could buy after paying her living out of that?" The argument was broken up by a third person, just at the point when Hamilton was rejoining to her antagonist that "it's nothing to do with the rich how the poor spend their money."[53]

As Hamilton saw a class dimension to this supposedly moral complaint, so too did a working-class woman munitions worker who expressed her feelings about class prejudice and her right to dispose of her own income as she chose in a letter to the *Daily Express* in November 1917. Referring to the common middle-class complaint that women factory workers were earning too much and spending it all on clothes, she defined the topic of her letter as "the censure which is levelled at me by some people for what

51. Ibid., 118. One wonders how she knew about their underclothes.

52. "How Wages Are Wasted," *Sheffield Weekly Independent,* 22 January 1916, 3. A guinea was a unit of currency equal to 21 shillings.

53. Peggy Hamilton, *Three Years or the Duration: The Memoirs of a Munition Worker, 1914–1918* (London: Peter Owen, 1978), 48.

is called my reckless extravagance in dress." Her reply to this censure, entitled "In Self-Defence, By A Munition Girl," ran as follows:

> Those who point the finger of scorn at me seem to me to be utterly without imagination. Let them put themselves in my place. Let them realise what it means, after a life of soul-suffocation, to find oneself suddenly able to breathe free air, to see the walls of one's prison house gradually crumbling, to feel the shackles of tyranny loosening from one's feet, to taste a tiny bit of ambition realised. Ambition is the same power in every walk of life, whether it aims at world dominion or the possession of a small article of flesh-coloured crepe de Chine. . . . If I, and thousands like me, stopped work and went back to my old bondage and unsatisfactory wage, who is there who could step in and take my place?
>
> Without wishing to judge unfairly, it seems to me that these critics grudge me this sudden improvement in my financial position. If I were to put every penny I make into war certificates there would still be those who considered it unseemly that I should be in a position to make such an investment. It is the old autocratic spirit, struggling in its death throes to make a last endeavour to assert itself. The same spirit which my efforts in war work are supposed to be helping to crush.[54]

This woman worker identified and challenged the political meaning embedded within the criticism of workers' extravagance, inextricably interwoven with the moral and cultural indictments.

The charge that women workers were spending on "unnecessary," exciting items rather than saving for the future, as social reformers urged, was not a new wartime phenomenon. Gareth Stedman Jones has pointed out that in the late Victorian and Edwardian periods, urban working-class people had constantly frustrated reformers by buying pictures for the front room, for example, rather than opening a savings account. Among factory girls in particular, he notes, savings in clothing clubs (which made fashionably cut dresses affordable) were much more prevalent than membership in friendly societies.[55]

Clothes were the outward, publicly visible form with which women could claim social mobility. As Carolyn Steedman has observed, far from being the trivial items of expenditure middle-class reformers usually thought, decent outer clothes were long known by working women and

54. "In Self-Defence, By A Munition Girl," *Daily Express*, 1 November 1917.

55. Gareth Stedman Jones, "Working-Class Culture and Working-Class Politics," in *Languages of Class*, 199. Maud Pember Reeves similarly commented on clothing clubs that allowed women to put small regular amounts of money toward the purchase of clothes, *Round About a Pound*, 62–63.

girls to be essential according to rules of social behavior.[56] Clothes were the main vehicle through which women workers could hope to demonstrate the respectability crucial to social status for the working class.

Criticism of working-class women's expenditure on clothes signified more than just social reformers' concern with habits of thrift. Accusations of women's aspirations to "finery" were made in a cultural context reaching back into the nineteenth century. As Mariana Valverde has shown through careful deconstruction of both historical documents and novels of the Victorian period, the wearing of cheap and gaudy clothes, termed "finery," was taken as a sign of the "fallen woman," the woman who had or could become a prostitute. Vanity and the love of finery were considered in themselves causes of women's descent into prostitution; and both finery and prostitution were associated with factory girls, whose low wages made them notoriously susceptible to means of quick earnings. Bourgeois construction of a moral code of dress was also particularly related to the fact that, later in the nineteenth century, domestic servants were increasingly attracted to "factory work or other more independent occupations, in which women could wear whatever clothes they wanted—at least in the evenings and on Sundays. In the context of 'the servant problem' (as ladies referred to it), dress codes were an important part of the mistresses' show of power over their maids."[57]

Criticism of women munitions workers' spending their wages on new, ostentatiously fashionable or expensive clothes, in this cultural context, suggested that, like their nineteenth-century forebears, they were behaving like prostitutes. Such allegations therefore were overlaid with moral condemnation and represented fears of women's sexual behavior. If women could afford to spend money on new clothes, it meant that they had attained a degree of autonomy, which in turn meant that they were less likely to be constrained by the middle class's desire for social and moral order. These fears had a basis in actual circumstances. Women munitions workers were enjoying not only higher wages but also greater physical mobility. It is likely that for many women, especially younger women, the freedom to choose to spend their money in these ways stemmed from the fact that they had left home to take up munitions work.

But the fears were not grounded in reality. As the accusations about

56. Carolyn Kay Steedman, *Landscape for a Good Woman: A Story of Two Lives* (New Brunswick, N.J.: Rutgers University Press, 1987), 89.

57. Mariana Valverde, "The Love of Finery: Fashion and the Fallen Woman in Nineteenth-Century Social Discourse," *Victorian Studies* 32 (Winter 1989): 182–83.

women's excessive drinking were found, upon examination, to be wildly exaggerated, so too were fears of uncontrolled sexuality among women munitions workers. At base, as "A Munition Girl" identified in her letter to the *Daily Express,* the issue was one of social hierarchy and power.

Clothing was a means by which women workers could assert their own cultural identity. On one hand, welfare supervisors and well-meaning reformers advised women munitions workers to wear sober clothes that would emulate the middle class.[58] The premise underlying such advice was that there was a "nice" way of dressing to which all working women should aspire, one that embodied virtues of modesty and simplicity. What such advice either refused to recognize or consciously countered was that women workers had their own codes and styles of dressing that their wartime incomes allowed them to express more fully.

Agnes Foxwell, a university woman who worked for six months as an overlooker at Woolwich Arsenal to do "her bit," was struck by the ingenuity with which women workers modified their drab uniforms. The regulation cap, she noted for example, was worn in such diverse and imaginative ways that it "would trick the uninitiated into thinking that there were at least a dozen different shapes of caps." During the summer and autumn women would come to work adorned with flowers, different workshops choosing their own special colors, even though these would have to be removed by the overseer in accordance with factory regulations and given back only at breaktime. When the frustration of having their flowers removed became too much, the cap shop women had a brilliant idea: they all appeared one morning having exchanged their government-regulation shoelaces for bright emerald-green ribbons. The envy and admiration they provoked that day was so much that the next day the fashion had spread throughout the whole factory, with shoe ribbons of blue, pink, white, and red appearing in various areas, even including the office clerks'.[59] Their off-the-job outfits may also have been marked by their own signifiers of fashion, in an expression of shared bonds in direct contra-assertion to attempts to impose a bourgeois dress code on them.[60] Women workers reconciled their concepts of respectability with their

58. For example "Jewelry and Trimmings," *The War-Worker* 1, no. 2 (July 1917): 28.
59. Foxwell, *Munition Lasses,* 42–44.
60. Maxine Berg has suggested that "time and especially money spent by the poor on cultural ritual, gifts, feasts and luxury consumer display were a form of 'social exchange', a means of strengthening bonds of neighbourhood and friendship." Berg, "Women's Work, Mechanisation and the Early Phases of Industrialisation in England," in *The Historical Meanings of Work,* ed. Patrick Joyce (Cambridge: Cambridge University Press, 1987), 93.

own choice of clothing style, but their buying and wearing of finer clothes revealed their social aspirations to respectability. For women, clothes and accessories were the main medium for indicating class status as well as for expressing fashion and personal style.

In contrast to complaints that men munitions workers were spending increased wages on the conspicuous consumption of motorcycles, hired cars, and outings, women workers' supposed extravagance centered on their own bodies. The pervasive cultural reduction of women to bodies and sexuality channeled criticism of women workers' autonomy into specific complaints. Expensive clothes not only implied aspirations to higher class status but also enhanced physical attractiveness. Women's alleged drunkenness signified their supposed indulgence in bodily pleasures and sensuality, clearly implying a sexual promiscuity that threatened to undermine both social order and the health of the troops. Charges of drunkenness and promiscuity raised the specter of prostitution, which had long been associated with women factory workers but which munitions wages in fact made unnecessary. These allegations and fears provided further justification for the introduction of women police and patrols specifically to control the social and sexual behavior of women workers. In this context, the expanded leisure activities of women munitions workers, reflecting both physical liberation and urban mobility, exacerbated fears of what their increased autonomy portended.

CHAPTER SIX

Off the Job

Leisure, Socializing, and Sex

It is becoming increasingly clear that the forces making for
social and economic change in the position of women have
received an immense impetus from the war, and that women
and girls in many nations have reached at a bound an
economic opportunity and a social freedom for which they are
scarcely prepared. . . .

But we have also to reckon with the fact now receiving
wide-spread recognition that there is a change not merely in
conditions but in the mental and moral attitudes of many girls.
The old conventions and restraints are thrust aside, and the
new sense of independence and freedom expresses itself in very
many on the one hand in a disavowal of religion, and on the
other in a reckless search for pleasure and excitement.

Letter from the President to Members
of the YWCA, 1 February 1917

LEISURE AND RECREATION

In the second half of the nineteenth century, leisure and recreational
options for working-class people expanded at the same time that some
older practices of rural popular culture were lost or transformed through
industrialization. By the early twentieth century, workers in their time
off, augmented by the increasingly common Saturday half-holiday, were
taking day excursions into the countryside, playing and watching football
matches, filling the recently enlarged music halls, walking on promenades
and piers, and of course spending time at the pub.[1] A plethora of clubs,
societies, leagues, and movements depended on working-class membership. While some, like the Clarion Cycling Club, had their origins among

---

1. On working-class leisure in this period see Hugh Cunningham, "Leisure," in *The
Working Class in England 1875–1914,* ed. John Benson (London: Croom Helm, 1985);
"Leisure and Culture," in *People and Their Environment,* vol. 2 of *The Cambridge Social
History of Britain 1750–1950,* ed. F. M. L. Thompson (Cambridge: Cambridge University
Press, 1990), esp. 310–20. Football is the British name for soccer.

the working class and the socialist movement, many others, including the YMCA and YWCA, were the product of middle- and upper-class drives to purify the masses of their baser habits and to inculcate in them the precepts of Christianity, nationalism, and imperialism. The social history of this period has focused on both the impact of the middle-class (and socialist) enterprise to reshape the cultures and values of workers on the one hand and the need to recognize the resilience of popular cultures and the agency of workers in making their own recreational choices on the other. It is the quest to find the right balance between these countervailing forces that has impelled the debate among historians about leisure, culture, and social control.[2]

Within the historiography on leisure, however, gender differences in working-class leisure are usually dismissed with the acknowledgment that young working women participated in a variety of pursuits but once they married it was, in the words of Preston women, "all bed and work."[3] Munitions workers of the Great War offer some insight into working-class women's participation in the mass leisure industry: their relatively high wages combined with their mobility and the turbulence of wartime allowed them unprecedented access to recreational pursuits. Significantly, they took advantage of these possibilities of urban leisure, both old (music hall) and new (cinema), at the same time that the welfare supervisors in their factories and the voluntary agencies ministering to them as patriotic workers facilitated their access to a range of activities that had once been available only to artisans and skilled workers. It was as though these women workers were allowed a taste of older privileges and practices just as those practices were being swallowed up in the vast, urban anonymity of the developing mass leisure industry. Moreover, the chances they were given to play sports were truly extraordinary for women of the working class at this time. While middle- and upper-class women had been playing tennis and hockey for decades, football teams of women munitions

2. For example, Peter Bailey, *Leisure and Class in Victorian England: Rational Recreation and the Contest for Control, 1830–1885* (London: Routledge & Kegan Paul, 1978), esp. ch. 4 and "Conclusions"; Gareth Stedman Jones, "Class Expression versus Social Control? A Critique of Recent Trends in the Social History of 'Leisure,'" *History Workshop* 4 (Autumn 1977), 162–70; Eileen and Stephen Yeo, "Ways of Seeing: Control and Leisure versus Class and Struggle," in *Popular Culture and Class Conflict 1590–1914: Explorations in the History of Labour and Leisure,* ed. Eileen and Stephen Yeo (Sussex: Harvester Press, 1981), 128–54; Cunningham, "Leisure and Culture," 2:326–30, 335–36. On socialists' failed attempt to remake working-class leisure, see Chris Waters, *British Socialists and the Politics of Popular Culture 1884–1914* (Stanford: Stanford University Press, 1990).

3. Cunningham, "Leisure," 149.

workers were a novelty that resonated with both gender and class significance (see figure 7). The experience of being on the cusp between old
and new was an important aspect of munitions workers' enjoyment of
the privileges from which they had been previously excluded, and it
enhanced their sense of new opportunities and identities. The range of
recreational possibilities was dependent on location: women in cities took
advantage of cinemas, mass transport systems, parks, and other urban
facilities, while those in remote areas like Gretna or even in smaller towns
were more dependent on factory-based social activities. Similarly, their
age and familial roles affected the amount of time they could spend
enjoying themselves away from work. Transcending these factors, their
time off the job was the inverse of their time on the job and thus was
shaped by the length of their shifts, whether they were working daytime
or nighttime, and sometimes whether there was a big push on at the
front and they had production levels to meet.

SOCIAL LIFE, SPORT, AND
RECREATION IN THE FACTORY

In munitions factories, particularly those owned or controlled by the
government, various social activities were arranged for women workers,
and they were encouraged to organize their own. Patrick Joyce has argued
that all aspects of life for late-nineteenth-century factory operatives were
part of the culture of the factory.[4] Certainly in World War I munitions
factories, the maternal (and paternal) roles of the welfare supervisor, the
burgeoning of factory canteens, and the quantity of social activities
arranged by and within factories created a factory culture that seemed to
subsume all aspects of life. The provision of social and recreational activities in munitions factories was one element of the Welfare Department's policy to keep workers' morale and therefore their productivity as
high as possible. While work dominated the waking hours of workers,
their leisure and social lives were their inspiration and focus.

Observers frequently commented on the fact that munitions workers'
wages, when available for nonessential items, often went toward the
purchase of pianos and gramophones for their homes.[5] Pianos were also

4. Patrick Joyce, *Work, Society and Politics: The Culture of the Factory in Later Victorian
England* (New Brunswick, N.J.: Rutgers University Press, 1980), xv–xvi.

5. For example MRC, "Minutes of the Commission . . . to Enquire into the Question
of Recreation as Affecting the Younger Women of Today, 1st Meeting," 14 March 1917,
YWCA Papers, MSS. 243/178. See also Cunningham, "Leisure and Culture," 326.

placed in the canteens or mess rooms of a large number of factories, and piano playing and singing accompaniment became a favorite mealtime diversion, especially for night-shift workers, who were most in need of diversions to keep them awake and had nowhere to go outside the factory. Mealtime concerts were popular, featuring the performances of both workers and invited artists; lectures were also given during dinner hours. Some factories provided magazines or games in the mess rooms or rest rooms. Munitions factories spawned social clubs, theatrical societies, operatic societies, musical bands, debating societies, and other organizations. Although these were often formed on the initiative of workers, welfare supervisors commonly provided facilities or encouragement. Such societies made accessible to women workers the culture of self-improvement that had previously been the prerogative of artisans and skilled workers.

Welfare supervisors also arranged dances or other evening social events that at least some workers attended enthusiastically; sometimes these events were held to raise money for their own benevolent funds or for the war effort. Classes were organized in particular skills or crafts, such as sewing and typing. One welfare supervisor in Wales made herself so popular by teaching classes in industrial history and other subjects to women workers that the men workers at the same company asked for a welfare supervisor too.[6] Film screenings, particularly about the war, were held. Some factories arranged day or half-day picnics or outings, depending on weekend work schedules. Welfare supervisors were also instructed to work with voluntary and charitable agencies in the provision of clubs and recreation facilities for women workers.

Welfare supervisors encouraged exercise as part of their emphasis on health, and although munitions workers were usually doing physically exhausting work for long shifts, sport became part of the cultural fabric of many factories. For working-class women this access to sport was a great novelty; it was clear to observers that they had no prior experience of team games or exercise for pleasure.[7] In the late Victorian and Edwardian periods sport had become part of the ethos of private schools for young women of the upper classes: girls played tennis, hockey and cricket, swam, ran, and did gymnastics. At the same time women began to

6. PRO, MUN 2/28, 15 December 1917, 20.
7. Richard Holt, *Sport and the British: A Modern History* (Oxford: Clarendon Press, 1989), 118. On the introduction and evolution of sport for women, see Kathleen E. McCrone, *Playing the Game: Sport and the Emancipation of English Women, 1870–1914* (Lexington: University Press of Kentucky, 1988).

participate in the new bourgeois activities of tennis, croquet, badminton, and golf. But women of the working class had access to little other than a few gym classes at school.[8]

In wartime munitions factories football, hockey, cricket, netball, gymnastics, tennis, swimming, and other sporting classes and clubs formed; some factories provided sports fields while others made arrangements for workers to use municipal facilities. Athletics days were held when managers and their wives attended and showed their interest in the workers, who eagerly participated. Football proved very popular among women munitions workers:

> The latest development in the social life of the S. F. F. [Scottish Filling Factory] is the Georgetown Girls' Football Club. Its inception is due to the Parkhead workers of Messrs. Beardmore issuing a challenge to our Factory to play them in their Sports. Georgetown has never yet shown the white feather, and although we possessed no football team, the challenge was at once accepted by our girls with enthusiasm. Preliminary practice has begun, and from all reports we have no doubt our team will give a good account of itself.[9]

That football should have become so popular is significant because it was a sport associated with the lower classes, in contrast to tennis or cricket; in the early twentieth century professional football matches drew thousands of spectators to each game.[10] It seems that young women workers were demonstrating class allegiance at the same time that they challenged gender constrictions: not only had football been a masculine preserve, but the players wore shorts, and the game itself involved more physical aggression than other sports, such as cricket or hockey.

Integral to the success of the social activities organized within the factory was the camaraderie that women workers often developed among themselves. Women workers had several ways of resisting the tedium, dangerousness, or oppression of their factories. By establishing a spirit of cooperation and comradeship among themselves, they could create a resilient cheerfulness that helped them endure their working day or night. Observers were frequently struck by the gaiety women workers displayed, larking about when they were on breaktime or when their shift was over. Young women workers in particular often gave vent to an exuberant energy that seemed improbable after such tiring work. A reporter de-

---

8. Holt, *Sport and the British,* 117–34.

9. *Georgetown Gazette* 2, no. 8 (May 1918): 248.

10. In the 1908–09 season the First Division games averaged a crowd of 16,000. Stephen G. Jones, *Sport, Politics and the Working Class: Organised Labour and Sport in Interwar Britain* (Manchester: Manchester University Press, 1988), 19.

scribed women workers at Woolwich Arsenal on the way to the canteen at midnight: "From every corner girls, gay as crocuses in their many-coloured caps and overalls, run fleetly to the staircase leading to the canteen, laughing and chattering cheerfully as they go."[11]

By singing, joking, and bending the rules, women workers imposed their own definitions on their working hours. The extent of the social activities, clubs, and sports that flourished in wartime munitions factories suggests that workers developed friendships, enjoyed the company of their workmates, and were eager to participate in both familiar and novel activities together. These off-the-job but factory-based pursuits must have enriched their working relationships and added multiple dimensions to their identities both as munitions workers (by, for example, competing against workers at other munitions factories) and as workers at their particular factory.

LEISURE OPTIONS BEYOND THE FACTORY

In the second decade of the twentieth century, women munitions workers, with their enabling wages, enjoyed many diverse forms of commercial entertainment in their leisure time. Cinema, dancing, theater, concerts, opera, and music hall were all available to women workers, and they availed themselves of them.

Music hall had grown and evolved in the nineteenth century from rooms in pubs and "free-and-easies" into a heavily capitalized cornerstone of the mass leisure industry, in often lavish theaters. At the same time it withstood the attacks of reformers who sought to remove the drinking, clean up the prostitution, and sanitize the acts or "turns" that constituted the programs. Even when reform attempts had the weight of licensing committees on their side, such as on the London County Council from 1888 to 1907, music hall emerged essentially unchanged.[12] A favorite form of entertainment for the working and lower-middle classes, with its popular songs, audience repartee, bawdiness, and spectacular variety, it was at its peak in the years before the war.[13] The Woolwich Hippodrome, for example, boasted the following program one week in January 1917:

11. "Midnight At Woolwich Arsenal," *The Times,* 1 September 1916. Also IWM, DSR, 000684/05.

12. Susan Pennybacker, "'It Was Not What She Said But the Way in Which She Said It': The London County Council and the Music Halls," in *Music Hall: The Business of Pleasure,* ed. Peter Bailey (Milton Keynes: Open University Press, 1986), 118–40.

13. James Walvin, *Leisure and Society 1830–1950* (London: Longman, 1978), 109–11.

Oswald Williams, the famous English illusionist and phantasist, supported by Miss Roo Warwick and company, presents a gorgeous entertainment of mirth and mystery in four parts, including an entirely new and original musical phantasy, "The Rose Girl." Sam Mayo, an old favourite, keeps the house roaring with his "One-man Band." Goodfellow and Grogson, in comedy tit-bits, are very good. The ever-welcome May Henderson, the famous comedi-enne, scores heavily. John Donald, Scotch baritone, presents his song scene, "The Clachan Inn," and is well received. Other "turns" include Mdlle. Yetta, the dancing girl on the wire, Hilda Glyder, revue artiste, the Quaint Q's, and the bioscope.[14]

Cinema grew out of music hall: starting in the 1890s as one of the variety genres that music hall boasted, it became so popular that it was launched on its own. "The pictures" were introduced in working-class neighborhoods in the Edwardian period and by 1914 there were on average twenty-two cinemas per town with a population over 100,000.[15] The war dramatically increased cinema-going. Ruth Bowley noted in 1935 that during the war "women began to flock to the cinemas. War-time conditions no doubt intensified this popularity, but the films them-selves had a real appeal to women, and the era of the 'stars' began. . . . The technique of the films improved and the range of subjects widened, the intrigues of society replacing the cowboy stories. By the end of the War the cinemas were the most popular indoor amusements in London."[16] Besides the increasing appeal of films to women, the higher wages that so many women workers were receiving must have been partially respon-sible for their increased attendance at the cinema.

During the war, local cinemas showed the latest movies and young women's magazines provided readers with reviews and gossip. "Saturday Night at the 'Pictures,'" written by "Polly o' the Pictures," was a regular weekly feature in *Our Girls,* offering "a weekly survey of all that's newest, brightest and best in the cinema world." The films that Polly featured in her reviews were patently romantic and yet they offered audiences female protagonists who were independent and powerful, an interesting fact in light of Bowley's testimony to their increased appeal to women. Mary Pickford starred in *The Eternal Grind* as a highly principled factory worker with a frivolous friend. Pickford's character captures the heart of the socially conscious son of the factory owner, saves her friend Amy's life by

14. "Local Amusements: Woolwich Hippodrome," *The Pioneer,* 5 January 1917.
15. Cunningham, "Leisure," 138.
16. Ruth Bowley, "The Pursuits of Leisure: Amusements and Entertainments," in *Life and Leisure,* vol. 9 of *The New Survey of London Life & Labour,* ed. London School of Economics and Political Science (London: P. S. King & Son, 1935), 44.

forcing the rake son of the factory owner to marry her and, for the denouement, forces the factory owner to improve conditions in the factory.[17] The cinema was introducing the British working class to American culture, and it was doing so all over the nation, right in their own neighborhoods. Its appeal as escapist entertainment and its importance in broadening working-class cultural exposure were both immense. Cinema audiences also saw films about the war, which showed them battle scenes, albeit in versions censored for propaganda effects.

The theater offered another form of recreation for women munitions workers, both as performers and audience. The King's Norton Club for women munitions workers at Abbey Wood, like other clubs for munitions workers around the country, had its own theatrical troupe known as "The Purple Poms," who performed for other club members (see figure 8).[18] Munitions workers sometimes engaged in local amateur theater. On 14 September 1916, women and men munitions workers performed in the production *The Empire's Honour* at the New Town Hall, Woolwich, in aid of the Red Cross and the League of Honour.[19] As audiences, munitions workers could attend local theater near most munitions factories, including productions that traveled after their seasons at the West End. Theater attendance boomed during the war.[20]

Munitions workers appreciated music in several forms. Concerts were regular events in urban working-class areas and country towns. When Lilian Miles left Exeter and lived in Coventry during the war as a worker at White and Poppe's and then at the Coventry ordnance factory, she frequently went to the opera: "I was very fond of opera because we had a very good opera house here. . . . They used to have all the good operas, in Ale Street. . . . I used to go there two or three times a week. I used to love the operas."[21]

Dancing was a passionate pursuit for many younger munitions workers, no doubt for its courtship potential as well as the joy of dancing. Dances were held by factories, clubs, hostels, local public bodies, and commercial dancing halls, so they were readily available on a constant basis. Lillah Bonetti, who doped and sewed aircraft wings and then worked as a clerk at the Pemberton Billings aircraft factory at Southampton during the war, recalled: "Oh, yes, I was dancing mad. Every night,

17. "Saturday Night at the 'Pictures,'" *Our Girls,* 29 July 1916, 264.
18. IWM, Department of Photographs, Photo. no. Q. 108251.
19. "Munition Workers as Actors and Actresses," *The Pioneer,* 8 September 1916.
20. Walvin, *Leisure and Society,* 133.
21. IWM, DSR, 000854/04, 10.

for a period, every night of the week including Saturdays and Sundays if I could get one in. . . . [T]he Pier was a very favourite—but that was mostly gala nights, when you put on your long dress or your silk dress against cotton, and the boys dressed up in their nice new suits."[22]

Cycling had achieved the proportions of a craze in the 1890s, offering independence and freedom of movement to more affluent workers, though for women it was commonly seen at the time as apocalyptic and was often read in sexual terms.[23] Bicycles were expensive for workers' budgets, yet the Clarion Cycling Club had eight thousand members in 1913, including women.[24] During the war some women workers rode to work, particularly in the Southampton area. Bonetti remembered that cycling was a favorite weekend activity that she shared with her workmates: "Well, we worked every day except Saturdays, of course, that was our only half day. So Saturday and Sunday we would either have our own boyfriends or girlfriends that had brothers, and we would . . . all get together with cycles. Our favourite place was Hamble, or Marchwood, anywhere where there was water and we could bathe. But it was always cycling. New Forest was another nice place."[25]

Day-long outings had become a factory custom, even where workers did not normally socialize together. Joan Williams recorded the details of an outing in the summer of 1918 by her coworkers at Gwynne's engine factory in Chiswick, even though she herself had shrunk from it:

> It began very early in the morning with a tram ride to Richmond, after which they all took steamer to Staines, having lunch on board. I gathered it was bitterly cold and they all shivered in their best muslins. At Staines they had a walk and then tea at an Inn where they made friends with some wounded soldiers and all danced and played games till supper and then went home by train. It sounded dreadfully exhausting. . . . However I always feel a shirker over the "outing" and feel it was an experience missed. My special 'factory-ites' ended up with drinks all round in a public house, nothing rowdy, just a convivial glass before parting and I always feel there would have been a savour in finding myself actually leaning over a bar and being treated to a 'three' or a 'half and half' or some other mysterious measure, by the man who swept up the floors.[26]

This account is redolent with the cultural differences separating munitions

22. IWM, DSR, 7436/02. Interview by Southampton Oral History Project.
23. Holt, *Sport and the British*, 122–23.
24. Jones, *Sport, Politics and the Working Class*, 32–33.
25. IWM, DSR, 7436/02.
26. Williams, "A Munition Workers' [*sic*] Career," IWM, DPB, 56.

workers from working-class and middle-class backgrounds, not least the fact that for Williams drinking in a pub seemed attractively unrespectable.[27]

SEXUAL MORALITY AND SEXUAL ACTIVITY

Although music halls, dance halls, cinemas, and theaters had been accessible to working-class women before the war, their wartime munitions wages enabled many young women workers to take advantage of them, as well as to indulge their tastes for fashion. It was within a social landscape of such places of entertainment, a landscape in which their steady wages provided the terra firma, that women munitions workers' social and sexual lives were played out. Because of the war, many thousands of women became migrants in an important sense. They left behind their families and the communities in which they had grown up and in which they felt the greatest social constraints on their behavior and reputation. In a new city or munitions settlement, they had a certain degree of anonymity at a time when everything seemed short-term and conditional anyway. Their wages, the proximity of new acquaintances of both sexes, and the social independence they had, despite having to dodge women patrols, policewomen and YWCA workers, must have been a heady concoction.[28]

That it seemed to shock concerned observers and reformers that women were behaving in ways they themselves had not previously seen does not by itself prove that the war caused social change. Clearly the war expedited changes that were already underway, but the profusion of commentary on the behavior of women suggests, moreover, that it accelerated the changes in particular ways. Vicars and journalists condemned young women's bad language and smoking, both of which, they contended, had been aggravated by the war and were particularly evident among munitions workers. Mary Macarthur, the most eminent of contemporary women's labor leaders, commented on the changing behavior

27. On women drinking in this period, see Charles Booth, *Notes on Social Influences and Conclusion*, final vol. of *Life and Labour of the People of London* (London: Macmillan & Co., 1903), 48; Jones, *Languages of Class*, 198. Judy Lown notes that some of the Courtauld women workers frequented public houses in the 1840s. *Women and Industrialization: Gender at Work in Nineteenth-Century England* (Cambridge: Polity Press, 1990), 144. Ellen Ross notes women's pub culture in London before the turn of the century. Ross, "Survival Networks," 10. See also Carl Chinn, *They Worked All Their Lives: Women of the Urban Poor in England, 1880–1939* (Manchester: Manchester University Press, 1988), 119–20.

28. On this topic for the U.S. see Kathy Peiss, *Cheap Amusements: Working Women and Leisure in Turn-of-the-Century New York* (Philadelphia: Temple University Press, 1986).

among young women in her regular column in *Woman's Life*. Responding
to a letter from a young woman who was incensed by a newspaper's use
of the term "Flaunting Flappers," Macarthur cast the problem as a
perennial one, the age-old conflict between generations. She did, however, concede that "the last three years have brought their own difficulties
and dangers. In many directions the restraints of more normal times have
been loosened." Moreover, she suggested, changes were occurring due to
women's employment: "A girl who has to work all day in an office or
factory, and to hang on on her way home to a strap in a tram packed to
suffocation, may lose something of her virginal shyness and diffidence,
may not have eyes that are downcast and sedate, may even be hardly more
alarmed by a bomb than her great-grandmother by a mouse."[29]

To some observers, there was no doubt that World War I was a time
of loosening sexual mores in Britain. Feminist Ray Strachey, from the
vantage point of 1936, considered both the change in sexual mores and
its cause indisputable:

> It was during the war, and after it, that the changing moral standards of
> women became definitely noticeable. Thousands of women had seen their
> actual or potential mates swallowed up in that ever-increasing wave of death
> which was the Great War. Life was less than cheap; it was thrown away. The
> religious teaching that the body was the temple of the Holy Ghost could mean
> little or nothing to those who saw it mutilated and destroyed in millions by
> Christian nations engaged in war. All moral standards had been submerged.
> Life and love were held for a short moment and irretrievably lost. Little
> wonder that the old ideals of chastity and self-control in sex were, for many,
> also lost.[30]

There is concrete evidence that welfare workers and others dealing with
women munitions workers were sufficiently concerned about their sexual
activity to believe them in need of stern warnings about the likely
consequences of sexual intercourse. Lillian Evans, a welfare superintendent who wrote an advice book *To Women War Workers,* felt it necessary
to conclude with the warning that "certain personal diseases have become
more widely spread through the war." Although she hastened to add that
"perfectly pure, innocent persons may be infected through the carelessness
of sufferers from the diseases," she nevertheless cautioned women workers
to "maintain your womanly dignity always. Be true to your sex. It may

29. Mary Macarthur, "The Flaunting Flapper," *Woman's Life,* no. 302 (17 November
1917): 202.
30. Ray Strachey, ed., *Our Freedom and Its Results* (London: Leonard & Virginia Woolf,
1936), 223.

be fun to 'pick up' for a time, but the after effects are, all too often, very bitter and sad."[31]

Dr. Beatrice Webb, a medical officer in a munitions factory, wrote a handbook for welfare supervisors on the *Health of Working Girls,* based on her observations. She felt compelled to point out two areas of special concern in sexual matters: masturbation, and the sexual consequences of drinking. She hoped that by describing the symptoms of the "sufferers from this habit" of masturbation, welfare supervisors might be able to recognize them and, treating them with "not scorn, but help," encourage them to desist. They could be identified because they "are often pallid, dull-eyed with dark rings round the eyes, morose and shy, and if children or young girls, often seem unable to look one straight in the face." Although it "would be disastrous to confuse with these the ordinary anaemic, shy, diffident girl," identification was important because "where the trouble is known to exist, as much help as possible should be given in the way of cold baths, swimming lessons, ample outdoor amusements, many interests, the cutting off for a time of meat, tea and coffee, the giving up of alcohol taken." Besides being partially to blame for exacerbating the tendency to masturbation, according to Dr. Webb, alcohol was responsible for "about half the crimes against morality," by which she meant "illegitimate births." In this area, she believed, welfare supervisors could have a marked effect.[32]

At the conference for welfare supervisors held at University Hall in Leeds in August 1917, Miss Newcomb, the welfare supervisor at Messrs. Hans Renolds Ltd., stated that her firm had decided at the beginning of the war not to employ married women and asked members of the audience for "expressions of opinions on the question whether the presence of married women lowered the moral tone in a factory."[33] In the light of Miss O. M. Taylor's reminiscences of her life as a munitions worker, Miss Newcomb was right to worry about the effect of young, unmarried women working side-by-side with married women. Taylor recalled vividly:

> It was in this factory that to my disgust I was told how babies were made. I refused to believe it and told those women in no uncertain terms what I thought of them, remarking, "My mum & dad would never do that!"

31. Lillian A. Evans, "To Women War Workers," IWM, Women's Work Collection, Emp. 45.18:10.
32. Beatrice Webb, M.D., *Health of Working Girls: A Handbook for Welfare Supervisors and Others* (London: Blackie and Son Ltd., 1917), 64, 83–84.
33. "Report of Conference Held At University Hall, Leeds, August 4–6, 1917," 4th session, MRC, MSS. 97/1/EC/1/1.

How those women laughed!

It seems hard to believe in these permissive days but women in the country had no idea of what was to happen to them when they married.

At one period while working in this factory I was employed in the Transit shed, and it was very embarrassing to find that my ignorance of sexual matters and what I thought of those women who talked of them had preceded me and the men called to each other, "Hey! here comes old Molly never had it." That became the name by which I was known.[34]

A striking feature of this story is that, although it is highly unlikely that Taylor was the only young, unmarried woman employed at the factory, she was sufficiently distinctive to be accorded the nickname "old Molly never had it."

Evidence of women munitions workers' actual sexual activity, as opposed to the opinions of commentators, is elusive. Of the women workers interviewed by the Imperial War Museum's Sound Records Department, none was so forthcoming as to discuss her sex life. Lilian Bineham, however, who worked in Woolwich Arsenal, as did her father's sister, who worked with TNT powder, made one reference to sexual activity. This particular aunt, Bineham recalled, whose French husband was away in the army, was one of the women who participated in the "good deal of carryings-on, you know, during the war, with the men away, the women left at home."[35] Similarly, Elsie Slater commented on the activities of some of her coworkers at the Barnbow shell factory:

There used to be a train go this way to Barnbow, a train go that way to York, and half of them that come from Castleford used to buzz on to York, with t' soldiers. There used to be no end of 'em forget to go to work and get on wit' t' soldiers. . . . Oh, they were fast, yeah. They never turned up.[36]

"WAR BABIES," ABORTION, AND INFANTICIDE

One reasonable way of determining the extent of sexual activity during the war, particularly for the working class whose access to and use of birth control at this time, though increasing, was more limited than that

34. IWM, DD, 83/17/1, Taylor.
35. IWM, DSR, 8778/2.
36. IWM, DSR, 000725/06. Historian Carl Chinn sees the war as having sexual significance for poor women. He argues that they acquired such autonomy that after the war they refused their men sex unless they wanted it themselves. My evidence does not extend to the postwar period and cannot shed light on this assertion, but it is certainly true that public discussion of women's sexual pleasure increased significantly after the war. Chinn, *They Worked All Their Lives,* 166.

TABLE THREE.   Births per 1,000 of
Total Population, 1913–20

	England and Wales	Scotland
1913	24.1	25.5
1914	23.8	26.1
1915	21.9	23.9
1916	20.9	22.9
1917	17.8	20.3
1918	17.7	20.5
1919	18.5	22.0
1920	25.5	28.1

SOURCE: G. Evelyn Gates, ed., *The Woman's Year Book 1923–1924*, 310–11.

of other classes, is to look at the birthrate.[37] Over the longer term, birth rates had been dropping in the late nineteenth and early twentieth centuries. This decline, combined with an increasing rate of infant mortality, had sparked a movement for the cause of infant health and welfare. These long-term trajectories—of declining birth rates and increased infant mortality—partly explain why birth rates dropped significantly over the course of the war. Other reasons, of course, were the many men overseas and the many among them who died.

The figures shown in table 3 do not substantiate the wartime claims that there was a vast number of "illegitimate" children or "war babies." It seems, instead, that there was an upsurge of "peace babies" when the troops returned after the war. According to Sylvia Pankhurst, however, there was a small rise in the percentage of births that were "illegitimate," although there was no rise in the overall birthrate. In the three years from 1911 to 1914, in England and Wales there had been an average of forty-three "illegitimate" babies for every thousand births, while the rate of

37. Diana Gittins, for example, in *Fair Sex: Family Size and Structure, 1900–39* (London: Hutchinson, 1982), 162–63, shows that in the years 1910 to 1919 60 percent of the middle class, 39 percent of the skilled worker class, and 33 percent of the unskilled worker class were using birth control. Of these, 15 percent of the middle class used birth control "appliances," compared to 11 percent of skilled workers and 5 percent of unskilled workers. A caution attached to these figures is that the working-class couples often did not consider coitus interruptus a birth control method, so their birth control use is probably underrepresented by these figures.

"illegitimacy" stayed consistent, albeit much higher, in Scotland. The rate in England and Wales rose to fifty-two in the years 1915 to 1918 and then sank a little to forty-nine from 1919 to 1922. Nevertheless, Pankhurst observed, the fuss about "war babies" was out of proportion to the figures: "Eight months after the War began, arose a great talk of War Babies. Dear! Dear! one might almost have thought that the business of the Army was to propagate infants!"[38]

Allegations about rampant "war babies" were usually made by middle- and upper-class observers scandalized by what they perceived as sexual license among the working class (and perhaps among some middle-class women). But working-class morality too condemned "illegitimacy." Caroline Rennles recalled the attitude she and her coworkers at the arsenal took toward those who were unmarried and pregnant: "We thought it was disgusting for girls to be pregnant in those times."[39]

With such a weight of responsibility for their families' as well as their own reputations, and the growing desire of married women to limit family size, women workers often tried to terminate a pregnancy if they could.[40] Dr. Beatrice Webb issued the following warning about abortive practices to welfare supervisors in munitions factories:

> Pregnant women should not be allowed to work in lead, as lead-poisoning leads to miscarriage. Women who wish to terminate a pregnancy in this way are well aware of the fact, and take lead compounds for the purpose—a most dangerous practice, for themselves as well as for the undesired child. A common practice is to buy diachylon plaster, sold for cuts and wounds, roll the mixture up into pills, and go on taking them till the miscarriage occurs. In such women a blue line will be found at the junction of the teeth and the gums, and this is a danger-signal which should lead to the women being persuaded to see a doctor. There are various other methods of procuring abortion which it will not come within the scope of the Welfare Supervisor to prevent, except in so far as she can bring moral influence to bear, and this she will do less by what she says than by what she is.[41]

Dr. Janet Campbell substantiated this information in her report on "The Health of Women in Industry" in December 1918. Expressing no surprise that some working women were dismayed by pregnancy, especially when

38. Pankhurst, *Home Front,* 175–76.
39. IWM, DSR, 000566/07, reel 02, 14–15. See also Robert Roberts, *The Classic Slum: Salford Life in the First Quarter of the Century* (Manchester: Manchester University Press, 1971), 30.
40. See Patricia Knight, "Women and Abortion in Victorian and Edwardian England," *History Workshop* 4 (Autumn 1977): 57–68.
41. Webb, *Health of Working Girls,* 63.

they already had several children, she observed that "the practice of taking abortifacients and the use of other means of preventing pregnancy are becoming more familiar to working women. The subject is difficult to investigate, but to quote the Medical Officer of the Local Government Board, 'there is reason to think that on a somewhat considerable scale attempts have been made in some of the textile towns to produce abortion, and it is clear that on a large scale anti-conceptive devices are employed.'"[42]

What the Medical Officer meant by "anti-conceptive devices" here is an interesting question. Rubber sheaths, a product of the vulcanization of rubber in the nineteenth century, were being adopted by working-class people, but tended to be expensive for their budgets, with prices in 1920 ranging from around 2s. a piece for durable ones to 4s. a dozen for the lesser variety.[43] The cervical cap had a very limited use among working-class women: even when women knew of it and could get hold of it, the crowded conditions of working-class life meant no privacy in which to insert it and no bathrooms with running water. Pessaries were less problematic and could be used by a woman without her husband's knowledge. The most prevalent means of birth control for working-class people were still coitus interruptus and abortion.[44]

According to Robert Roberts, the illegitimacy rate had been declining steadily in the late nineteenth and early twentieth centuries because of the spread of knowledge of birth control techniques. The spread of literacy, he asserts, facilitated the spread of birth control knowledge through the publications of birth control societies before the war and Marie Stopes's publications after the war. Working-class women, he contends, had "for generations" used such homemade preventives as oiled sponges attached with tapes and pessaries compounded of lard and flour. It seems that literacy and pragmatism won out over fatalistic resistance to contraceptives.[45]

Women munitions workers, like other women, resorted to abortion when they found themselves in an unwanted pregnancy. Laura Verity began working at George Bray and Company in Leeds before the war, when she was 13 years old, making uprights for gas lighting burners.

42. Dr. Janet Campbell, "Memorandum: The Health of Women in Industry," *Report of the War Cabinet Committee on Women in Industry,* 231.

43. Barbara Brookes, "Women and Reproduction, 1860–1939," in *Labour and Love: Women's Experience of Home and Family 1850–1940,* ed. Jane Lewis (Oxford: Basil Blackwell, 1986), 159.

44. Ibid., 158–60.

45. Roberts, *Classic Slum,* 33–35. Cf. Elizabeth Roberts, *A Woman's Place,* 83–100.

During the war, the company undertook munitions work on contract for the national shell factory of Greenwood and Batley's at Armley. Verity recalled some of her coworkers at Bray's going to Bradford for "illegal" operations: "They didn't have it done in Leeds because they were frightened of somebody getting to know, besides one of my best friends her sister did one in Sackville Street . . . got two years for doing one, you see. Oh, they used to, oh no you could see folks going to have [*sic*] because you knew where they did them. . . . There used to be often girls die of abortion. But they called it illegal operation in those days." Several of her coworkers at Bray's who needed to go to Bradford to procure an abortion asked Verity for a "loan" of money to pay for it. Verity would then approach her father, a relatively well-off fishmonger who was known for his generosity to his neighbors, for the money: "I've a few five quids out that I've given to girls. But I don't want them back."[46]

For women munitions workers who endured an unwanted pregnancy but were too frightened, or did not know how, to have an abortion, there was another way out: infanticide. Although, like abortion, it was a traditional solution to an age-old problem, it is extremely difficult to estimate how commonly this occurred.[47] Through the war years, *The Pioneer* reported a few cases of infant bodies being found in the Thames in the Woolwich district. For women munitions workers who lived in hostels, however, the problem of disposing of the evidence was more complicated than for women who were not subject to the intrusion and inspection of maids and matrons. Two munitions workers at Woolwich were found out this way, even though they managed to have full-term pregnancies and give birth in apparent secrecy.

In May 1917, Grace Goodwin, a twenty-three-year-old munitions worker from Tunbridge Wells who lived at the King's Norton Hostel in Abbey Wood, was charged with "the wilful murder of her newly-born female child at the hostel." Early one Saturday morning, the hospital nurse at the national filling factory where Goodwin worked was called to examine Goodwin, who had been found ill. Subsequent examinations and a doctor's visit resulted in Goodwin being told to go home, which she refused to do, asking instead to be sent to lodgings. A corridor maid at the hostel who helped Goodwin to pack was puzzled by a soft, heavy

46. IWM, DSR, 000864/08, 68–71. "Quid" is slang for a pound. On abortion, see also Campbell, "Memorandum," *Report of the War Cabinet Committee on Women in Industry,* 231; Gittins, *Fair Sex,* 160–61, 164; "Illegal Operations," *The Times,* 12 September 1916.

47. See Lionel Rose, *The Massacre of the Innocents: Infanticide in Britain 1800–1939* (London: Routledge & Kegan Paul, 1986).

bundle, which Goodwin had previously explained to the nurse as being "dirty linen." The maid opened the bundle and discovered its contents. She called the nurse, who then noticed that the baby's mouth was stuffed with a cloth and its neck and knees tied together with a cord. The factory management testified to Goodwin's "excellent character" at work at the Woolwich police court trial, during which she nevertheless was found guilty of willful murder and committed for trial at the Old Bailey (the central criminal court). This court found her not guilty of willful murder but committed her to trial on a charge of concealment of birth.[48]

In September 1917, May Smith, a twenty-year-old arsenal worker who lived at a women's hostel on the Well Hall Estate, was charged in the Woolwich police court with the concealment of the birth of her child. The baby had been born in June, and the superintendent of the hostel stated that she had noticed nothing suspicious about Smith's condition. It was only in September, when a "most objectionable odour" was noticed (presumably by a maid) coming from a suitcase in Smith's room, that the child's body was discovered. The policewomen who were immediately called to deal with the incident questioned Smith that night. They discovered that she had become pregnant by a soldier who was married but had been billeted in the house where she was a domestic servant. He had since been killed in action. From her description of the birth, it appeared that the baby had been stillborn; the doctor at the Royal Arsenal Women's Hospital stated that it was impossible to know the time of death because of the decomposition of the body. Smith explained that at the time of birth she was too frightened to do anything, so just put the baby's body in a box in her cupboard.

The police court committed Smith for trial and the chief superintendent of ordnance factories paid her bail. The court was told that Smith had no relatives and no friends, and that Lilian Barker, the "lady superintendent" at the arsenal, was at present keeping her at her own expense.[49] Clearly, Smith had left her domestic service position while pregnant to take up a munitions job at the arsenal. If she knew she was pregnant when she changed jobs, perhaps munitions work seemed an anonymous refuge, in contrast to the threat of dismissal from her service position

48. "Discovery at Munition Workers Hostel," *The Pioneer*, 4 May 1917; "'Wilful Murder' Against a Munition Girl," *The Pioneer*, 18 May 1917; "Munition Girl Committed for Trial," *The Pioneer*, 1 June 1917, 5; *The Pioneer*, 22 June 1917.

49. *The Pioneer*, 21 September 1917; "Alleged Concealment of Birth," *The Pioneer*, 5 October 1917, 5; *The Pioneer*, 12 October 1917, 1; *The Women Police Service: A Report of Work Accomplished during the Year 1918–1919* (n.p., n.d.), 27–30.

when her pregnancy became obvious. Further, perhaps munitions work offered the chance to save a little money, which, in her circumstances, she may well have needed.

LOVE AND MARRIAGE

The war interfered with women's relationships with their sweethearts, fiancés, and husbands by putting distance, both geographical and emotional, between many couples. For women whose loved ones were in the armed forces, the exigencies of war rendered the whereabouts, duties, and well-being of the loved ones unknowable at most points in time. Worse, the incredible magnitude of the carnage at the battlefronts meant that hundreds of thousands of women lost their men or had them return home as amputees, disfigured, shell-shocked, or alienated. Even when the man was alive and well, the knowledge that he might meet such a fate must have put a searing tension into a relationship. For women involved with civilian men, the war may have challenged their sense of their partners' masculine identity on grounds of their opposition to or exclusion from the war. For all too many heterosexual women, the war cut off their chances for marriage.

Vera Brittain noted the emotional wounds inflicted by the war in her grief-suffused elegy to both her fiancé and her brother, *Testament of Youth*. Writing of her fiancé's mother, Brittain observed: "Love, for her, was something to be gloried in and acknowledged; like so many others, she had not seen enough of the War at first hand to realise how quickly romance was being replaced by bitterness and pessimism in all the young lovers whom 1914 had caught at the end of their teens."[50] To women of all classes and ages, the war was a hard dose of reality that tested their notions of marriage and sexual morality; many determined to grab what they could while they could.

Marriage held diverse meanings for young women workers, including independence from their natal families, domesticity, children, and leisure time centered on the home. Perhaps above all else, for many it sharply marked the end of their working years and thus meant relief from the grind of a wage-earner's existence. Not all women workers were able to leave their jobs after marriage, however, especially during the war, nor did all women want to do so. Yet the ideal of staying at home was

50. Vera Brittain, *Testament of Youth* (1933; reprint, n.p.: Wideview Books, 1980), 184.

common enough that *The Girls' Friend* included a piece in its advice section urging young women to keep working rather than succumb to marriage as protection against the world:

> To the girl who must earn her own living, I say go bravely to the call of duty in which your path may lie before you, and falter not. . . . Don't look to marriage to help you get out of working, for if you marry some honest young fellow who has none of this world's goods, and only his strong, sturdy hands and willing heart, you will find you have got into a labyrinth of work a hundredfold harder and more wearing than that for which you received a regular and snug little stipend, which you could have for your very own, to spend just as your fancy willed.[51]

This advice served the interests of the state well during the wartime crisis.

Nevertheless, the consensus of public opinion was that many wartime couples rushed into marriage to grab what time together, and "legitimate" sex, they could. A YWCA report for 1915 solemnly noted: "A goodly number of our young women have entered the state of holy matrimony. We earnestly hope and trust that their married lives will be happy. The War marriages on the part of some girls have given us deep concern, as undoubtedly many married in haste, and we hope that they will not have to repent at leisure. In some cases it is sadly probable that they will never meet their husbands again."[52]

The statistics in table 4 show that there was something of a rush into marriage, but only in 1915 in England and Wales. There, the marriage rate leapt upward in 1915, dropped dramatically in 1916, sank further in 1917, and jumped again in 1918. In Scotland, meanwhile, the rate was slightly lower, and only a small increase occurred in 1915. In all three countries, 1919 witnessed a veritable boom in marriages, no doubt owing to marriages delayed until the war was over.

Regardless of the YWCA's hopes that their women would not have to "repent at leisure," separation and divorce terminated a proportion of those wartime marriages not ended by death. As one writer recorded in 1920: "In the first year of the war the number of cases heard in the divorce court rose from 289 to 520, which was the highest figure then on record. Last season the number had sprung up to 775, while on the present term's lists there are nearly 800 cases, showing the exceeding

51. "The Girl Who Must Earn Her Own Living," *Girls' Friend*, no. 951 (26 January 1918): 27.

52. YWCA, "Homes for Working Girls in London: The Work of the Year 1915" (London, n.d.), 13. Also Caine, *Our Girls*, 79.

TABLE FOUR.   Marriages per 1,000 of
Total Population, 1913–20

	England and Wales	Scotland
1913	15.7	14.2
1914	15.9	14.8
1915	19.4	15.2
1916	14.9	13.1
1917	13.8	12.6
1918	15.3	14.4
1919	19.7	18.3
1920	20.2	19.3

SOURCE: G. Evelyn Gates, ed., *The Woman's Year Book 1923–1924,* 310–11.

increase on the pre-war rate. A large percentage of the marriages which are dissolved by the court have been contracted since August 1914."[53]

Yet divorce was too expensive for many workers. A *Punch* cartoon commenting on the subject showed "Munition Kate" leaning over a counter to the "Puzzled Income-Tax Official" who was querying whether her separation from her husband was a legal one. She replied, "I dunno about 'Official.' All I knows is as when 'e comes to our 'ouse we calls the police and they chucks 'im out."[54]

According to Charles Booth's 1903 survey of life among London's laboring poor, marriage was not as socially necessary in the working class as it was in the middle or upper class. Although most working-class people got married in early adulthood, many of these marriages ended in separation (but not divorce because of the expense), which was followed by nonlegalized cohabitation with another partner. Such cohabitation was socially acceptable, and it was "said of rough labourers that they behave best if not married to the women with whom they live."[55] Despite this tolerance of cohabitation, marriage was made a significantly more attractive prospect during the war by the fact that a legal wife could claim a separation allowance when her husband was serving in the armed forces, whereas a de facto spouse could not.

In December 1918, the Ministry of Labour was concerned about the

53. Hartley, *Women's Wild Oats,* 98.
54. *Punch,* 9 October 1918, 225.
55. Booth, *Notes on Social Influences,* 41–42.

domestic abilities of war brides who had spent the duration working in industry. It estimated that nearly 400,000 women had married soldiers during the term of the war, that 300,000 of these had no children, and that many of them had been in the work force. At the suggestion of the Women's Trade Union League, they decided to institute classes in which "the girls will be given lectures and practical demonstrations in all kinds of domestic work, infant welfare and sewing." Courses were to be established around the country to be made open to all women registered as unemployed. Thus the ministry hoped to reconcile women who had been expelled from their wartime jobs to their fate of marriage, domesticity and motherhood. For those who were neither war brides nor patient fiancées, an alternative scheme was considered to resettle "munition girls" into domestic service.[56]

CLUBS AND HUTS FOR MUNITIONS WORKERS

Women reformers and their organizations chose an aggressive approach to what they saw as working-class women's susceptibility to the unsettling social effects of the war. By offering positive counter-attractions to the temptations of street life and pubs, they believed they could draw women away from "vice" and moral danger and bring them within their own protective reach. Very quickly after the start of the war, therefore, the YWCA, the Church Army, the Girls' Friendly Society, and the women patrols of the National Union of Women Workers (NUWW) expanded their existing efforts and launched a network of social shelters for women around the country.[57] Rest huts on the grounds of munitions factories and clubs in working-class neighborhoods provided places where women could rest, socialize with other women, find nonalcoholic drinks, and enjoy wholesome recreational pursuits under the supervision of a reform worker. Some of these shelters encouraged women to bring their men friends along on special occasions for supervised socializing. Most were motivated in good part by the hope of coaxing working-class women further into the fold of Christianity. The heaviest concentration of YWCA

56. "Munition Girls' Future: 400,000 War Brides," *The Pioneer,* 20 December 1918, 6.

57. On the work of settlement house women to provide clubs for young working women before the war, see Martha Vicinus, *Independent Women: Work and Community for Single Women 1850–1920* (Chicago: University of Chicago Press, 1985), esp. 232–41. On the girls' club movement in the late nineteenth and early twentieth centuries, see Carol Dyhouse, *Girls Growing Up in Late Victorian and Edwardian England* (London: Routledge & Kegan Paul, 1981), 104–14.

clubs and huts was in London, but they were also located in virtually every county of England as well as seven sites in Wales.[58] By November 1916, the YWCA claimed six thousand members in their clubs for women.[59]

Not all clubs and huts catered to women munitions workers: others were for Land Army workers, VADs, the WAACs, or other paramilitary groups, and many described their clientele as simply "girls and soldier friends," a rubric under which munitions workers certainly fell.[60] Those that catered to munitions workers believed that they were performing an important national service. One YWCA propagandist described the problem with which they dealt:

> There is the very difficult problem of how best to help this army of hundreds of thousands, with its new wealth and its new freedom, to spend its scanty leisure at least not injuriously, and if possible with profit. This is where these Rest Rooms (they might just as well be called clubs) come in. There are so many girls—very many of them girls who had never left home before and are quite unarmed against city dangers—who have nowhere to go out of work hours except a dingy little room shared with a mate in some dingy lodging house. There are the streets and there are the picture palaces, of course. . . .[61]

One "hut leader" made it clear that evangelizing was an integral function of the rest hut: "In huts and canteens we do our utmost to reach the girls in the short time we are with them. We believe that much former opposition to Christianity has gone."[62] Some women munitions workers, however, must have been deterred from using YWCA and other organizations' huts and clubs when the religious mission was too overtly pushed. Disagreement over the social activities permitted at many clubs split the YWCA at the end of the war.[63] A splinter group left to form the Christian Alliance of Women and Girls, comprised of disaffected YWCA members who felt that there had not been sufficient emphasis on the religious mission of the association in its war work.

Like the YWCA, the Girls' Friendly Society (GFS), an organization begun in 1874 under the aegis of the Church of England to protect and

58. MRC, YWCA Papers, MSS. 243/62.

59. Evidence of Mrs. Piercy before the Women's Service Committee, 23 November 1916, IWM, Women's Work Collection, Mun. 18.1, 72.

60. "List of Y.W.C.A. Centres for Special War-Time Work," MRC, MSS. 243/62.

61. Hugh Martin, *The Girl He Left Behind Him: The Story of A War-Worker* (published for the YWCA, London: Witherby & Co., 1916), 11.

62. *Newsletter* (YWCA, November 1918), 68.

63. "To the Countess of Portsmouth: National President of the Young Women's Christian Association of Great Britain," MRC, YWCA Papers, MSS. 243/14/23/8.

help poor girls and young women, saw the war as an opportunity to cast its net still wider. The GFS launched a public appeal for ten thousand pounds with which to provide accommodation, clubs, recreation rooms, and canteens for working women, especially munitions workers. Raising even more than the desired amount, it erected hostels, clubs, and huts in England, Wales, and Scotland. To an even greater degree than the YWCA, it stressed the evangelical nature of its work and commonly incorporated small chapels or prayer rooms as part of hostel and club buildings. The GFS also participated in a campaign of spiritual work carried out by the Church of England in munitions areas. Its own special contribution was the printing and distributing of small cards inscribed with a biblical message: "The little Card with its printing in red and black became a familiar feature in many of the cubicles of the working girls in those times, as it hung by its slender ribbon, bearing on its face the words of Christ, from St. John xv. 14, 17, and a simple daily prayer."[64]

Brian Harrison contends that World War I "confirmed the GFS in its backward-looking puritan values. Its periodicals grew thinner but no less dull: its war-work consisted of organizing a massive campaign for thrift, prayer and purity." Despite its own tremendous pride in the success of its fundraising campaign, and the new facilities that it completed, the society lost 6,537 associates and 38,326 members.[65] Like the YWCA, it too was split between the pragmatism of its active leaders and the unswerving convictions of its ideologues.

The Women Patrols Committee of the NUWW also opened clubs for young working women. "The object of the Patrol movement is to draw young girls away from the dangerous atmosphere of the streets," it asserted. "It is therefore essential to provide for them a place where they can meet members of the other sex under good conditions, and under healthy influences which will serve to counteract the restless excitement of the present time."[66] In a March 1916 report to Home Secretary M. G. Carden, the honorary secretary of the Women Patrols Committee informed him that the clubs the committee had opened were "of great value" because "the girls have only the streets and open places for recreation." The patrols, she reported, directed their energies toward "the

64. M. H. Stubbs, *Friendship's Way: Being the History of the Girls' Friendly Society, 1875–1925* (London, 1926): 100.

65. Brian Harrison, "For Church, Queen and Family: The Girls' Friendly Society 1874–1920," *Past and Present* 61 (November 1973): 137.

66. Liverpool Women's War Service Bureau, *Report August 7th, 1914–August 7th, 1915* (Liverpool, 1915), 45–48.

rough girls" whom they wanted to draw off the streets. One tack that they had found successful was to create clubs specifically for these "rough girls," who often refused to go into existing clubs.[67]

Often enough in these clubs middle-class women reformers were confronted by the cultural chasm separating them from their sometimes reluctant flock.[68] *Punch* captured the problem in an exchange between a befurred and upright volunteer and the group of rowdy young working women whom she sought to uplift with her advice. When she admonished them, "Of course you know, dear girls, ladies never talk to gentlemen unless they have been properly introduced?" to the delight of her friends, one young woman replied, "We knows it, Mum, and we feels sorry for yer" (see figure 9).[69]

In an unusually honest assessment of the proceedings at a typical club in "a large North-East Coast town," one volunteer described the trials she and her covolunteers faced even after the initial battle of persuading some "factory girls" in "their dark shawls" to attend. With the best of intentions, they tried to employ a "self-governing" method in which the women decided on their own entertainment and generally considered it a success. Nevertheless,

> the girls were so easily satisfied, so hostile to innovations. They wanted dancing—their own sort of dancing, not ours; they wanted, also, to "do something for the soldiers"; they did not wish for singing, apart from outbursts of impromptu ragtimes; they did not wish to learn new dances, nor songs, nor games, nor to have anything read aloud while they sewed. They would unite in attacking or opposing anything or person they disliked, but they were slow to combine for purposes of pleasure or work.

Despite feeling that she and her coworkers had dealt patiently with these problems and bravely endured incidents such as when "a kindly and accomplished singer" was received with only "blank silence" immediately followed by "loud and discordant voices burst[ing] into, 'Pack all your troubles in an old kit-bag, and Smile, Smile, Smile,'" the writer could only conclude that "our success is difficult to gauge."[70]

In the face of such difficulties, clubs for women workers spread around the nation, reflecting the faith of social workers in the value of their

67. PRO, HO 45/10806/309485/74, 15 March 1916.

68. On difficulties and strategies of girls' club leaders see Vicinus, *Independent Women*, 232–33.

69. *Punch,* 23 January 1918, 59.

70. Margaret Weddell, "My Friend Sarah," *Common Cause,* 9 March 1917, 632. See also *The Pioneer,* 25 May 1917, 4.

efforts and the zeal that middle- and upper-class women had to do something for the war effort. Rest huts for munitions workers provided a welcome facility, a warm place where workers could relax or socialize on their dinner break. Clubs created their own clientele among munitions workers by offering recreation and a social life where other alternatives were short. Particularly when they were situated near the munitions factory, hostel, or area where women lodged, they constituted a strong attraction to many women. The Girls' Club in the Cow Lane Rooms, Coventry, opened in the autumn of 1917, was soon "crowded to its utmost capacity" because of its offerings of "excellent rooms, well furnished, where girls can spend their time reading, writing, or playing quiet games." Besides "an excellent canteen," it also provided "a large hall, which is in constant use for dancing, physical exercises, and entertainments" including a weekly dance to which members were allowed to bring male friends.[71]

Some clubs, such as one started in the basement of the welfare supervisor's office at a munitions factory, appealed to workers by providing them with their own space and the autonomy to do as they wished with it; these were more in the tradition of workingmen's clubs than the clubs run by reformers. This particular one, the supervisor reported, had the strength of its own informality:

> This Club is managed by a Committee of girls who are all workers. They have the use of the room at all times when they are off duty, and I find they freely use it. There is hot water and they are able to wash blouses etc. they have a set of irons, a sewing machine, a piano (hired) there is a gas ring and they make tea or coffee whenever they like, supplying their own. . . . The tone and standard are entirely in their hands and the Committee is responsible for all arrangements. There is room for about 10 couples to dance in an outer hall. . . . The members have so far been busy getting together furniture, decorations, etc. Their plan is to have "Industrial" mornings when their time off falls then, and they have musical and social evenings alternate weeks.[72]

No doubt the appeal of this club included its relative lack of supervision and absence of a reformist agenda, but it also provided facilities that at least some women did not have in their homes, lodgings, or hostels.

The success of the club movement was due in part to the central organizational structures promoting it. The National Organisation of Girls' Clubs, which worked in connection with the NUWW, saw clubs

71. "Workers' Welfare: What Coventry Is Doing," *Midland Daily Telegraph*, 18 May 1918.
72. IWM, Women's Work Collection, Mun. 18.9/13, app. B.

as integral to a comprehensive scheme for improving the lives of young working women.[73] By 1917 the Ministry of Munitions, through the extramural welfare workers of its welfare and health section, recognized the importance of providing recreational facilities for workers. Worried that the "insufficiency of wholesome recreation was leading to industrial unrest . . . and to public disorder," they came to the conclusion that "clubs were needed for the health and happiness of the workers, and to keep them off the streets."[74] Like the rational recreation movement of the nineteenth century, high hopes were held by many associated with the club movement for the legacy it would bestow on the postwar world.[75]

Patrick Joyce has argued in relation to the late nineteenth century that it was the working class's own consolidated leisure pursuits and options that did much to confound the middle-class reform effort; workers gained access to the city and were lost to reformers.[76] I would argue that the significance of women munitions workers' leisure and recreation is that they gained better access to the mass leisure industry at the same moment that they were exposed to a full if belated barrage of rational recreation options and reformers' suasions and lures. That they mingled both, and that they were so obviously resistant to the reformers, show that their rejection of reformers' agendas arose from their own choices as well as from the options provided by mass transport and the mass entertainment industry.

Women were at best subordinate objects of the rational recreation movement in the nineteenth century and were left out of most of the self-improvement enterprise of mechanics' institutes and workingmen's clubs.[77] Finally identified in the First World War as workers of national importance, ministered to by welfare supervisors and a myriad of reform associations, they encountered the full force of reform when the growing secularism of the working class inured them to much of its message. Working-class men's participation in reform societies in the nineteenth century and their development of modes of respectable manhood consti-

73. "Problems and Prospects of the Working Girl," *Christian Commonwealth,* 29 September 1915.

74. Dr. E. L. Collis, "Welfare Work Outside Factories," 18 April 1918, PRO, MUN 5/ 94/346/39:8.

75. IWM, Women's Work Collection, Mun. 18.9/13, 3 (1918). On the rational recreation movement, see Bailey, *Leisure and Class.*

76. Joyce, *Work, Society and Politics,* 286, 337–38.

77. June Purvis, *Hard Lessons: The Lives and Education of Working-Class Women in Nineteenth-Century England* (Cambridge: Polity Press, 1989), pt. 3.

tuted part of their negotiated relationships with masters and employers. For wartime women workers, their negotiated relationships with women of the middle and upper classes included conditional acceptance of the clearly useful facilities voluntary workers provided. This occurred within the context of their massive escape from the deference of the mistress-servant relationship for the duration. But it also occurred in factories that were the site of significantly expanded opportunities for middle-class women. Thus munitions factories became the venue for new interclass relationships among women.

CHAPTER SEVEN

Class Relations among Women

How else can we explain that amazing outburst in August
1914, when the daughters of educated men who had been
educated thus rushed into hospitals, some still attended by
their maids, drove lorries, worked in fields and munition
factories, and used all their immense stores of charm, of
sympathy, to persuade young men that to fight was heroic[?].
. . . [The educated man's daughter] would undertake any
task however menial, exercise any fascination however fatal
that enabled her to escape. Thus consciously she desired
"our splendid Empire"; unconsciously she desired our
splendid war.

Virginia Woolf, Three Guineas, *1938*

Women in the munitions factories were a heterogeneous cohort comprising working-class women who performed skilled and unskilled labor in a vast array of capacities; patriotically inspired middle- and upper-class "war workers" in for the duration; middle-class women who saw the war as a momentous opportunity for women to establish themselves in professions and careers from which they had previously been excluded, such as engineering and policing, or in which they had been marginalized, such as medicine; a greatly increased number of (middle-class) women welfare supervisors; and other middle-class women who sought to make their contribution to the war through the work of charitable organizations such as the YWCA, particularly through the welfare, and the control, of women workers. For women of the working class, class differences among women were not only a matter of dealing with the "ladies" who were suddenly in their midst but also of coming to terms with that other army of women in positions of authority above them, including welfare supervisors, overlookers, and chargehands (although sometimes these were of their own class), women police on the factory floor, women patrols on the streets outside, and women volunteers running the canteens, rest huts, and hostels that often were the only amenities available.

Relationships among women in wartime munitions factories underscored their relative class positions. Middle- and upper-class women maintained authority over working-class women, although the public nature of the factory environment significantly altered these relations. Women who once faced each other as servant and mistress now found themselves interacting as worker and welfare supervisor, worker and policewoman, worker and canteen or rest-hut volunteer. In domestic service, the code of employer-employee relations had been based on wealth and class deference, with interaction occurring in relative isolation and without recourse to an arbitrator. On the factory floor, women interacted publicly and with a certain degree of anonymity, according to lines of authority ostensibly defined by job description alone. Especially in the engineering, metal, and chemical trades, the codes of the factory were male-defined. Not only the products of convention, they bore the weight of law, state regulation, and agreements between unions and government.

At this intersection, where it was theoretically possible for women to join together in their newfound roles and power, their class identities obstructed gender-bonding. Rather, the tensions between women underscored their class identities and strengthened their realization of cultural definitions of class. Workers were freed from the servility of domestic service, worked together in large numbers in the same space rather than within isolated households, and bonded in recognition of their shared status as workers, a development clearly reflected in the leaps in women's union membership during the war. They recognized and resented the maternalist and professional attitudes that welfare supervisors, women police, women patrols, and others adopted, using their age, education, and expertise to augment authority based on class hierarchy. The motivations and ideologies of the middle- and upper-class women who worked in these capacities were inevitably diverse, shaped differently by religion, political commitment, empathy, and altruism. Certainly at least some wanted genuinely to help improve the lives and conditions of working-class women. However, women in official and semiofficial capacities were not trying to befriend or entertain working-class women. Their roles centered around organizing, disciplining, and controlling women workers.

Middle- and upper-class women who availed themselves of wartime professional opportunities dramatically pushed forward the process (begun on a small scale in the 1870s and 1880s) of women entering the professions. In so doing, they engaged in the transformation of the power that middle- and upper-class women held over their working-class sisters, from a moral authority based on the social construction of genteel femininity to a professional authority based on education and expertise. As professional "experts" they participated in the maintenance and shaping of the dominant social and cultural order, through their authority over women workers whose wartime autonomy posed challenges.[1]

While some feminists addressed themselves to the subject of women munitions workers and were interested in the significance of the vast expansion of employment for women during the war, there was no transcendent feminist analysis of the subject or its ramifications.[2] A major reason for the relative lack of feminist focus on women munitions workers was the opposition of many leading feminists to the war effort and therefore to women's participation in it. The middle- and upper-class feminists who had led the prewar suffrage movement in its diverse factions were bitterly divided by the war, with some opposing the war on the basis of a pacifism they believed integral to their feminist convictions and others supporting the war cause and believing that patriotic involvement would further women's inclusion in the political system. For the suffragists who opposed the war and the war effort, and who threw their energies into the women's peace conference held at The Hague in April 1915 and the founding of the Women's International League (later the Women's International League for Peace and Freedom), opposition to the war was entirely consistent with their prewar emphasis on internationalism and with their determination not only to get the vote but to redefine politics radically. This group of feminists included more than half of the executive committee of the National Union of Women's Suffrage Societies, who resigned their positions because of the union's decision to support the war effort.[3]

1. Here I am drawing on T. J. Jackson Lears's explication of Gramsci's concept of cultural hegemony, which shows how officials and experts participate in shaping the values and attitudes of society. "The Concept of Cultural Hegemony: Problems and Possibilities," *American Historical Review* 90, no. 3 (June 1985): 572.

2. Interest in the subject was sufficient that articles on women munitions workers appeared in periodicals such as *The Englishwoman, Common Cause,* and *Nineteenth Century* throughout the war.

3. On the split in the suffrage movement over the war, see Jo Vellacott, "Feminist Consciousness and the First World War," *History Workshop Journal* 23 (Spring 1987): 81–101; Johanna Alberti, *Beyond Suffrage: Feminists in War and Peace, 1914–28* (New York: St. Martin's Press, 1989); Catherine Marshall, C. K. Ogden, and Mary Sargant Florence, *Militarism Versus Feminism: Writings on Women and War* (1915), rev. ed., ed. Margaret Kaminer and Jo Vellacott (London: Virago, 1987); Jill Liddington, *The Road to Greenham Common: Feminism and Anti-Militarism in Britain since 1820* (Syracuse, N.Y.: Syracuse University Press, 1991). The term "suffragette" was used by those who were self-consciously militant in the suffrage cause. Those who believed in peaceful, constitutional tactics called themselves "suffragists."

The prewar feminists who believed in internationalism and were antimilitarist included women of the working class as well as the middle and upper classes. But, as Jill Liddington has shown in the case of radical feminist and pacifist Selina Cooper, for working-class feminists it was not easy to take a principled stand for internationalism and pacifism. Having to maintain an income was a sheer necessity.[4] As Agnes Smith, an unemployed weaver, wrote to Virginia Woolf in 1938 in response to *Three Guineas:* "You say glibly that the working woman could refuse to nurse and to make munitions—and so stop the war. A working woman who refuses to work will starve—and there is nothing like stark hunger for blasting ideals."[5]

Sylvia Pankhurst was an important exception to middle-class feminists who preferred not to focus on women making munitions of war: although she opposed the war effort she was strongly interested in conditions for women workers. Her newspaper the *Woman's Dreadnought* (later the *Workers' Dreadnought*) monitored conditions and issues in munitions factories throughout the war. Among those who supported the war effort, Emmeline and Christabel Pankhurst expressed no interest in working-class women's issues; Eleanor Rathbone used them as a vehicle for arguing for family allowances (already framing the argument that would cause a major split among feminists in the 1920s); and Millicent Garrett Fawcett saw in women munitions workers evidence of great promise for improvement in women's status, perhaps unsurprisingly, given that she had alienated so many of her suffrage allies by her support for the war effort.[6]

Thus the feminist-suffragist movement, dominated as it was by middle-class women, failed to offer much leadership or support that could be of use to women munitions workers. It was the feminist activists (many of whom were also suffragists) who had devoted themselves to the issues of women workers before the war—such as Mary Macarthur, Margaret Bondfield, other women labor leaders, socialists, and women factory inspectors—who were of most assistance to women munitions workers

4. Jill Liddington, *The Life and Times of a Respectable Rebel: Selina Cooper 1864–1946* (London: Virago, 1984), 264–65.

5. Letter from Agnes Smith, Holmfirth, Yorkshire to Virginia Woolf, 7 November 1938, Virginia Woolf Correspondence Collection, University of Sussex Library. I am grateful to Brenda Silver for this note.

6. Eleanor F. Rathbone, "The Remuneration of Women's Services," in *The Making of Women: Oxford Essays in Feminism,* ed. Victor Gollancz (London: George Allen & Unwin, 1917), 100–127.

in improving their wages and establishing some control over their working conditions.

The multiple emblems of class status, such as language, accent, dress, recreational interests, and standards of housing, all operated in the relationships between women of different classes in the workplace. The friction that resulted, and the close proximity in which different classes of women worked during the war, on an unprecedented scale, contributed to the class polarization that characterized politics in Britain in the 1920s and into the 1930s. It is often asserted that the male experience of trench warfare was a politicizing one: the fallibility of their officers and leaders showed men of the lower classes weaknesses in their social superiors, and the terrible degree of sacrifice exacted from those who survived to return home politicized them into higher levels of involvement after the war.[7] I contend that women on the factory floor were politicized by the public recognition of their work, through their union organization, their anger at demobilization, and class interaction with other women. That politicization provided impetus in the postwar period not to feminist but to class-based movements.

AUTHORITY ON THE FACTORY FLOOR

Like most organizations, munitions factories operated by a hierarchical system of authority. Workers were subject to the orders of chargehands, overlookers, foremen or forewomen, welfare supervisors, women police and other security personnel, and whatever managers the firm employed. Increasingly during the war, the jobs of chargehand, overlooker, and foreman were given to women, either women of superior education or class background or responsible workers promoted from the ranks.[8]

---

7. Eric J. Leed has described the high levels of anger and violence among the veterans returning from the front at the end of the war, anger at the society that had impelled them to undergo such horrors. *No Man's Land: Combat and Identity in World War I* (Cambridge: Cambridge University Press, 1979), 193–204.

8. In at least two munitions factories, both in Scotland, women rose to senior levels of management. At the Georgetown National Filling Factory, Agnes Borthwick, who held an M.A. degree from Glasgow University and had studied in the U.S., became works manager at the age of twenty-seven. McLaren, *Women of the War,* 29–31. At the Galloway Engineering Co. Ltd., which produced parts for airplane engines in Kirkoudbright, Scotland, the determination of the owner to train women as engineers was such that women employees were treated as proper engineering apprentices and women held several of the managerial positions, including that of works superintendent. Helen Fraser, *Women and War Work* (New York: G. Arnold Shaw, 1918), 123–24.

Middle-class women were recruited into munitions factories specifically to be trained and employed as overlookers, on the assumption that their education and class advantage suited them for the job. Apart from the authority, one of the incentives to become a chargehand, overlooker, or forewoman was the better rate of pay. At Georgetown National Filling Factory, for example, while ordinary workers were receiving a rate of 25s. a week, chargehands earned 27s. 6d. a week, overlookers 30s. a week, and sectional forewomen 35s. a week.[9]

A chargehand was responsible for a small gang of fellow workers. She ensured their attendance to factory rules governing hours, uniforms, and safety; encouraged workers to move quickly on and off at each shift; and reported illness or trouble to the welfare supervisor.[10] Another responsible position was that of inspector of pieces produced; women who were skilled enough to be promoted to inspection also received a higher rate of pay. An overlooker was the next rank up from chargehand, responsible for the supervision of a whole "shop," that is, a building or area of workers. Elsie McIntyre (née Bateson), who remembered well how her uniform became more attractive with each promotion, recalled also the clear indication of the status each level was accorded: "I was Elsie as a worker, Elsie as a chargehand but went to Miss Bateson when I was an overlooker."[11] The overlooker was responsible for the training of new workers as well as their supervision.

Within the ranks of workers on the factory floor, distinctions of authority, status, and wages were significant even among women of the same socioeconomic background. The fact that women of the middle and upper classes who chose to work in a munitions factory were automatically considered more eligible for positions as chargehand and overlooker underscored existing class tensions.

WELFARE SUPERVISORS

The relationship between women workers and women welfare supervisors was ambiguous at best. Welfare supervisors had grown from sparse novelties before the war to accepted agents of wartime efficiency because of their placement in munitions factories by the Welfare Department of the Ministry of Munitions. The amenities and comforts that the welfare

9. Ministry of Munitions, *Scottish Filling Factory,* 149.
10. "Duties of Chargehands," IWM, Women's Work Collection, Mun. 21/37.
11. IWM, DSR, 000673/09, 7.

supervisor brought in her wake meant that she was met with some gratitude on the part of workers. The dimension of her job that included moral supervision and discipline, however, provoked simultaneous resentment and suspicion on the part of workers.

The trade union movement was flatly opposed to, or at best deeply wary of, welfare supervisors. On the one hand, they objected to the ambiguous position of the welfare supervisor: while purporting to work in the interests of women workers, in fact she often was being paid directly by the employer and functioned as a part of the management, with the clear aim of high productivity. To the hard-line unionist or socialist, welfare work was amelioration, an attempt to soften the systemic conflict of interests between employer and employed. Mary Macarthur, representing the National Federation of Women Workers, testified to the War Cabinet Committee on Women in Industry in October 1918 that

> the very word welfare sticks in the nostrils of the women workers. . . . Last August we had a bi-ennial Conference. Our work women were there from the bench and factory from all parts of the country. We sat two days discussing all sorts of subjects. . . . [T]here was no more caustic debate than that on Welfare. All the women were on their feet at once to say how much they hated it. . . . One woman got up and in the same tone of triumph as she might have said "We are doing a skilled man's job and getting his rate". She said "We have no Welfare in our factory". That was the atmosphere of that Conference.[12]

The relationship between women workers and women welfare supervisors (who were almost exclusively middle class) was suffused with class tension.

The fact that welfare supervisors were employed as much for the purpose of controlling workers as for any promotion of their well-being is reflected by their alternative name, that of "lady superintendents" (see figure 10). In many factories, welfare supervisors had the ultimate control over women workers, the hiring, firing, and meting out of punishment for bad timekeeping or other misdemeanors. There were several possible attitudes that could work adversely for the supervisor. The *Woman's Dreadnought* complained that the welfare supervisor at the filling factory at Abbey Wood was the wife of the manager, and that, not unnaturally, she refused to listen to complaints against the management.[13] Another supervisor made a disastrous beginning on her first day at work by telling

12. Evidence heard by the War Cabinet Committee on Women in Industry, 1918. IWM, DPB, Women's Work Collection, Emp. 70/1.
13. "An Insult to Honest Working Women," *Woman's Dreadnought*, 22 July 1916, 515.

the workers that they ought to have a club because their homes were so overcrowded and dirty; the women threw their lunch at her.[14]

In contrast, the senior welfare supervisor at Woolwich Arsenal was considered a great success even by those who opposed welfare work in general. Lilian Barker was later made a dame of the British Empire in recognition of her work at Woolwich and afterward in women's prisons. Barker was stern and authoritarian at times and puritanical about some issues. If she saw a woman worker with makeup on, she would order her to "go and wash that muck off your face." Always urging on the women the patriotic importance of their work, she constantly railed against absenteeism and preempted strikes if possible.

Yet Barker established a rapport with the workers at Woolwich. Her accessibility was such that there was "a constant throng of workers" gathered around her office, for whom she did her best to straighten out any work, financial, or even emotional problems.[15] She visited sick workers at home or in the hospital; when one woman was blinded in a work accident, Barker kept in touch with her as she recuperated, took her for drives on her tours of the arsenal, and encouraged her to cope with her impairment.[16] When one of her welfare supervisors asked her when to interrupt workers embracing, she replied, "When you see a man with one arm round a girl, look the other way, but if he's got two arms round her, it's time to intervene."[17] She once upset some clergymen speaking on a platform with her when she described unmarried motherhood as "a very human, even a generous sin" compared to others, and shocked male workers at the arsenal by refusing to dismiss an unmarried woman who became pregnant unless the man in question was also dismissed.[18]

Barker's successful rapport with workers was due in part to the fact that she was born in near-poverty, the daughter of a former butler. Her work was sufficiently distinctive that even the *New Statesman*, when it published a piece condemning welfare work in general, called her the "Florence Nightingale of this war" and hailed her work as "brilliantly and consistently successful." Welfare supervisors in general, it charged, were "meddlesome" women of the "lady bountiful" type, not truly concerned with the health and comfort of employees. "The lady-bountiful supervisor

14. *Aberdeen Journal*, 3 April 1918.
15. McLaren, *Women of the War*, 10.
16. Elizabeth Gore, *The Better Fight: The Story of Dame Lilian Barker* (London: Geoffrey Bles, 1965), 73–74.
17. Ibid., 77.
18. Mitchell, *Women on the Warpath*, 250.

is more concerned with the worthiness of the recipients of her bounty than with the worthiness of her bounty. She has to discover, not merely whether the workers for whom she is responsible are physically fit for their work, but also whether they are morally deserving of her patronage."[19]

Welfare supervisors sometimes met with suspicious resistance when they first entered a factory, and unless they were tactful enough to diffuse the tension, strikes could result. Some welfare supervisors badly failed to understand the realities of working women's lives; many had never encountered working women at close range before. The *Woman Worker* complained that welfare supervisors "in the West Country" were sending women home with minor illnesses and telling them not to return until the doctor allowed them to: what they didn't understand was that these women would have preferred to stay at work ill, because at home they could not earn the money they needed for sheer survival.[20] For most welfare supervisors, the class barrier between themselves and the women workers in their charge exacerbated the tension inherent in a relationship based on control and authority.

"THE BEAT" INSIDE AND OUTSIDE THE FACTORY: WOMEN POLICE AND PATROLS

Also in an ambiguous position in factories were the women police: members of the newly founded Women Police Service (WPS) and its rival organization the Women Patrols Committee of the National Union of Women Workers. Women police, a wartime novelty that they themselves hoped would be the beginning of admission of women into regular constabulary jobs, were employed by munitions factories during the war to discipline and control the female work force (and men too in some instances). To women workers, they were a comforting presence when accidents or emergencies did occur, but on a daily basis they represented authority, the state, and the law. The fact that they were women confused the issue, because compared to "bobbies" they seemed unorthodox and therefore interfering, meddlesome in the same way that women social reformers were wont to be. They represented, thus, yet another way in which middle-class women were seeking to promote themselves into official positions over their working-class counterparts.

19. "Welfare Work In Its Proper Place," *New Statesman,* 22 September 1917, 582–83.
20. Margaret Bondfield, "Welfare in the West Country," *Woman Worker* 14 (February 1917): 1.

In the years before the war, there was a growing conviction among reform circles in Britain that women ought to be employed in the police force. Women police were needed, reformers contended, to help prevent young women from falling prey to prostitution and white slavery (the kidnapping of women into prostitution, which was believed to be widely practiced). Reformers urged, further, that women police should be employed to conduct inquiries in cases involving women and children, particularly when there was sexual assault, and to be present when women were arrested, on trial, or in prison. In June 1914 Lord Henry Bentinck of the Criminal Law Amendment Committee proposed an amendment to the Criminal Justice Administration Bill before Parliament that women constables be adopted in every county, but the amendment failed.[21] On 16 July 1914 a deputation organized by the National Vigilance Association was interviewed by the Home Secretary on the same issue.[22] This and other efforts were without success because of the police force's patriarchal attitudes and conservatism.

Nevertheless, within months the nucleus of a force of women police had formed, grasping the opportunity of the social turmoil and anxiety caused by the war, combined with the belief that men should be freed from jobs at home.[23] Unfortunately, for the sake of a movement that aspired to launch a career for women beyond wartime, it began with three different groups that were at times mutually competitive and antagonistic. In September 1914 the Women Police Volunteers were formed by Margaret Damer Dawson and Nina Boyle, who had joined together after founding separate groups, but they split again in February 1915 over the question of whether their cooperation with male police and military surveillance of women was in the women's interests.[24] Damer Dawson took the majority of the membership to form the WPS, and the Women Police Volunteers (WPV) dwindled away. Also in September 1914, the NUWW (later the National Council of Women) formed

21. Chloe Owings, *Women Police: A Study of the Development and Status of the Women Police Movement* (New York: Frederick H. Hitchcock, 1925), 4.

22. "Delegates to Deputation *Re* Appointment of Women Police," PRO, HO 45/10806/309485.

23. A fuller analysis of women police during the war is Philippa Levine, "'Walking the Streets in a Way No Decent Woman Should': Women Police in World War One," *Journal of Modern History* (forthcoming March 1994).

24. Lucy Bland expresses the view that the women police movement was dogged throughout the war by this issue, wanting out of principle to protect women but needing to cooperate with the male police force in order to win official recognition. "In the Name of Protection," 23–49.

voluntary women patrols, whose members were part-time in contrast to the full-time women police of the WPS, and who were less vociferous about their career ambitions, yet who finally received coveted official recognition in September 1918. Both groups sought official recognition as soon as they formed. Separately, they approached Sir Edward Henry, commissioner of the Metropolitan Police Force, and received his approval in the form of authorized identity cards and promises of cooperation, but initially neither group was incorporated into the police force or given official monies. Both groups began with donations from private supporters and relied on these to a certain extent throughout the war. The WPV (later WPS) had also received permission for its members to wear a blue uniform, an official-looking female version of the familiar policeman's uniform, with a hat and badge; the women patrols, however, limited themselves to armbands.

Both groups began with the goals of working with women and children in streets and public places and suppressing prostitution and white slavery. Beyond that, however, their aims diverged. The WPS was intent on incorporating women in all police procedures, such as the power of arrest, taking of evidence, attendance at trials, and supervision in prisons: they sought full police powers with the aim that women should be full police officers. The women patrols sprang from a widespread public concern about the behavior of young women in public places, especially in areas where large numbers of troops were stationed, and a more general concern about the state of morality in a time of crisis and unrest. The NUWW had been conducting rescue work among young working-class women since the 1870s; its patrols were middle-class women of a moral, reforming bent, doing part-time work on a local basis. The WPS, in contrast, enrolled women who wanted to work full-time and were prepared to move around the country.

Both groups had suffragist connections. Ironically, several of the WPS had been militant suffragettes in the Women's Social and Political Union (WSPU), the bane of the Metropolitan Police Force before the war. Mary Allen, who became subcommandant of the WPS and was voted leader when Damer Dawson died soon after the war, had been a member of the activist core of the WSPU and had been imprisoned three times and force-fed twice. The daughter of the manager of the Great Western Railway, she was thrown out of home when she decided to become a suffragette. For Allen, there was a logical connection between suffrage activism and the WPS: like the suffragettes, the early women police were pioneers in an important movement, and both were part of "a women's rebellion."[25] The NUWW, too, had close ties to the suffrage cause through the National Union of Women's Suffrage Societies, but they were not as assertively feminist.[26] The ideological differences between the NUWW's women patrols and the WPS were apparent, for example, on the issue of prostitution: the WPS contended that men were equally as guilty for patronizing prostitutes as prostitutes were for soliciting. The Women Patrols Committee did not share this point of view.[27]

The WPS received two lucky breaks during the war that gave it financial viability as well as roles to play. The first break came in November 1914, when it was invited by the military authorities at Grantham to send two of its members to help keep social order (meaning the control of inter-action between troops and local women) in a situation in which a military camp of twenty-five thousand troops had been stationed just outside a town of twenty-thousand inhabitants.[28] They met with success and local official approval, which paved the way for them to be invited to perform a similar role in other towns and areas.[29] When the policewomen thus invited proved their worth to a local constabulary, they were taken onto the local police payroll. The Police, Factories &c. (Miscellaneous Provisions) Act of 1916 was passed, in part, to establish policewomen's status as public servants so that women police and women patrols could be paid as desired. The next break came in 1916 when, on the recommendation of Sir Edward Henry, the WPS was invited by the Ministry of Munitions to train women police to take jobs in munitions factories employing large numbers of women.

Both the WPS and the women patrols emphasized training for the job and set up schools around England, notably in Bristol, Liverpool, and London. The WPS supplied trained police for a variety of work during the war, including the control of drug trafficking and espionage.[30] Throughout the war, they provided seventy inspectors, sergeants, and constables to towns and boroughs; nineteen to private societies such as

25. *The Women's Who's Who 1934–5* (London: Shaw Publishing Co.), 40; Mary S. Allen, *Lady In Blue* (London: Stanley Paul & Co., 1936), 13–14.

26. Joan Lock says that the women patrols' suffragist origins were reflected in the way they organized and were well known to the police. *The British Policewoman: Her Story* (London: Robert Hale, 1979), 33. Bland speaks of the "largely feminist police and patrols"; "In the Name of Protection," 23.

27. F. Stanley, "Report of Work of Women Patrols: May 26th to June 30th," PRO, MEPOL 2/1748 (1917 or 1918).

28. Owings, *Women Police*, 11–13.

29. Mary Allen was one of the first two policewomen sent to Grantham and recorded her impressions in her memoir *Lady In Blue*, 29–33.

30. Allen, *Lady In Blue*, 38–39.

the YMCA and public places such as Victoria Station; and eighteen to large, private, nonmunitions factories. The bulk of their trained recruits, however, went to work for the Ministry of Munitions: the WPS supplied altogether 985 women police to royal factories, national filling factories, controlled establishments, and government hostels during the war.[31]

The Minister of Munitions wanted policewomen to control the growing numbers of women workers in munitions factories. The WPS agreed to train and equip 140 women, without any payment from the ministry for the first six months as a trial period.[32] The first batches of women police were sent to factories at Queen's Ferry, Gretna, Waltham Abbey, and Pembrey under agreements drawn up with the ministry. The WPS's investment was well rewarded. On 26 January 1917 Damer Dawson and Allen, as leaders of the WPS, signed an agreement with the Ministry of Munitions that they would train as many recruits as the ministry wanted and receive 25s. or 30s. (depending upon "the class of recruit engaged") per week for each recruit plus third-class rail fares for travel required in the monthlong training. Further, the ministry would pay the recruits once trained at the rates of £2 per week for a policewoman, £2 5s. per week for a sergeant, and £2 10s. per week for an inspector; the ministry would supply accommodation at a reasonable charge but each policewoman would have to provide her own uniform.[33]

The WPS reported of munitions factories that:

> The duties of the policewomen consist in checking the entry of women into the factory; examining passports; searching for contraband, namely, matches, cigarettes and alcohol; dealing with complaints of petty offences; patrolling the neighbourhood for the protection of women going home from work; accompanying the women to and fro in the workmen's trains to the neighbouring town where they lodge, serious cases of annoyance to the girls being frequent; appearing, in necessary cases, at the Police Court and assisting the magistrate to deal with such cases.[34]

The overriding reason for the employment of women police in factories was to control the workers, both by settling quarrels and breaking strikes.[35]

31. *The Women Police Service* (London: WPS, 1919), 13–18.
32. Lock, *British Policewoman*, 48.
33. PRO, HO 45/10806/309485.
34. *The Women Police Service: An Account of Its Aims with a Report of Work Accomplished During the Year 1915–16* (London: St. Clements Press, 1916), 13. See also "H. M. Factory, Pembrey: Duties of Women Police," IWM, Women's Work Collection, Emp. 43/103.
35. Diary of Miss G. M. West, 9 September 1917, IWM, DD, 77/156/1.

The reaction of women's organizations to the role of women police in munitions factories was mixed, reflecting their dual tasks of control and protection. The *Woman's Dreadnought* protested that "the practice of introducing police into the factories seems to us a dangerous one from the workers' standpoint."[36] The *Common Cause,* however, representing another suffrage organization, demurred:

> We claim there is no war-work undertaken by women more patriotic in character than that of the Women Police. . . . To maintain order and ensure the protection of her working sisters, to help them to avoid the many temptations which beset them seems to afford a large field to those women who would combine an independent profession with doing their bit for their country.[37]

Mary Allen's view of the effects that women police had on women workers highlights the interaction between women of two classes and two cultures:

> On various occasions at their first appearance threats were made to mob the policewomen; but when the latter stood their ground, proving that they were able to maintain order, and to insist on work being resumed, the excitement invariably calmed down. At the end of a few weeks the beneficial results brought about by the presence of uniformed policewomen became evident to the dullest eye. . . . The conversation among the workers had been frequently appallingly coarse, young girls of nineteen and twenty using the most profane language. Continued remonstrances, grave but kindly, were in the end effectual, and in consequence the whole tone of the factory was raised. Habitual loitering had also to be attacked with energy. The policewomen found girls hiding away from their work in all sorts of strange places, or trying to escape from the shops on all manner of trivial pretexts.[38]

Women police combined the reformers' agenda of helping and improving the working class with a newfound professional role. The basis of their new relationship with women workers was that of their authority over them. Although they were at times genuinely helpful and received workers' gratitude, they were establishing themselves in a career position and asserting authority that they believed concomitant with their class status. In their new uniforms, expediting the work of munitions factories, they were also taking a role that they knew to be of patriotic importance. Although there is no record that any policewoman was killed or injured in a munitions factory, the work was intrinsically dangerous. Policewomen

36. *Woman's Dreadnought,* 3 February 1917, 663.
37. "Women Police Service," *Common Cause,* 13 October 1916, 340.
38. Mary S. Allen, *The Pioneer Policewoman* (London: Chatto & Windus, 1925), 72–73.

were most often employed in factories processing dangerous explosives, and although they apparently did not suffer from exposure to poisons, they did patrol among powerful fumes. More to the point, because their purpose in the factories was partly to keep control in times of crisis, they were expected to take command when there was a fire, explosion, air raid, or accident, which meant being at the center of the danger.

Women patrols, on the other hand, were unambivalently resented by women workers. When the patrols saw women behaving in ways they considered immoral or inappropriate (such as intimate physical contact with a man) they would approach the woman in question, appeal to her that she should not be where she was but safely at home, and even forcibly escort her home. Unsurprisingly, women who received these unwanted interferences (usually young, working-class women) deeply resented them.

Occasionally women patrols worked in conjunction with the WPS, such as in Hull in 1915, and a number of them were employed on police work in munitions factories, at Holton Heath Cordite Factory and at Woolwich Arsenal from late 1917 onward.[39] On the whole, however, women patrols were concerned with preventive moral guidance rather than such traditional police activity as the apprehension of criminals. The Women Patrols Committee operated by selecting and training paid organizers, who were then dispersed to the scattered towns where there were NUWW branches interested in taking up patrol work. The paid organizers there recruited and trained volunteers, who became the bulk of women patrols. By December 1914 sixty-two organizers had been taken on, twenty-six in London and thirty-six elsewhere; and by October 1915 there were 2,301 women patrols at work in 108 places in Britain and Ireland, including 425 at twenty different places in Scotland.[40] The patrols extended to South Africa, invited by the Capetown branch of the NUWW, who were concerned about relations between local women and the troops stationed there.

Gradually, increasing numbers of women patrols were paid for their efforts, either by the police constabulary under whose supervision they worked, or by another employer. By 1918, there were 2,338 women

39. National Council of Women of Great Britain and Ireland, *The History of the Official Policewomen* (London, 1922), 5.

40. Report of the Central Women's Patrol Committee, NUWW, 5 December 1914, PRO, HO 45/10806/309485; "Women Workers in Conference: More Female Police Demanded: Problem of the 'Flighty Girl,'" *Daily Chronicle,* 6 October 1915; Report of the Women Patrols Committee for Scotland, NUWW, November 1915, PRO, HO 45/10806/309485:1.

patrols working in seventy-two places in England and Wales.[41] Women patrols included within their beats streets, parks, and public places such as cinemas, music halls, and dancing halls. On the lookout for criminal, moral, or unseemly behavior, especially involving women, they were ready to call a constable for an arrest, help maintain order in a crisis, give information or sensible help, or move along or take home any young women they thought at risk. In some instances, munitions factories were in the same town or area as a troop camp, and in such cases the separation of women workers from troops became a long-term job for women patrols. When in May 1916 it came to light that there was a plan to build a hut settlement for women munitions workers in close proximity to an Australian troop camp, the *British Australasian* raised an alarm as to the likely social and sexual consequences, and the cry was taken up by others. The horror increased when it was discovered that the Australian troops were soon to leave and the camp was to be taken over by Indian troops. The *Common Cause* railed that women would never have allowed such a plan: "The advice of a few practical women, taken NOW, will save any amount of preventable misery and misdoing. And that is a far more satisfactory way, as well as less expensive, than first creating evils and then appointing special police, women missionaries, and a vast amount of social salvage apparatus to deal with a situation that ought never to have arisen."[42]

Part of the rationale for women patrols was concern about women acting other than demurely in the streets. Women munitions workers were undoubtedly part of this criticized group, although older women workers had too many domestic responsibilities and too little energy to be able to act wildly in the streets. That young women workers yelled exuberantly at each other, or ran about in the streets, was a fact of working-class life. It is likely, moreover, that the tension and drama of the war added to the pitch at which many people lived. For many young women workers, however, letting off steam in the streets was simply a reaction to having been in one place all day, concentrating hard over a machine or process.[43]

Women munitions workers confronted women patrols in several situations. First, women patrols were employed at or around some munitions factories in the same capacity as women police. Besides those

41. *Handbook and Report of the National Council and Union of Women Workers of Great Britain and Ireland, 1917–1918* (London, 1918), 130–31.

42. "The Hut Folly," *Common Cause*, 26 May 1916, 94.

43. Webb, *Health of Working Girls*, 51–52.

employed at Woolwich Arsenal, there were a few stationed in Woolwich itself who patroled streets and public places. In the month of October 1918, the women patrols at Eltham, next to Woolwich, reported that they had "shifted" forty-five couples in the vicinity of the Well Hall Hostels.[44] At Croydon, women patrols were sent to deal with the neighborhood around a government munitions factory, which employed both men and women and was adjacent to a military hospital. A report on the work of patrols in Croydon noted:

> Four Patrols daily on whole time duty at varying hours in vicinity of Government Factory. Ten part-time workers on street duty all without Constables. When Patrols commenced work around the Factory they found numbers of men and girls coming from work paired off and retired to surrounding lanes and [sic] where they lay about in suggestive attitudes. At the end of a month's work Patrols report great improvement in behaviour of such pairs.[45]

Besides watching out for women patrols in their off-work hours in the neighborhood of their factory, women munitions workers had to keep an eye out for them in a variety of public places. If a woman worker chose to take a stroll in Hyde Park or on Hampstead Heath in her free time, perhaps on a Sunday afternoon, she encountered patrols there, ever vigilant for misconduct between couples. In London and all other cities, towns, or areas where they were stationed, women patrols considered parks, squares, riverbanks, streets, and other public places their domain in which to guard against danger to women, protect men from prostitutes, and otherwise control vice and uphold what they considered proper, moral conduct. In so doing they were imposing their own moral code. But it was also the case that middle-class women simply did not understand the way in which poor people's lives were carried on in the street as well as in their homes, which lacked any privacy. Women munitions workers were also likely to encounter women patrols in the clubs for young working women that the NUWW established as a counter-attraction to the streets and to provide a venue for entertainment and sociability under the supervision of middle-class women volunteers.

The fact that both the WPS and the Women Patrols Committee had strong suffragist connections, even though the women patrols were not as assertive in their feminism as the WPS, adds a powerful irony to the

44. F. Stanley, "Report on Work of Women Patrols for October 1918," PRO, MEPOL 2/1748.

45. F. Stanley, "Report of Work of Women Patrols: May 26th to June 30th," 1917 or 1918, PRO, MEPOL 2/1748.

evidence of the primacy of class interests over gender solidarity during the war. That these groups of organized feminists, who sought to open the career of policing to women, were prepared to use women of the working class as objects for their own ends was a harsh assertion of their priorities.

The class origin of many members of the WPS is revealed in the simple fact that many of them could speak French, in contrast to the "ordinary London 'Bobbies,'" and were therefore useful with the flood of Belgian refugees in late 1914 and early 1915.[46] The NUWW claimed that they "have all social grades among the Patrols, but the majority are educated women."[47] Interaction between women police and women patrols on the one hand and women munitions workers on the other was dominantly that of middle-class women adopting new roles through which to control and discipline women workers. Both more official and more professional than social reform work, the role of women police allowed middle-class women to invoke the weight of the law in their dealings with women workers in and around munitions factories during the war.

CLASS TENSION AMONG
WOMEN MUNITIONS WORKERS

Women of all classes worked in munitions factories in World War I, but even when women of different classes performed the same job on the factory floor their experiences were essentially different. A middle- or upper-class woman producing munitions as her contribution to the war effort for the duration, even when she worked harder than she had ever previously imagined possible, knew that she could choose to leave and that her work was sustained by her commitment to patriotism or her desire for vengeance. But for a woman of the working class who simply had to work to stay alive and for whom this was the best-paid job available, even though she might also be fired by patriotic inspiration, work was far more a daily necessity than a patriotic choice. Awareness of their class differences was a constant factor in relations between women "war workers" or patriotic volunteers and their working-class coworkers.

Throughout the war, women were subjected to a barrage of exhortations regarding what they ought and ought not be doing for the war

46. "The Woman In Blue," *Woman's Life,* 6 February 1915, 202.
47. PRO, MUN 5/93. Interviews with Mrs. Stanley, Supervisor of Women Police Patrols, 2 and 7 July 1918.

effort. These exhortations came from all quarters, but it is likely that they weighed more on the consciences of middle-class women who were in a quandary as to how best to make themselves useful than on the minds of working-class women for whom necessity and convenience were at least as powerful determinants.[48] One much-publicized group that recruited women of the leisured classes to relieve women workers one day a week in munitions factories was the Women Relief Munition Workers' Organisation formed by Lady Moir and Lady Cowan and registered as a private company in July 1915. The organization arranged with Vickers Ltd. to train women for three weeks at Vickers' factory at Erith to turn out shells on lathes, after which they could be used as weekend workers to help keep the factory running seven days a week. The scheme was sufficiently successful that it spread to Glasgow, Newcastle, and elsewhere. They became known as "relief," "weekend," "voluntary," or just "war" workers.[49] Reports of their patriotic efforts stressed the striking contrast between their presence in the factory on a weekend and the usual weekday scene: "In the ranks of the industrial hands there are nursemaids, inn-keepers' daughters, laundry girls, Belgian peasant women, dressmakers' apprentices; while in the ranks of the week-end relief workers are found artists, authors, generals' wives, dukes' daughters, hunting women, ministers' wives, golfers, women drawn from every branch of the educated classes."[50]

Other women of the middle and upper classes took up munitions work full time. While they were given the limelight by the press, in fact these women were a tiny proportion of the women working in munitions. One of the favorite topics of wartime journalists was the presence of "ladies" in the factories, roughing it along with their working-class sisters and proving themselves paragons of patriotic effort. They took every chance they could to report incidents such as when Lady Victoria Cavendish-Bentinck's apparent anonymity in the aircraft factory in which she worked was betrayed the day the king came to visit the factory and greeted her with warm recognition.[51]

The critical problem that employers and the Ministry of Munitions had to solve was how to replace skilled workers. Initially, unskilled men were promoted. However, as unskilled and semiskilled men were drained

48. For example *The Suffragette*, 16 July 1915, 213; *Woman's Life*, 22 April 1916, 135.

49. IWM, Women's Work Collection, Mun. 17.2/3, 17.2/8; *Daily News and Leader*, 26 July 1915; *Common Cause*, 17 March 1916, 646.

50. "The Sunday 'Shift': The Women Who Save The Workers' Health," *The Times*, 29 April 1916.

51. *Sheffield Daily Telegraph*, 31 December 1914.

by conscription, especially from 1916 onward, the need for women to do semiskilled and skilled work became increasingly apparent. To trade unionists such as the Amalgamated Society of Engineers, better-educated, middle-class women who would not want to continue with factory work were a nonthreatening proposition much more attractive than trained working-class women who would constitute long-term competition. For the woman worker, acceptance of "ladies" in the factory was not eased by the fact that upper- and middle-class women were much more likely than they to be able to take advantage of the courses suddenly available for training in skilled engineering work, such as fitting and turning, machine-setting, and oxyacetylene welding. Already-privileged women therefore commonly secured jobs of higher status, were paid more, and were more likely to be selected as forewomen, chargehands, and overlookers.

While the presence of middle- and upper-class women in the factories suited the ministry and men trade unionists, it resulted in friction between women of different classes on the factory floor. Caroline Rennles recalled one incident that reveals the resentment felt by women of the working class toward those more fortunate:

> Oh yes; yes, we had two girls their father was a Northampton big boot manufacturer. Well, some of the girls I worked with they could use some lovely language, you know, and these two girls they used to have some lovely high-legged boots and everything which we never had, and I know they were passing through in the factory one night and one of the girls I was working with said something lovely about 'em, and they turned round and they let out such a lovely string of swear words themselves. They said 'Look, don't think because we've come from rich people that we don't understand swear words, because we can use them as well', you know, and it took this girl back because she thought that because they were posh, you know, that they'd never heard a swear word in their life before. Yes, I can remember that, yes.[52]

Some war workers were from the ranks of women who had devoted their energies before the war to improving the lives of working-class women, such as two members of the Women's University Settlement Committee who became munitions workers in 1916.[53] But, as Martha Vicinus has described, even devoted settlement house workers commonly failed to overcome the cultural gaps between themselves and working-class women.[54] Resentment of "ladies" in munitions factories often included the women

52. IWM, DSR, 000566/07, 39–40.
53. Women's University Settlement Thirtieth Annual Report, March 1917, 6. Fawcett Library, Women's University Settlement Collection, 5/WUS/R/29.
54. Vicinus, *Independent Women*, 238–41.

who volunteered to run factory canteens. Peggy Hamilton, a middle-class worker at Woolwich Arsenal, recalled how absurdly patronizing the attitude of some of the volunteers in canteens could be. One day when she and a friend were having their lunch "a woman paused beside us and said, 'You're having rather a treat today aren't you? You see that lady playing the piano, she is the Duchess of . . . and I'm Lady . . . , gooodbye [sic].'"[55] Where canteens were staffed by middle- or upper-class women "doing their bit," workers could easily feel patronized or uncomfortable.

CLASS OVER GENDER IN THE POSTWAR WORLD

Jane Marcus has posited that the middle- and upper-class women who participated in the war effort as nurses, ambulance drivers, and munitions factory workers and partook of the popular culture of the war through its songs and music hall routines were consciously doing so in an attempt to be "democratic" for the duration. This "dilution" or leveling of culture, she suggests, was part of their patriotic efforts for the cause, only given up after the war with the return of class and gender polarities.[56] Some contemporary observers cherished the belief that class distinctions had become insignificant in munitions factories: "The *esprit de corps* amongst the women is splendid, titled ladies, university girls, and housemaids sitting side by side. This war is a great social leveller."[57] As Marcus suggests, the imperative of the war demanded such democratic avowals.

Whatever leveling of class or culture occurred among women during the war in munitions factories, it was a temporary phenomenon, as superficial as their factory uniforms. The close, unfamiliar environment in which women of different classes worked together for the war effort did not produce class harmony or understanding. Class tensions were starkly shown rather than dulled by factory coexistence.

One clear consequence of working-class women's experience as munitions workers for class relations in the postwar world was a marked aversion to domestic service. Domestic service was in a state of gradual decline in the early twentieth century; while it remained the single largest employer of women after World War I, the war had shown its fragility,

55. Hamilton, *Three Years or the Duration*, 33–34.
56. Jane Marcus, "Afterword," in Irene Rathbone, *We That Were Young* (1932; reprint, New York: Feminist Press at CUNY, 1989), 475–76.
57. Mrs. Ellis Chadwick, "Women to the Rescue: A Visit to a Great Munition Arsenal," *Wesleyan Methodist Magazine*, November 1916.

and World War II sounded its death knell. It was vanquished by a combination of improved education for girls, the availability of alternative work, the mechanization of household work, and the desire for greater social equality on the part of the working class.

Estimates during the war suggested that 100,000 women had left domestic service to take wartime jobs, most of which, presumably, were munitions jobs.[58] The attitude that large numbers of women munitions workers expressed toward the prospect of taking domestic service work after the war was a powerful reflection of the changes they had undergone in their wartime jobs. There was a widespread reluctance to consider domestic service employment at all, but even when women were prepared to consider it, they firmly enunciated a standard of expectations as to conditions of work.[59] Having experienced munitions wages, domestic service wages seemed appallingly low, and this was an important sticking point. Less definably, women munitions workers had enjoyed an autonomy that domestic service jobs did not provide, especially in live-in jobs. Many women conceded that they would return to domestic service if they could do so on a daily rather than a live-in basis, or at least could have more free evenings a week. The lack of social autonomy in domestic service work was a new stumbling block, but there was also the issue of servility. In a munitions factory, although they had had to work hard and obey rules and orders, women workers had been accorded some respect and dignity; in domestic service, a degree of obsequiousness was unavoidable.

The low wages proffered by domestic service had much to do with its unpopularity but were far from being the whole explanation. As the *Manchester Guardian* pointed out, "Very few girls will go into domestic service after experiencing the freedom of limited hours and their own home."[60] Even deeper than the question of hours was that of autonomy and deference. Journalist Ward Muir cast some light on the underlying issues in a piece in the *Daily Mail* entitled "Why Mary Won't Come Back." Purporting that his Aunt Matilda (Mrs. Egerton-Browne of the Garden Suburb) was gloating that her "general" maid Mary would soon be back from her stint on munitions work and would be grateful for the good home and wages that she offered, Muir demurred:

58. "The Passing of the 'Servant,'" *Woman's Dreadnought,* 10 February 1917, 671.
59. "Dismissal of Munition Workers: 15,000 Girls Idle in Newcastle," *Newcastle Daily Journal,* 20 December 1918; "Women's Peace Work," *Bulletin,* 9 January 1919; "Domestic Service: Certain Considerations," *The Englishwoman* 41 (March 1919): 109.
60. *Manchester Guardian,* 22 March 1918.

For one thing, Mary has lost, for ever and ever, the "respectfulness" which—well, which made her imagine that to wait on Mrs. Egerton-Browne, who had been too stupid ever to earn a penny in her life, was the natural and proper fate for a clever girl in Mary's "position"—that is, without the means to be as idle as her mistress.

And as for the comforts which Mary lacks by having left Aunt Matilda's roof—

I have had glimpses of those comforts. When doing odd-job carpentry in my aunt's house I have seen Mary's bedroom, furnished with a "servant's set." I have seen the bare little kitchen in which Mary wasn't allowed to receive admirers . . . but in which she was supposed to sit very contentedly for six evenings of the week. And I don't think that Mary will come rushing back to these havens of luxury.[61]

Unfortunately, however, "Mary" often lacked an alternative to domestic service. After her out-of-work benefit expired, she had to survive by some means. If she was offered a job by the labor exchange at which she was registered, she refused it at the peril of losing her benefit. Given the wide demand for domestic servants, the odds were stacked against those who hoped to stay away from such employment.

Those who did return to domestic work out of necessity could at least take comfort in the discussion about the nature of domestic service that resounded through the demobilization period. There was a general feeling that domestic service must change. Even a representative of the Ministry of Labour conceded in the House of Commons that the conditions of domestic service must be improved, although he hoped that this could be achieved voluntarily through agreement between organizations of the mistresses on the one hand and of the servants on the other.[62] Lilian Barker observed, referring to the future of the women leaving Woolwich Arsenal, that thousands of them would enter domestic service: "But they would want better conditions and more freedom than had been usual. They had learned the dignity of labour, they had been working under carefully considered conditions; there had been a wonderful organisation for their welfare both inside and outside the workshops, and they would no longer be content to work for inconsiderate mistresses."[63]

Labor organizations took up the subject of domestic service seriously. The *Labour Woman*, published by the Labour Party, suggested a Domestic Workers' Charter that would cover a minimum wage (namely, 35s. a week

61. Ward Muir, "Why Mary Won't Come Back," *Daily Mail*, 8 November 1918.
62. "The Domestic Worker and the Unemployed Women," *Labour Woman* 7 (March 1919): 26.
63. *Manchester Graphic*, 21 November 1918.

minus the cost of food and lodgings, estimated at 25s. a week) and stipulate the hours to be worked.[64] It advocated that, wherever possible, domestic service should be on a daily rather than a live-in basis; live-in workers should have autonomy over their bedrooms; the domestics' working day should be twelve hours including four unpaid hours for meals and rest, and their working week should not exceed fifty-two hours; they should have two weeks' holiday every year and should be paid overtime if they worked on Sundays or public holidays.

By 1920, although domestic service was still held in low regard by women workers, a Domestic Servants' Union had been formed in Birmingham by Julia Varley, the Birmingham organizer of the Workers' Union. The new union succeeded in gaining an adherence among servants as well as exercising persuasion over mistresses. Besides stipulating conditions such as the hours of work (6:30 A.M. to 10 P.M.), four and a half hours off daily, half a day weekly, alternate Sundays off, two weeks' holiday a year, a minimum wage just under thirty-five pounds a year, and the provision of both a comfortable kitchen and a bedroom, there were two other novel items on its list of conditions. One was that the mistress should bear the large part of the cost of the servant's uniform, no small item to a working woman needing a job. The other was that, in marked contrast to the tradition that a mistress simplified a servant's name if she thought it too fancy (so that "Marjorie" would be called "Jane" or "Ellen"), mistresses now agreed to call the servant either by her proper "Christian" name or by her surname, whichever the servant chose. This, too, was a significant development in recognizing the servant's self-respect.[65]

Cross-class interaction among women in munitions factories was not simply a relationship of power or hostility. Some accounts demonstrate that women bonded as individuals working together in often oppressive and close environments, helping each other, joking, and sharing details of their personal lives. Mary Allen testified that even within the disciplinary work of policewomen there was room for friendliness, albeit maternal: "The routine official work in the factory included searching, patrolling,

64. "The Domestic Worker and the Unemployed Women," *Labour Woman* 7 (March 1919): 26.

65. "New Era For Domestics: Trade Union To Be Formed; Minimum Wage; Clubs, Dancing and Music," *Daily News*, 27 January 1920; "Servants' Paradise is- Birmingham: Club the Envy of Their Mistresses; Jazz & Shopping Teas," *Daily Chronicle*, 31 January 1920; "The Passing of the 'Servant,'" *Woman's Dreadnought*, 10 February 1917, 671.

and the keeping of order. The unofficial work included every conceivable form of consultation, from the settlement of family quarrels to giving advice in affairs of the heart."[66] Middle-class war workers' accounts reveal too that proximity with working-class women challenged them both personally and politically. Naomi Loughnan, for example, wrote in the midst of the war that

> laughter, anger, acute confusion, and laughter again, are constantly changing our immediate outlook on life. Sometimes disgust will overcome us but we are learning with painful clarity that the fault is not theirs whose actions disgust us, but must be placed to the discredit of those other classes who have allowed the continued existence of conditions which generate the things from which we shrink appalled.[67]

Ultimately, however, the personal confidences and the occasional insights were less significant than the sum of the relational inequalities between women of different classes.

Subject to the discipline imposed by middle-class welfare supervisors, the control and authority of women police, the out-of-hours interference by women patrols, and the proximity of a handful of members of the privileged middle and upper classes at work on the factory floor, the class identity of women workers in munitions factories was confirmed on all sides during the war. In the postwar world, with women over thirty newly enfranchised as voting citizens, women's political allegiances were even more important than before the war. They were energetically courted by the major political parties, who played on their class interests in wooing their votes. For women workers, the decision of the organized women's union movement to merge with the men's labor movement strengthened the political dimensions to their identity as workers. In 1921 the Women's Trade Union League and the National Federation of Women Workers dissolved themselves by merger with the Trades Union Congress General Council and the National Union of General Workers respectively, in a clear subordination of the interests of women as a sex to class solidarity. The Women's Engineering Society relinquished its aspirations to represent working-class women as professional engineers within its ranks. Women welfare supervisors became increasingly professionally self-conscious in the struggle to retain as many jobs as they could

66. Allen, *Pioneer Policewoman*, 64.
67. Loughnan, "Munition Work," 38.

and to maintain their hold on the field while merging with male welfare supervisors in an association that would become the Institute of Personnel Management. In the politically polarized atmosphere of the 1920s and 1930s, class identity overwhelmed any gender bonding among women of different classes. The experience of women in World War I munitions factories cemented rather than challenged the primacy of class.

CHAPTER EIGHT

"On Her Their Lives Depend"

Gender, War, and Women
Munitions Workers

And in the munitions factories, in the handling of heavy and
often difficult machinery, and in adaptability and inventiveness
and enthusiasm and steadfastness, their achievement has been
astonishing. . . . They have revolutionized the estimate of their
economic importance, and it is scarcely too much to say that
when in the long run the military strength of the Allies bears
down the strength of Germany it will be this superiority of
our women . . . which has tipped the balance of this war.

Those women have won the Vote. Not the most frantic
outbursts of militancy after this war can prevent their getting
it. The girls who have faced death and wounds so gallantly in
our cordite factories—there is a not inconsiderable loss of
dead and wounded from these places—have killed forever the
poor argument that women should not vote because they had
no military value. Indeed, they have killed every argument
against their subjection.

H. G. Wells, in Ladies Home Journal, *June 1916*

EFFECTS OF THE WAR ON WOMEN'S STATUS

The greatest symbolic change in the status of women that occurred during
the war was the granting of the vote to women householders and
university graduates over thirty under the Representation of the People
Act in 1918. Other legal breakthroughs soon followed, such as the Sex
Disqualification (Removal) Act of 1919, which gave women the right to
hold most public offices and prohibited bars against their entry into
professions.[1]

One of the paramount questions about World War I for British
women's history is that of its significance in the granting of the partial

1. Stella Newsome, *Women's Freedom League 1907–1957* (London: Women's Freedom
League, n.d.), 12–13.

suffrage. Following the rhetoric of the politicians of the day, especially such wartime converts to suffrage as H. H. Asquith, most historians have accepted that the vote was a token of gratitude for women's critical role in the war effort. Indeed, some contemporary commentators perceived that the suffrage had been granted to women as a reward for their devoted participation in the war effort, notably in taking over men's jobs. *The Tatler,* for example, ran a cartoon in April 1917 (by which time the likelihood of women's suffrage was becoming evident) called "The Key of the Situation," in which a woman in a munitions uniform was unlocking a door to the Houses of Parliament labeled "The Vote." She had just laid down an axe marked "Militancy" and was now using a key marked "National Work." Meanwhile John Bull, inside the door, was greeting her with this admonition: "It was no good axe-ing for it, but now you've worked for it and earned it, it's a different matter."[2]

This interpretation, although it identified the role of munitions workers as central to wartime changes for women, denigrated the importance of the long, hard suffrage campaign, inferring that it had achieved nothing, whereas bending to the national cause had achieved all. Sandra Stanley Holton's close study of the political campaign of the constitutional suffragists before and during the war, however, has shown that in fact the issue was near political resolution in 1914 and that the war, while possibly even delaying the granting of the vote to women, did little other than to dismantle the antisuffrage opposition lobby by removing their grounds for argument.[3] The obvious way in which the war contributed to the suffrage in 1918 was by necessitating reform of the basis of male suffrage and thereby precipitating the bill that suffragists insisted had to include women.

The partial suffrage was a highly important breakthrough for women of all classes, and it was significant that working-class women were involved in the suffrage campaign in Lancashire, Yorkshire, East London, and elsewhere.[4] It is impossible to know how many munitions workers were feminists or suffragists. We do know, however, that during the war organizers of the National Union of Women's Suffrage Societies campaigned specifically among women munitions workers, obtaining at least

2. "Pictorial Politics: The Key of the Situation," *The Tatler,* 11 April 1917, 40.

3. Sandra Stanley Holton, *Feminism and Democracy: Women's Suffrage and Reform Politics in Britain 1900–1918* (Cambridge: Cambridge University Press, 1986), 130.

4. See Jill Liddington and Jill Norris, *One Hand Tied Behind Us: The Rise of the Women's Suffrage Movement* (London: Virago, 1978), and Sandra Stanley Holton, "The Suffragist and the 'Average Woman,'" *Women's History Review* 1, no. 1 (1992): 9–24.

hundreds (and probably thousands) of signatures on petitions for the vote. The Manchester Federation reported that women munitions workers expressed "annoyance" at being left out of the bill that gave the vote to women over thirty.[5] For women munitions workers, the age restriction (designed to ensure that there were more men voters than women) was of great import. Although women of virtually all ages worked in munitions factories, the dominant age group was under thirty, a fact that challenges the idea that the vote was a token of gratitude for wartime work. Even if women were not given the vote as a reward, in an important sense, as Bonnie Smith has suggested, women who worked in patriotic solidarity with men for the war effort took over from suffragists as the most visible public image of womanhood.[6] Women workers' visible dedication to the national cause, while not as explicit as suffragists' demands, constituted an implicit claim to women's citizenship.

In the aftermath of the war, the victory of partial suffrage was countered by the widespread demobilization of women, as women were asked to make way for the returning soldiers. Even so, many observers continued to believe that the war had changed the status of women workers. To Robert Roberts, at least, looking back to his childhood observations of the women around him in the poor working-class neighborhood where he grew up, the vote was low on the list of transformations wrought on women's status by the war:

> Whatever war did to women in home, field, service or factory, it undoubtedly snapped strings that had bound them in so many ways to the Victorian age. Even we, the young, noticed their new self-confidence. Wives in the shop no longer talked about 'my boss', or 'my master'. Master had gone to war and Missis ruled the household, or he worked close to her in a factory, turning out shell cases on a lathe and earning little more than she did herself. Housewives left their homes and immediate neighbourhood more frequently, and with money in their purses went foraging for goods even into the city shops, each trip being an exercise in self-education. She discovered her own rights. The pre-1914 movements for her political emancipation, bourgeois in origin and function, meant very little to the lower-working-class woman. In the end the consequences of war, not the legal acquisition of female rights, released her from bondage.[7]

Carl Chinn, in his work on poor women in Birmingham, confirms

---

5. Liddington, *Respectable Rebel*, 271–72.

6. Bonnie Smith, *Changing Lives: Women in European History Since 1700* (Lexington, Mass.: D. C. Heath and Co., 1989), 372.

7. Roberts, *Classic Slum*, 162.

Roberts' view by identifying the war as the watershed in the first half of the twentieth century: "In many respects it was shown that their men were not needed; women were doing men's jobs and, for the first time, they were openly in control of their own destinies. With their return, men found it harder to reimpose the old *status quo* whereby overt power was in their hands and covert power was in the hands of the women."[8] Many women workers left their munitions jobs only under pressure. One survey of three thousand women munitions workers, probably taken in 1917, reported that twenty-five hundred of those questioned preferred to stay in their wartime factory jobs rather than return to their prewar occupations.[9]

Given that society's valuation of an occupation is directly expressed in the wage attached to it, it is to be expected that workers who suddenly receive a fatter pay packet enjoy a concomitant growth in self-esteem. Clementina Black, on behalf of the Women's Industrial Council, made this point to the War Cabinet Committee on Women in Industry when she asserted: "The lower payment of women leads them to hold cheap their own work which they see held cheap by others. It thus lowers their standard of work, and the lower standard appears, in turn, to justify the lower wage."[10] When women workers were earning around three times their prewar wages on munitions, then, they gained not only the where-withal to buy new or nicer clothing and to eat better and pay their household bills but also an increased degree of self-esteem and self-satisfaction.

Other commentators, too, hailed the industrial, psychological, and social gains made by women workers during the war. Americans Irene Andrews and Margarett Hobbs commented of British women workers during the war: "The development of the woman industrial worker . . . may prove to be one of the most important changes wrought by the conflict."[11] Millicent Garrett Fawcett, the preeminent suffragist who had supported the war effort, asserted in 1920: "The war revolutionized the industrial position of women. It found them serfs and left them free. It not only opened to them opportunities of employment in a number of

8. Chinn, *They Worked All Their Lives,* 165. See also "The Women's Share: What the Future Has in Store," *Daily Mail,* 13 June 1916.

9. Daggett, *Women Wanted,* 194.

10. "The Women's Industrial Council: Miss Clementina Black," in *Report of the War Cabinet Committee on Women in Industry,* app. B, 16.

11. Irene Osgood Andrews and Margarett A. Hobbs, *Economic Effects of the War Upon Women and Children in Great Britain* (New York: Oxford University Press, 1918), 172.

skilled trades, but, more important even than this, it revolutionized men's minds and their conception of the sort of work of which the ordinary everyday woman was capable."[12]

An assessment of the impact of the war on women who worked in munitions factories must include, indeed value above all, the women's own understanding of its bearing on their lives. In particular, women munitions workers' views of the war's effects on the system of gender roles in which they participated are crucial to an analysis of those effects. Women workers' perceptions of the gendering effects of war include their views of their role in the war effort compared to that of the men in the armed forces; their relationships with their male coworkers; and their own evaluation of the war as an experience in the longer term of their lives.

VIEWS OF THEIR OWN ROLE IN THE WAR

To approach an understanding of the impact of the war on gender distinctions, it is necessary to attempt to reconstruct women munitions workers' views of their own role in the conduct of the war. Inherent in such views are the degree of pride they felt in their contributions toward prosecution of the war and their estimation of the import of their role in terms of its military value.

To cheer themselves during the long monotony of their shifts, especially on night shift, women munitions workers sang the songs of wartime popular culture. Some of the songs they repetitively sang were the same as those sung by soldiers while marching. In addition, women munitions workers took well-known tunes and made up new lyrics that featured themselves as heroines. Part of the purpose of these was to commemorate their own work group or unit, to distinguish themselves from the women workers in the next shed, factory, or process. In the lyrics they invented, however, they often portrayed themselves as performing a direct, heroic role in the business of the war, in the bloodshed and the vanquishing of the enemy. The songs indicate a vivid awareness of the nature of munitions work and of the war at the front, as well as a desire to valorize their own role in it. A song from an explosives factory at Faversham in Kent went as follows:

12. Millicent Garrett Fawcett, *The Women's Victory—And After: Personal Reminiscences* (London: Sidgwick & Jackson, 1920), 106.

The Girls with Yellow Hands

The guns out there are roaring fast, the bullets fly like rain;
The aeroplanes are curvetting, they go and come again;
The bombs talk loud; the mines crash out; no trench their might
  withstands.
Who helped them all to do their job? The girls with yellow hands.

The boys out there have hands of red; it's German blood, and warm.
The Germans know what's coming when the English swarm—
Canadians and British, and the men from Southern lands.
Who helped them all to do their job? The girls with yellow hands.

The boys are smiling though they rush against a barb'ed trench;
The girls are smiling though destruction hovers o'er their bench;
And when the soldiers sweep along through lines of shattered strands,
Who helped them all to do their job? The girls with yellow hands.[13]

Lyrics to such songs often referred specifically to working with TNT and its emblematic yellowing, presumably to arrogate whatever glamor was possible to a discoloration that must have been a social embarrassment as well as an indication of poisoning. The song below is from the south of Scotland:

Give honour to the Gretna girls,
Give honour where honour is due,
Don't forget the Gretna girls
Who are doing their duty for you.

And when they are in the factory
Midst the cordite and the smell,
We'll give three cheers for the Gretna girls
And the others can come as well.

Come boys and do your little bit,
We'll meet you by-and-by

13. Percival, "Faversham Gunpowder Industry," 25. Another song that referred specifically to TNT yellowing was sung by workers at Woolwich Arsenal: "Where are the girls of the Arsenal? Working night and day; Wearing the roses off their cheeks / For precious little pay. Some people style them 'canaries,' But we're working for the lads across the sea. If it were not for the munition lasses, Where would the Empire be?" *Daily Express,* 19 August 1918. Interestingly, Amy May, who worked at Woolwich Arsenal, remembered what was presumably the same song, sung by the "canaries" working on TNT, but her recollection of the lyrics places emphasis on the equality of the patriotic importance of the women and soldiers: "'Same as the lads across the sea, if it wasn't for us, our munition girls, where would the Empire be?'" IWM, DSR, 000684/05. Deborah Thom has noted another song sung by women at Woolwich Arsenal, with the first verse as follows: "Way down in Shell Shop Two / You'll never find us blue / We're working night and day / To keep the Huns away." "Tommy's Sister," 151.

> Every girl in the fighting line
> Is willing to do or die.[14]

By suggesting, even facetiously, that the men at the front were doing only their "little bit" for the war, women workers were aggressively asserting their own importance to the war. Similarly, in the first song, the equation of the "boys . . . smiling though they rush against a barb'ed trench" and the "girls . . . smiling though destruction hovers o'er their bench" is a claim to not only equality of contribution but also equality of courage and patriotic fearlessness. It is apparent from these lyrics that women munitions workers saw themselves as critically involved in the war effort and as being vitally linked to their men at the front. To some of them, the danger involved in their work was a positive attribute because it proved their courage and their patriotism. Caroline Rennles, for example, recalled that she and her friends, despite being severely discolored from their work with TNT, blithely disregarded the physical injury the work was doing them. Even when the train conductors on their way to work direly predicted that they, the young women workers, had only two years to live, they replied: "'Well, we don't mind dying for our country.'"[15]

For a working-class woman, munitions work was an available means of patriotic participation. The conscription of men into the armed forces proved an extended and highly controversial political issue in Britain, yet after conscription was introduced in January 1916 the possibility of an equivalent system for women was raised.[16] This idea never gained currency, however, largely because it was unnecessary. Women entered industry, shifted to munitions jobs, took up charitable works, and joined the paramilitary forces with resolution and energy. Economic forces, patriotic propaganda, and the loosening of trade union restrictions and employers' prejudices successfully resulted in the massive entry of women into the necessary areas of industry. The power of imperialist and nationalist discourse was so strong in the prewar years that many more women saw the war as a great opportunity than opposed it on the basis of antimilitarist principles.[17]

Women working in munitions had the satisfaction of knowing they

14. A song sung by women cordite workers on night shift at H. M. Factory Gretna, Scotland. Kinnaird, *Reminiscences,* 162.

15. IWM, DSR, 000566/07, 9–10.

16. *Parliamentary Debates, Commons,* 5th ser., 108 (11 July 1918): 490. On the issue of conscription for men, see R. J. Q. Adams and Philip P. Poirier, *The Conscription Controversy in Great Britain, 1900–18* (Columbus: Ohio State University Press, 1987).

17. Liddington, *Road to Greenham Common,* 60–61.

were directly helping the armies fighting at the front, or the navy or air force, by providing them with critically necessary ammunition, weapons, or equipment. "My husband is fighting at the front, and I should like to make cartridges for him," one soldier's wife wrote to the *Daily Telegraph*.[18] Another worker, interviewed by the *Sunday Times,* said: "Dad's in the Navy, and I applied for work in a danger room, where I tie the cordite, for I feel that with every day I work I am helping him. Lots of the girls whose men are out there want to do work that will help to kill Germans and end the war."[19]

To underscore for workers the direct connection between the shells they made and the war at the front, factories displayed posters of aerial photographs of German trenches on the western front before and after bombardment, with the caption "Munition workers see the effect of your work!"[20] In repeatedly assuring women munitions workers of the national importance of their work, such propaganda was critical in forging a shared sense of participation in the war effort and consequently a belief that they had played an important public role.

Workers' zeal was not fired by any one motive alone. It is important to keep in mind the overriding need to work for most of these women, but any one of them could also feel a patriotic urge, or desire a new experience or an excuse to get away from home. Some simply lived in a neighborhood where a munitions factory was established. One writer found a combination of three different motives when he toured a factory making wooden boxes to carry shells to the front, in which all the joiners were "girls":

> Never was there a brighter scene. The girls seem to have a sense of doing big things with a blow and a swing—not tinkering with feminine trifles. They love their work. It is said that not long ago a theatrical company, playing a rather foolish revue, came to a neighbouring theatre, and some of the ladies of the chorus lodged at the same house with one of the female joiners.
>
> "I'm surprised at you, my dears," said the munition girl, "kicking your legs over the footlights when you might be earning more money in our shop, and doing something for your country." "Well, that's worth thinking about," answered the ladies of the theatre; and on the Friday night following, the whole chorus presented themselves at the factory and were engaged.[21]

18. *Daily Telegraph,* 23 March 1915, quoted in *Common Cause,* 26 March 1915, 777.

19. Mary Macleod Moore, "Women As Munition Workers," *Sunday Times,* 23 July 1916.

20. Amy Eleanor Mack, "Oiling the Human Wheels," *Pearson's Magazine* 43, no. 7 (February 1917): 140–41.

21. Hall Caine, "Feeding the Arsenal: Tasks British Women Are Doing," *Nottingham Guardian,* 28 October 1916.

The attractions of munitions work apparently included an excitement peculiar to younger women workers, perhaps only teenagers. One instance of this was the February 1916 report, cited in the Introduction, in which Elsie Davey's mother explained that the seventeen-year-old was "mad on munitions."[22] To Davey's mother, munitions work seems to have symbolized both an excitement about the novelty and the significance of munitions work and the freedom and pleasure made possible by decent wages.

For some women, munitions work was a way of proving their strength. Miss O. M. Taylor related her feeling that "though small I considered myself equal to any man, having carried, occasionally, sacks of wheat weighing eighteen stones [*sic*]. . . . I had always wished I had been born a boy and never more so than at this period. I really wanted to be a soldier."[23] After working in munitions for a while, she joined the WAACs, an option that became available only in 1917.

The WRNS and the WRAF, formed in 1917 and 1918 respectively, recruited women from the middle and upper classes rather than from the working class. Although some of the women in these paramilitary organizations were sent to serve in France, their work consisted of clerical and support services, and food preparation. The chiefs of the military services made it abundantly clear that the point of allowing women in auxiliary capacities was to free men from support work for the front lines. Women who joined these services were not under any delusion that their role was more than subordinate, but it did allow them some sense of participating in the military forces and gave them the opportunity to serve abroad.[24]

Only a minority of women in munitions factories consciously sought the franchise or argued that because of their work they deserved full citizenship rights. Yet women munitions workers believed themselves to be discharging their duty to their country and, in so doing, to be pulling their weight as well as any men. Such equality of participation in the national effort, they assumed, established some claim to consideration of their interests in the future. It was the blatant disregard of this claim in

22. *Pioneer and Labour Journal,* 4 February 1916. See also *Our Girls,* 4 March 1916, 4.
23. IWM, DD, 83/17/1.
24. See Crosthwait, "'Girl Behind the Man,'" 161–81; Jenny Gould, "Women's Military Services in First World War Britain," in *Behind the Lines: Gender and the Two World Wars,* ed. Margaret Randolph Higonnet et al. (New Haven: Yale University Press, 1987), 114–25. See also Anne Summers, *Angels and Citizens: British Women as Military Nurses 1854–1914* (London: Routledge & Kegan Paul, 1988).

the process of demobilization and the immediate postwar period that so angered many women who had been munitions workers.

RELATIONS WITH MEN IN THE ARMED FORCES

Given that women could not join the armed forces and that women's paramilitary organizations did not exist until the latter stages of the war, we must read women workers' stance on the war from their attitudes toward men who fought as well as toward their own involvement in munitions making. Women munitions workers considered themselves linked to the fighting forces in both public and private ways. Publicly, the weapons and ammunition they made directly supported the troops. Privately, a woman participated vicariously through her enlisted husband, lover, father, sons or brothers; as Tommy's sister, she was intimately related to Tommy. Much social prestige flowed through the status attached to a man who was serving in the armed forces. Not surprisingly, women munitions workers, despite the agony of fear that it entailed, were proud of their soldier, sailor, or airman brothers, sweethearts, and husbands.[25] A slightly caricatured version of this pride appeared in a piece in *The Englishwoman*, depicting life in a working-class neighborhood: "Hester Ball is with us once more, after a week of crowded, glorious life in and about the munition works. She tells the street that she has a chap 'over there,' and that a wedding is imminent. 'But I place no faith in *that*,' says Potter; 'just talking to do the grand, that's what I put it down to.'"[26]

It seems that at least some working-class women shared in the zeal that motivated middle- and upper-class women to publicly shame male noncombatants by thrusting a white feather on them. Caroline Rennles, for example, recalled that being "very patriotic in the First War" included "if you saw a chap out in the street you know, you'd say 'Why aren't you in the army?', you know. Oh, we thought it was marvellous to go to the war."[27] She drew a sharp distinction between the men with whom she worked at her first job as a shell filler at Slades Green, who had returned wounded from the war and then taken munitions jobs, and her male coworkers at Woolwich Arsenal who had never enlisted or had been

25. On women's relationships with their combatant brothers see Angela Woollacott, "Sisters and Brothers in Arms: Family, Class and Gendering in World War I Britain," in Cooke and Woollacott, eds., *Gendering War Talk*.

26. C. M. Verschoyle, "The Street Again," *The Englishwoman*, 32 (October 1916): 72. See also Caine, *Our Girls*, 73–74.

27. IWM, DSR, 000566/07, 10.

exempt from conscription. Referring to the latter, she recalled "I tell you they used to swagger around . . . they was earning pretty good money. . . . Oh, I used to go mad, I used to call them all the white-livered whatsonames I could lay my tongue to." Her retrospective judgment of her own behavior was that it was her youth that had made her unaware of what war was like for the men who fought; in the Second World War, in contrast, she would not "have told anybody to go."[28]

Women workers in munitions factories devised ways of showing the troops at the front their support. Some workers made a habit of enclosing notes in the items they made, knowing that a British, dominion, or allied soldier at the front would receive each one. Kate Luker, for example, wrote a note to "My dear Tommy," on the back of the instructions for the gas respirator she was working on, wishing the receiver luck and asking for a "line" in reply.[29] Not infrequently, a correspondence began in this way. Amy May established correspondence with two or three soldiers after putting notes with her name and address in the fuses she made, but she was horrified when one of them announced he was coming home on leave and wanted to see her. She was too apprehensive about his expectations to go out with him herself, but resolved her dilemma by having her mother take him out for a drink.[30]

Amid the national alarm over German advances in the spring of 1918, the women workers at the Georgetown National Filling Factory made a powerful gesture of support for the air force: they decided to raise enough money among themselves to buy a "battleplane" and present it to them. By staging a fair, concerts, film screenings, and a fancy dress ball and by collecting donations, they raised the remarkable sum of twenty-five hundred pounds in short order. On 15 April 1918 a check for that amount was signed by Marion Howie of the shell painting department and Marion Rennie of the 4.5-inch cartridge section and forwarded "'with the love and best wishes' of Scottish Filling Factory girls to the Secretary of the Air Ministry for the purchase of the 'Georgetown Battleplane.'" The plane, when delivered to the Royal Air Force, was named *Georgetown* and inscribed with the words "Presented by the Munition Workers of the Scottish Filling Factory."[31]

28. Ibid., 36. See also George Truphet, IWM, DSR, 000693/07.
29. IWM, DD, misc. 103, item 1609.
30. IWM, DSR, 000684/05.
31. PRO, MUN 5/ 154/1223/30. *Georgetown Gazette* 2, no. 7 (April 1918): 208–13; *Georgetown Gazette* 2, no. 9 (June 1918): 280; *Georgetown Gazette* 2, no. 11 (August 1918): 340.

Women munitions workers also actively supported wounded soldiers who had returned to Britain. Factories frequently held charity drives to collect money to donate to wounded soldiers, often as a gift to a specific hospital or rest home. All over Britain, as part of the organized recreation attached to munitions factories, women enthusiastically entertained wounded soldiers. Sometimes they visited the local hospital or rest home and took out those who were fit enough for afternoon tea or a meal. Other forms of entertainment included organized functions such as dances and concerts. These events were sometimes charged with sexual tension because of the women's determination to convince the men that they were attractive despite their injuries.[32] On 5 March 1917, for example, when sixty wounded soldiers were entertained by women from the case factory at Woolwich Arsenal, "the girls, who were fully determined to give the Tommies a real good time, greeted them upon their arrival at the club with smiling faces and in the best of spirits. The Tommies soon realised they were in for a good time, and quickly made themselves on the best of terms with the girls, who suddenly, and almost unconsciously, found themselves linked hand in hand for a game at kiss-in-the-ring, as a good start for the afternoon. This pastime was a real enjoyment to the guests—and also the girls."[33]

Some women munitions workers were insulated from the war, caught up in their own lives, and unaware of military developments. Asked if she and her friends at Woolwich Arsenal discussed the war together at work, Lilian Bineham replied, "No, no. 'Cause being young, y'see, you wasn't really interested. It didn't appeal to us or anything like that. It was all their boyfriends and all the rest of it they were talkin' about."[34] But others took a serious interest. Elsie McIntyre, who was an overlooker at the Barnbow factory, recalled taking her "girls" to the Clarion Cafe to celebrate either a victory in France or a productive period in the factory.[35] Age may have been a decisive factor in awareness of the events of the war.[36]

Whether or not they kept informed about the particular events of the

32. On women's sexual versus their maternal powers to restore masculinity to disabled veterans, see Sonya Michel, "Danger on the Home Front: Motherhood, Sexuality and Disabled Veterans in American Postwar Films," in Cooke and Woollacott, eds., *Gendering War Talk.*

33. *The Pioneer,* 16 March 1917. See also "Wedding Bells," *Georgetown Gazette* 3, no. 13 (October 1918): 12; PRO, MUN 5/154/1223/30.

34. IWM, DSR, 8778/2.

35. IWM, DSR, 000673/09, 57.

36. IWM, DSR, 000613/08, 19.

war, women munitions workers believed themselves vitally involved in the war effort through their own work, through the troops whom they did not know but whom they supported emotionally and financially, and through the war participation of men to whom they were related or attached. Most were not pacifists. Some were in fact capable of enjoying thinking about the firing of the weapons they were creating, such as the "Detonator Plug Girl" who imagined the life span of a detonator plug she made, called it "a dear little thing," described "his" creation in quasi-sexual terms, and told the end she foresaw for "him" in which "many were sent to their last, long rest" and "what remains of him lies alone unknown and forgotten in a foreign land."[37] Such belligerence is not surprising, considering that they had been imbued with the imperialist and nationalist political and moral code of the Edwardian and prewar years, as had their men who went off to fight.[38] The majority of the working class in this period expressed an imperialist patriotism that easily lent itself to militarism.[39] As Deborah Thom has pointed out, the numerous visits of the king and queen to munitions factories gave them specific images of the state to which to relate.[40]

After the powerful initial war fervor of the late summer of 1914 subsided, they too, like the soldiers who volunteered or were conscripted, endured the war as a grim, patriotic necessity. Workers were given stern reminders of the patriotic importance of their work, including notices hung on factory walls and harangues by welfare supervisors and others that any shortfall in productivity was helping the enemy and harming their men. One commentator explained women workers' preparedness to work through a holiday by quoting a woman worker: "We know what it's for. We know where it goes."[41] The lyrics of the songs they sang suggest that they were well aware of their role in the war effort, but at times the men in the armed forces reminded them of it. Monica Cosens

37. "Fuze 106: The Adventures of a Detonator Plug," by a Detonator Plug Girl, in Perivale, *The War-Worker* 2, no. 4 (September 1918): 66.

38. Michael Blanch describes the institutionalized ways in which young working-class people were imbued with these ideas in "Imperialism, Nationalism and Organized Youth," in *Working-Class Culture: Studies in History and Theory*, ed. John Clark, Chas. Critcher, and Richard Johnson (London: Hutchinson, 1979), 116–20.

39. Hugh Cunningham, "The Language of Patriotism," in *History and Politics*, vol. 1 of *Patriotism: The Making and Unmaking of British National Identity*, ed. Raphael Samuel (London: Routledge, 1989), 78–82; John Keegan, *The Face of Battle: A Study of Agincourt, Waterloo and the Somme* (London: Penguin, 1978), 221–23.

40. Thom, "Tommy's Sister," 154.

41. "Woman in Industry," by a Woman Worker, *The War-Worker* 1, no. 3 (August 1917), 44.

recalled the power of a gesture made by wounded soldiers at a VAD hospital in Tiverton to the munitions workers at her factory. One day there were bunches of yellow primroses on all the tables in the factory canteen, picked and sent specifically for them by the wounded soldiers. Explaining how much fresh flowers meant to those who were confined in a grease-covered factory, she commented: "Here was real proof that Mr. Tommy Atkins thought about us. It made us feel we were sharing the war with him. It drew us together, and we felt for the first time we were working *with* our soldiers and not *for* them."[42]

RELATIONS WITH MALE COWORKERS

The hostility toward women on the part of the male craft unions, especially in the engineering trades that were at the heart of munitions industries, guaranteed difficult relations between women and men coworkers. When women first entered male-dominated engineering factories in large numbers early in the war, they were met with a variety of responses from coolness to curiosity. Women frequently commented that at first they were made to feel like oddities. Where the men strongly resented the encroachment of women (either because they were intruding on their trade or because they were in effect sending men to the front), instances of hostility occurred, such as men hiding a woman's tools, handing her poor or incorrect tools with which to do a job, giving her erroneous instructions, or even sabotaging her equipment. Deborah Thom has noted that women at Woolwich Arsenal were met with physical violence and verbal abuse.[43] One woman, who was sent by the Ministry of Munitions into a factory as a tool fitter to prove to the men on the shop floor that women could perform skilled work, recalled later that "at the end of three weeks my spirit was broken." She had endured general antagonism, deliberately false directions from the foreman, silence from her male coworkers, and acts of blatant hostility such as her drawer being nailed up and oil poured into it through a crack. On the point of quitting, she decided to stay when told that the manager had sent in a good report on her, noting that he had expected her not to last more than three days.[44]

As the novelty of women workers wore off, and the men were assured

42. Cosens, *Lloyd George's Munition Girls*, 67–68.
43. Thom, "Tommy's Sister," 148.
44. Mrs. H. A. Felstead's account of her war work, written in 1919 and cited in Arthur Marwick, *Women At War 1914–1918* (London: Fontana, 1977), 62–63.

that women would not undercut their pay, these tensions lessened but never disappeared. Sarah Wilkie, who worked as a welder from 1917 to 1920 at Beardmore's shipyard at Dalmuir, Clydebank, recalled that her male coworkers continued to be chauvinist and resentful, albeit in a subtle, polite manner. She and the other woman welder in her area, however, developed their own method of retribution: when they saw a man approaching who had been particularly unpleasant, they would "hotwire" one of the ubiquitous puddles of water, not enough to hurt him but enough to make him jump.[45]

The sexual harassment with which women had to contend was another dimension to this campaign to expel women workers. However, it is impossible to estimate how prevalent such harassment was.

No doubt at the beginning of the war, it was common for men workers, especially the skilled, to be skeptical of women's ability to perform the jobs in which they themselves took so much pride. As more and more women received training and opportunities on the job during the war, this skepticism was perforce broken down. Those administering the process of dilution were at some pains to undermine these attitudes: as the Ministry of Munitions had staged an exhibit of women's work, so did the technical section of the labor exchange department of the Board of Trade.[46] Those who had been prejudiced at the start of the war had thus to revise their thinking. Nevertheless, as is implicit in the name "dilutees," women workers were only accepted by most male unionists as stopgaps, coworkers for the duration of the war and no longer.

Despite these tensions, male workers were often civil, even friendly, to the women who appeared in their factories as coworkers. Women munitions workers happily walked out with or became romantically involved with men who worked in their factories. Of the women munitions workers interviewed by the Sound Records Department of the Imperial War Museum, several had had boyfriends or met their husbands among their male coworkers. None of the women indicated any embarrassment or regret that these men had not been in the fighting forces. Munitions work was essential to the war effort, a fact no doubt relevant to their feelings. Moreover, it was consistent with their estimation of their own essential role in the war effort to see their male coworkers as equally patriotically involved. In the later stages of the war, a high proportion of

45. Interview with Mr. James Wilkie, Sr., and Mr. James Wilkie, Jr., husband and son of Sarah Wilkie, 14 May 1986, two months after Sarah's death.

46. Fraser, *Women and War Work,* 116–20.

the men in munitions factories had been in the forces and discharged due to injuries or unfitness. These men in munitions factories were thus also "Tommy."

The Pioneer occasionally reported fights that occurred in Woolwich Arsenal when they ended up in the local police court; sometimes these were cross-sex conflicts. In July 1917 Victor Boyle, nineteen years old, was charged with assaulting Florence Perfect at the Plumstead National Filling Factory: he had punched her in the face when she threatened to report him for swearing at her.[47]

Prior to the war, women's exclusion from skilled work and segregation into unskilled or semiskilled areas had been clearcut. Women were determined to perform wartime munitions jobs to the best of their abilities. One effect of the war was to make them very aware that their prior exclusion had been based on prejudiced judgments of their abilities and on social conceptions such as the idea of the man's wage as a family wage. Women workers' experience in the war called both sets of assumptions into question and fostered women's confidence in their own abilities, including the ability, if allowed, to earn a self-sufficient, perhaps even family-sufficient, wage.

REPRESENTATIONS OF THE
WAR'S IMPACT ON THEIR LIVES

A source that could possibly provide some insight into women workers' thoughts or perceptions of their lives, and the impact that the war made on them, is the fiction they chose to read. As the mood of an epoch is often best evoked in its literature, so too do people read fiction to understand themselves, their culture, and their experience more fully.

Contemporary observers commented that women munitions workers always carried a penny novelette, one of the constant items in the bags they took to the factory. Education reform resulted in compulsory schooling for girls from the 1870s onward, but the double standard in parental and educational authorities' attitudes meant that girls did not receive as good a grounding in scholastic skills as boys. Nevertheless, by the late nineteenth century, working-class women, especially young women, were more literate than ever before. It is not surprising, therefore, that one writer commented of working-class women in 1908: "Some girls and women are assiduous devourers of weekly papers of the novelette kind,

47. *The Pioneer,* 20 July 1917.

but comparatively few take advantage of the public libraries. . . . [L]iterature, in the strict sense of the word, is unknown in the vocabulary of women factory workers."[48]

The literature of the late nineteenth and early twentieth centuries, the cultural domain of the middle and upper classes, was marked by the emergence of a new figure. The New Woman, as she was known then and today, represented the social changes occurring as a result of the feminist movement. Women who sought careers, questioned marriage, demanded their own identities (even if in tortuous ways), and asserted their rights in debate had made their appearance in the pages of novelists such as Olive Schreiner, Thomas Hardy, and George Gissing.[49] Yet there seems to have been no translation of the New Woman into the cultural lexicon or reading material of women workers.

Even more than middle- and upper-class women, women workers were positioned during the war to experience the kind of occupational liberation that Sandra Gilbert has emphasized in her reading of World War I literature.[50] It is difficult, however, to find evocations of this liberation in the reading material of women munitions workers.

Apart from newspapers, which some observers said women workers read during the war more than they ever had, it seems working women read mostly romance stories, in the form of novelettes and short stories. Romance fiction, a genre then as now almost exclusively written and read by women, provided women readers with an escape from the monotony, the anxiety, and the hard grind of their daily lives through vicarious adventures and imaginary love affairs.[51] Weekly papers such as *Our Girls, Girls Weekly,* and the *Girls' Friend,* which aimed at a wide, popular audience among young working women, fed workers with adventure and romance stories about young women like themselves, occasionally adding an aristocratic heroine to appease their appetites for fantasy. It is perhaps

48. Priscilla E. Moulder, "Woman's Sphere," *Christian Commonwealth,* 4 November 1908. See also Margaret Weddell, "My Friend Sarah," *Common Cause,* 9 March 1917, 632; Minutes of Commission . . . on Recreation, 11 July 1917, MRC, YWCA Papers, MSS. 243/178.

49. For a discussion of the New Woman in literature see, for example, Patricia Stubbs, *Women & Fiction: Feminism & The Novel 1880–1920* (London: Methuen, 1981).

50. Sandra Gilbert, "Soldier's Heart: Literary Men, Literary Women, and the Great War," *Signs* 8, no. 3 (Spring 1983): 422–50.

51. See for example Janice A. Radway, *Reading the Romance: Women, Patriarchy and Popular Literature* (Chapel Hill: University of North Carolina Press, 1984), esp. ch. 3, "The Act of Reading the Romance: Escape and Instruction."

surprising, though, that the weekly papers and monthly magazines published for the same audience by the YWCA and women's trade unions also provided them with a liberal number of romance stories. Such stories were very probably by middle-class writers, who were nearly all women in the case of the YWCA and union papers.

In the later years of the war, a portion of these stories figured munitions workers as heroines. Some provided their heroine with the patriotic determination to enter a munitions factory and work her hardest to do what she could for the "boys" in the trenches. Several stories finally allowed their heroine, after much uncertainty and difficulty, a happy ending to her romance with a respectable young man, almost always a soldier or a sailor. Typical examples of this genre include "The Aeroplane Girl" and "The Lady of the Lathe."[52]

A few stories narrated problems specific to their readers' lives. In "The Man Who Couldn't See," the heroine Molly Devon had been a housewife before the war, but when her husband, fighting in France, was wounded and captured, she found her household in a financial crisis. The demand for women workers in shell factories seemed to her a chance sent by "Heaven itself," so she entered a factory and worked hard. All was well until one day she looked in the mirror and noticed that her hair and face were both decidedly yellow. She had become one of the TNT workers dubbed "canary girls" because of this manifestation of TNT poisoning. When she suddenly received a wire that her husband would be home soon in an exchange of prisoners, she panicked and fled to a small flat. He tracked her down, but she needn't have dreaded his seeing her so discolored: he was blind.[53] Thus "canary girls" were assured that there were worse fates than TNT poisoning and that one's appearance was but a small sacrifice to the national cause.

The 1918 novel *Munition Mary* by Brenda Girvin represented its heroine as battling for the acceptance of women workers in the "men's work" of factories. Mary, who is "sweet-faced" with long golden hair below her waist, finally overcomes the prejudice of armaments-factory owner Sir William Harrison when she rounds up four enemy saboteurs

52. "The Aeroplane Girl," *Girls' Own Stories*, 12 June 1919, 9; Christine Jope-Slade, "The Lady of the Lathe," *Woman At Home* (September 1917): 206–14. At least one woman munitions worker appeared as a character on stage, in the wartime play "Smith, V.C."

53. Mrs. Alfred Praga, "The Man Who Couldn't See," *Woman's Life*, 21 July 1917, 74–78. See also Christine Jope-Slade, "Orange Hands: A Story of Eastbourne," *Woman's Life*, 27 July 1918, 83–85.

in the factory. Clinching the owner's conversion, Mary finally breaks down in tears, thus proving to him that she is still a gentle woman at heart and that therefore factory work is not antithetical to femininity.[54]

That these stories never progressed beyond this muffled blow struck for women's participation in the work force, and were far from having heroines who were thrilled to be in charge of powerful machinery or excited by driving electric cranes, shows that the writers either were not such women or were not in favor of women breaking through such boundaries. This fiction propagated the image of a woman worker who accepts her economic and social position and hopes at most to receive a proposal of marriage from a man somewhat above her own class, but who knows at heart it would be better to marry a man of her own class who is more suitable for her.

Presumably some of this message, specifically the focus on hopes of a happy marriage, resonated with the lives of some munitions workers. Yet, from their statements in interviews, women workers do not seem to have been preoccupied with the hope of marrying someone above their socio-economic status; rather, this seems more a preoccupation of the middle class. Even in the stories that constituted their reading material, women munitions workers had to contend with middle-class, unrealistic, and stereotypical images of themselves and their experiences. They read the stories because they filled their need for entertainment and diversion and perhaps gave them a chance to indulge in some wishful thinking about their lives. However, this fiction does not provide any insight into women workers' thoughts about their lives or their wartime experience, primarily because it was written for them, not by them. To find any such direct testimony, it is necessary to look to other sources.

There are, fortunately, a few written records by women munitions workers about their own experiences. Besides the accounts by middle-class women, there are several extant accounts by working-class women.[55]

54. Mary Cadogan and Patricia Craig, *Women and Children First: The Fiction of Two World Wars* (London: Victor Gollancz, 1978), 61.

55. Barker, "My Life as I Remember It"; Charlotte Meadowcroft, "Bygones," MS, 35 pp.; and Annie Lord, "My Life," MS, 12 pp., all in the Brunel University Library. For these I am indebted to John Burnett, David Vincent, and David Mayall, eds., *The Autobiography of the Working Class: An Annotated, Critical Bibliography, Vol. II 1900–1945* (New York: New York University Press, 1987). Among the unpublished accounts held by the Imperial War Museum are A. Darter, "Woolwich Arsenal 1917–18," Library 323.1 K.48004 and several in the Department of Documents. The published accounts include that of Rosina Whyatt in John Burnett, *Useful Toil: Autobiographies of Working People from the 1820s to the 1920s* (Harmondsworth: Penguin, 1984), 125–32; that of a "female munitions worker" in Charles

Occasionally a working women's magazine or a factory held an essay-writing competition, coaxing the workers to write of their experiences as munitions workers. It would seem that the writers of essays for these competitions either were truly fired by patriotic ideals or at least thought the prize would go to someone who claimed to be. When the YWCA magazine *Our Outlook* held such a competition in December 1916, one entry they published exuded nationalistic spirit. Claiming that she was a proud member of the YWCA, the essayist continued:

> Monotony is out of the question. It is wonderful to see the thousands of girls coming and going in the changing of shifts; a more good-natured, whole-hearted, livelier set of girls and women you could not meet anywhere. Each one is bent on doing her bit for King and country. . . . I am sure every worker has the same principle as myself, each one knowing she is needed to push on the mighty work of bringing this dreadful war to an end. . . . Patriotism and liberty in the truest sense were my motive in becoming a munition worker.[56]

The richest sources for women workers' own testimony available to the historian are oral history interviews. Historians interested in women's roles in wartime are indebted to the Sound Records Department of the Imperial War Museum, which has been systematically interviewing since the mid-1970s. The women interviewed in the 1970s who had worked in World War I munitions factories were quite young at the time of the war and quite old when they were interviewed, both of which factors set up certain biases or problems. One obvious bias is that the experiences they relate are preponderantly those of young, single women, whereas many of the workers were older, married, and had children. A problem is that another war had intervened, adding a whole other set of war memories that could become entangled.

Listening to the thirty-one interviews of World War I women munitions factory workers in the collection of the Sound Records Department, an overwhelming impression is of the absence of general, philosophical, or political statements about the whole experience. Perhaps this is a result of the women's perceptions of what the interviewers wanted, or perhaps it is simply a product of viewing one's youth from the distance of old age. Regenia Gagnier's analysis of autobiographies led her to conclude that,

---

Forman, *Industrial Town: Self-Portrait of St. Helens in the 1920s* (London: Granada Publishing, 1979), 83–84; and two very short pieces in Marwick, *Women At War*, 67–68.

56. "The Life of a Munition Worker," *Our Outlook* (YWCA) 9, no. 104 (December 1916): 234. Another such essay was written by Nellie Rooke who worked at Napier and Sons, Acton Vale. "Prize Competition: Awards," *Woman Worker*, 4 (April 1916): 14.

while working-class writers are often at variance with bourgeois, liberal, individualist subjectivity, they themselves present a range of subjectivities from the commemorative to the political.[57] The women munitions workers' recollections are given in disparate images, rather than in strong or summary statement, which indicates that they did not place their own development as the central reference point, perhaps because they were more inclined toward familial rather than self-identification. It is significant, of course, that these were responses to interviewers' questions, not their own deliberate writing. In proffering the minute details and circumstances of their lives, without judgments such as whether or not they felt themselves transformed by war experience, they emphasize the critical importance of short-term survival to workers and the relative unimportance of self-analysis and introspection.

Nevertheless, some of them expressed an emotional summation of the experience. Grace Bryant worked on gun inspection and cleaning at the Southampton Docks, and then as a machine operative at the Canute aircraft factory: "I went round to the Canute aeroplane works. . . . I was an engineer's mate first, filin' away at plates, and from there I wanted to get across the other side, because there was machinery. I'm rather interested in machinery, I was in those days. So I used to go over there and watch the capstans work. . . . [A]nyhow, there was a job goin' on what they call the milling machines. . . . It was very, very interesting. . . . [T]he happy times, it was really lovely."[58] Beatrice Lee also enjoyed her job as a driver of an overhead electric crane at the Copper Works in Leeds:

> I was on [an] average weekly wage. Two pounds 10 shillings, from 1916 to 1919, and we worked from six in the morning 'til six at night, and we had to be up in those conveyors at five minutes to six, not five past. We had to be up in those conveyors for when the buzzer went, we had to be ready to sail out. . . . [T]here was a control at one side for carrying ropes, and a driving control on this side and we used to drive all around the factory. . . . [I]t was a very happy life. It was very sad about the lads getting killed and all that, but as far as the work conditions it was a very 'appy life. It really was 'appy, I enjoyed being there.[59]

Remembering their war jobs as happy times must surely be significant. It could signify that the times were emotionally charged, perhaps, or that the work was more satisfying than jobs they held before or after the war.

57. Regenia Gagnier, *Subjectivities: A History of Self-Representation in Britain, 1832–1920* (New York and Oxford: Oxford University Press, 1991), esp. ch. 4.
58. IWM, DSR, 7433/02.
59. IWM, DSR, 000724/06.

Certainly it must have been related to the fact that they were earning more money than ever before, and despite rationing and shortages, many of them were enjoying a standard of living previously unknown. Perhaps above all else these women recalled the camaraderie they experienced, which, especially for those used to being isolated in domestic service or housework, must have been a singularly pleasurable part of their lives. For women interviewed in later life, the war may well have stood out in retrospect as being the most purposeful and most sociable of their working years. The contrast between the tones in which they describe their experience of the war and the unspeakable horrors that some of their male counterparts were experiencing at war is stark.

Manuscript and published accounts and oral interviews all leave wide gaps of meaning, or significance, between the fixed points of the details of the daily existence of women munitions workers. These gaps can be filled, to a certain extent, by interpreting women workers' actions, such as their protesting in the streets against demobilization, their vociferous stand against returning to domestic service, and their increased membership in trade unions. Such actions speak to women workers' increased sense of self-worth and greater self-confidence, acquired from the fact of their munitions jobs, from their improved wages and conditions, and from the appreciation they were shown for participating in the national effort and undertaking new and skilled tasks. Regardless of the scarcity of their verbal testimony to these psychological and emotional developments, the evidence of their experience left in the record of their actions bears out the views of others who saw such developments in them. Knowing this, it is possible to accept with greater confidence the judgments of observers who, though not women munitions workers themselves, saw them at sufficiently close hand to perceive changes.

MUNITIONS WORK:
A MASCULINIZING EXPERIENCE?

The gender implications of women's extraordinary wartime roles and experiences have recently become contested grounds for debate among literary critics. Sandra Gilbert has drawn on the wartime and postwar writing of the male and female literati to argue that while men were emasculated by the paralyzing terror and horror of trench warfare, women were empowered and exhilarated by their novel roles, chances to have adventures, and greater remuneration. While men were losing lives and limbs, entombed in ghastly trenches and suffering injuries that rendered them impotent, women were experiencing freedom and excitement as an erotic release and exulted in new social behavior and the chance to ride a motorbike, drive a car, or be at the front. She sees the result of these divergent experiences of the same war as a barrier or alienation between the sexes by which women achieved a victory, a conquest over men. The postwar result of this inversion, she contends, was a backlash combined of antifeminism in male writings and a debilitating guilt among women.[60]

Other literary critics have responded vehemently to Gilbert's thesis.[61] Gilbert describes the women ambulance drivers of the "forbidden zone" in France as "swoop[ing] over the wastelands of the war with the energetic love of Wagnerian Valkyries," a description that would astound any reader of Helen Zenna Smith's Not So Quiet . . . Stepdaughters of War.[62] Yet while Gilbert's characterization of ambulance drivers may be inappropriate, the point that women were exhilarated by controlling, especially driving, previously taboo machinery is valid for many women on the homefront. At some remove from the horrors of the battlefront, women who took charge of trucks, cranes, cars, and motorbikes in Britain during the war did find it thrilling. Margaret H. Adams recaptured in a short story her experience as a truck driver during the war: "With a feeling of great exhilaration and sense of adventure ahead, Joan made her way first along narrow roads and even a country lane. . . . Most people had probably not yet breakfasted while roads were almost empty. Pushing back her cap Joan savoured the cool rush of air through the front of the 'cab'."[63] P. L. Stephens recalled a proud moment when, having moved around the country on her secondhand Triumph motorcycle between munitions jobs, she finally applied for a position as a motorcyclist with the RAF. When

---

60. Gilbert, "Soldier's Heart."

61. Jane Marcus, "The Asylums of Antaeus; Women, War and Madness: Is There a Feminist Fetishism?" in The Difference Within: Feminism and Critical Theory, ed. Elizabeth Meese and Alice Parker (Philadelphia: John Benjamins Publishing, 1988); Claire Tylee, "'Maleness Run Riot'—The Great War and Women's Resistance to Militarism," Women's Studies International Forum 11, no. 3 (1988): 200. Marcus and Tylee share a central objection to Gilbert's suggestion that women experienced a sexual thrill from male death, an idea that Gilbert proffers with rhetorical questions such as "Does male death turn women nurses on?" "Soldier's Heart," 212.

62. Gilbert, "Soldier's Heart," 214; Helen Zenna Smith, Not So Quiet . . . Stepdaughters of War (1930; reprint, New York: Feminist Press at CUNY, 1989) is a pseudonymous novel of ambulance driving in France. Written by Evadne Price and based on Winifred Young's diaries as an ambulance driver, it shows that experience to have been a hellish one, in which nauseated women ambulance drivers drove their screaming cargo along atrocious roads as slowly as possible.

63. Margaret H. Adams, "The Visitor," IWM, DD, P348 W/W/1 T.

the sergeant who interviewed her told her to get into his sidecar for the trip to the camp, she replied: "'No, you hop in the side-car, & I'll drive you to Scampton'—So I was signed on, & found myself the only girl amongst some few hundred men."[64]

This debate among literary critics has overlooked the deaths and the suffering of women during the war. In the munitions factories women were killed, injured, and poisoned, while other women in support services behind the lines were vulnerable to bombs and to infection. It is important both to acknowledge this part of women's experience of the war and to recognize its small scale compared to the war experience of men. Gilbert's argument of women's empowerment and gains during the war is partly based on socioeconomic developments. Here, as distinct from her argument about the libidinous effect of male death, her evocation of female emancipation by the war is substantiated by the experience of women munitions workers. In refuting this side of her argument, Gilbert's critics are basing their interpretations on two small groups of women, the active women's peace movement and the women who nursed behind the lines or drove ambulances in France. They find pacifism, objection to the war, and a negation of hope in these women's accounts and assume these attitudes to be representative of all women.

The fact that women in a number of war-service roles wore uniforms during World War I was a subject of much social commentary (see figure 11). Women who wore uniforms frequently became the butt of derision by conservative segments of society and, more disconcertingly, their own menfolk. Objections were that women who wore uniforms were exaggerating their own importance to the war effort and consequently the role of women in the national crisis and that they were attempting to become just like men. Mrs. Wilby recalled that her then fiancé, an ambulance driver in East Africa, wrote to her and instructed her firmly that she must not wear trousers at work because it wasn't feminine.[65]

Despite opposition, uniforms pervaded numerous occupations that women undertook in the war years, from the Women's Land Army to the municipal tramways to Barclay's bank at Chelmsford, where Rev. Clark observed that the women clerks were "now all dressed in green overalls."[66] For women in the paramilitary corps, or the Women Police Service, the uniform was an important emblem of status and identity in the

64. P. L. Stephens, "My War Service during World War I—1914–1918," IWM, DD, "P"348 W/W/1 T.

65. IWM, DSR, 9356/2.

66. Munson, *Echoes of the Great War,* 192.

national effort. One observer claimed in late 1918 that "to-day, [a woman] may smoke, she may wear trousers, she may crop her hair short, she may live alone in flats, she may walk in the streets in khaki and salute other khaki-clad beings, for all the world as if she were a man."[67]

Although neither smart nor intended to be worn in public, uniforms acquired a similar emblematic quality for women munitions workers, as the bridesmaids in munitions uniform apparently felt (see chapter 2). Originally, however, they were worn purely for practical purposes. Munitions workers' uniforms consisted of a large dress-like overall made from heavy cotton, or trousers and three-quarter length jacket. Some women objected to wearing trousers, such as Mrs. Wilkinson who was fired from her job in Sheffield for refusing to wear them, but the majority did not object and may even have enjoyed a certain liberation.[68] Trousers or puttees (cloth bound round the legs) were found to be necessary for women crane drivers, who had to climb up and down, and were also adopted in situations where skirts could get caught in machinery. Thus women munitions workers were outwardly adopting masculine style, allowing for some greater physical freedom, at least at work. Before long, women would begin to wear trousers for casual occasions.

Some commentators expressed their abhorrence of women making the weapons of death, seeing this as conflicting with "women's nature" as mothers and nurturers. To contemporary poet Mary Gabrielle Collins, for example, the act of women engaged in making munitions "Taints the fountain head, Mounts like a poison to the Creator's very heart."[69] Similarly, popular writer Hall Caine lamented: "It is difficult to think of [woman] as a maker of weapons of death. . . . [W]oman is the life-giver, not the life-destroyer, and in her heart of hearts ten thousand slain, whether friend or foe, are ten thousand mothers' sons, each of them a man born of a woman and suckled at her breast."[70]

The inverse view was that women were fulfilling their maternal nature and function by making their death-dealing "babies" (see figure 12). One journalist expressed his admiration for women workers with this exclamation: "One might almost think that the girls looked on the shining

67. Amy Lester-Garland, "Should Women Imitate Men?" *The War-Worker* 2, no. 7 (December 1918): 102.

68. "Wouldn't Wear Trousers," *Woman Worker* (April 1917), 2.

69. Mary Gabrielle Collins, "Women At Munition Making," in *Scars Upon My Heart: Women's Poetry & Verse of the First World War,* ed. Catherine Reilly (London: Virago, 1981), 24.

70. Caine, *Our Girls,* 66–67.

shell-cases as babies, so keen is their pride in turning out work as perfect as possible."[71] As Claire Culleton has noted, other commentators have also drawn this parallel between munitions making and maternal functions.[72] The image of munitions makers as parents of their manufactures, however, was also applied to men workers.[73]

Women who were personally deprived by the war, losing their husbands, sons, lovers, or fathers, were susceptible to feelings of revenge or of wanting to take their place. In the view of one commentator, it was the spirit of grief-stricken participation in munitions making that was the key to resolving the conflict between women's generative role and their involvement in making weapons of death:

> And as I watched the busy scene it seemed an unnatural and awful thing that women's hands should be busied thus, fashioning means for the maiming and destruction of life—until, in a remote corner, I paused to watch a woman whose dexterous fingers were fitting finished cartridges into clips with wonderful celerity. A middle-aged woman, this, tall and white-haired, who, at my remark, looked up with a bright smile, but with eyes sombre and weary. "Yes, sir," she answered above the roar of machinery, "I had two boys at the front, but—they're a-laying out there somewhere killed by the same shell. I've got a photo of their graves—very neat they look, though bare, and I'll never be able to go and tend 'em, y'see—nor lay a few flowers on 'em. So I'm doin' this instead—to help the other lads." . . . I saluted the spirit of noble motherhood ere I turned and went my way.[74]

Only one of the women whose accounts are available expressed having felt perturbed by the nature of her work. Concluding a descriptive essay about her experience as a munitions worker, this woman fervently exclaimed that "once this war is over, never in creation will I do the same thing again, and let us hope that this is the last, and concentrate all thoughts on a worlds [sic] peace, and let us be one united world, and help to educate humanity to a higher and nobler standard of living when war will be impossible."[75] On the whole, however, most women workers usually dismissed from their minds the horrific potential of the objects they were making, beyond believing in their efficacy in the cause of

71. *Illustrated London News*, 23 September 1916.
72. Claire A. Culleton, "Gender-Charged Munitions: The Language of World War I Munitions Reports," *Women's Studies International Forum* 11, no. 2 (1988): 109–16.
73. "The Big Push," *Punch*, 2 August 1916.
74. Jeffery Farnol, *Great Britain At War* (Boston: Little, Brown, 1918), 8–9.
75. "My Experience of a Few Months in a Munition Factory," by "A Munition Girl" employed at the Armstrong Works, Alexandria, September 1916, IWM, Women's Work Collection, Mun. 24/15.

victory. When Mrs. Wilby's then fiancé found out that she had taken a job in a munitions factory as a lathe worker, he "was disgusted. He said, 'Fancy a nice girl making things to kill people. You was made to produce, not kill.' And he didn't like it at all." She, however, was unperturbed by his concerns, "didn't take any notice," she laughingly assured the interviewer, and "just carried on, to the end."[76] The issue of real gender significance is that by making the weapons of war women were directly participating in the war effort. In marked contrast to the women who were nurses, VADs, and ambulance drivers, they were neither healers nor pacifists. Rather they were the makers of war at its first stage of production.

While thus performing what could be characterized as part of the masculine propagation of war, women munitions workers did not articulate a sense of becoming either more masculine or less feminine. They did not challenge the division of labor that gave them primary responsibility for the household and childcare, despite arduous work shifts. Yet enhanced self-esteem and self-confidence, their satisfaction in their work, and awareness of their contribution to the national war effort all carry gender implications. Women knew that they had undertaken jobs considered "men's work," that they had performed these jobs creditably well, and that in so doing they had contributed significantly to the war effort, which could therefore not be considered solely men's undertaking. They knew they had executed work critical to the conduct of Britain's war campaign and that they had done so regardless of the inherent danger. They saw themselves as "the girls with yellow hands," who were "in the fighting line, willing to do or die." By playing an important, publicly acclaimed role in the first war to be conducted as a nationwide effort, a "total war" in which distinctions between the armed forces and the civilians at home were less sharp than ever before, women workers laid a claim to citizenship and to more equal treatment in the work force.[77]

CONCLUSION

The recent consensus among scholars studying women and the world wars has been that, despite gains made by women during wartime, the reconstruction of gender in the postwar worlds not only negated those gains but produced an antifeminist backlash. Focusing on official postwar

---

76. IWM, DSR, 9356/2.
77. For an evaluation of the concept of "total war," see Ian F. W. Beckett, "Total War," in Clive Emsley, Arthur Marwick, and Wendy Simpson, eds., *War, Peace and Social Change in Twentieth-Century Europe* (Milton Keynes: Open University Press, 1989), 26–44.

discourses, or even feminists' realignment, however, can obscure the meaning of the war experience for large numbers of women. For the masses of women who participated in the Great War as makers of munitions, their involvement was a temporary experience that revealed new possibilities. The perspective of women belligerents in World War I helps us to trace the path of women's increasing engagement in war in the twentieth century. It also contributes to breaking down the binary conception of women as the passive observers of war—pacifists or healers—in opposition to men warriors. While British women were drawn into munitions work because of its relative lucrativeness and its ubiquity amidst disrupted trade and industry, in World War I, unlike World War II, they voluntarily chose to become the makers of the weapons of war, active agents in its propagation. It is important for historians of women to reconstruct the experience of female actors in significant historical events rather than to see it through the circumlocutions of other actors such as governments, officials, or male unionists.

War accelerated rather than originated changes in women's social behavior, but wartime changes occurred both rapidly and within a context of involvement in military action, the quintessentially masculine sphere. Thus women's adoption of uniforms and other masculine emblems was seen as part of women's claims to participation in the heart of the nation's business. Performing "men's work" and adopting masculine clothing and emblems were only part of women's experience of war, however. It is inadequate to see the war as either masculinizing women workers or giving them access to some remote and diluted version of men's experience of war. We need to identify women's experience of war as valid and distinct. In exploring the options newly opened to them by the dislocations and demands of war, and by valorizing their own crucial involvement in the waging of war, women munitions workers actively participated in World War I in a way that contravened assumptions that the propagation of war was the exclusive domain of men.

Munitions work offered women unprecedented mobility and financial autonomy, thus fostering the ambition, independence, and assertiveness that were reflected in their desire to emigrate at the end of the war, their higher level of labor organization, and their refusal of the prewar conditions and servility of domestic service. Moreover, their improved health through their better diet, the evidence of the improved health and clothing of children in working-class neighborhoods, and women's pleasure in controlling an at least adequate family budget all constituted a challenge to the system of the family wage. Women's capability and relish at being fully remunerated breadwinners questioned the premises underlying the system of gendered wages, despite the continuation of unequal pay. At the same time their capability as workers in industry did much to persuade employers of the advantages of employing cheaper female labor.

While analysis of the literature of the war has underscored the emotional and psychological distance it put between the men who fought and the women on the homefront, the war affected relations between women and men of the working class through the quashing of women's temporary employment gains by male unions and workers at the war's end. Perceptions of class difference in the 1920s and 1930s may have been strong, but simultaneously cutting against class unity for workers was women's bitter awareness of their reduced options. Bernard Waites has argued that the emergence of concepts such as "equality of sacrifice" and "profiteering" in the latter part of the war indicate a new consciousness on the part of the working class of "the roots of inequality in capitalist market society."[78] The unionization of women workers during the war, the newfound assertiveness so widely commented on, and their public anger during demobilization all suggest a new conception of their own interests as distinctly different from those of men workers (and those of middle- and upper-class women). Their awareness of the importance of their efforts to the national cause gave them a basis on which to ground their expectations for future consideration.

With the growing political representation of labor, the expanded unionization of both male and female unskilled workers, the burgeoning of the mass leisure industry, and the new affordability of consumer goods, class relations in the decades following World War I were radically altered from those of the nineteenth century. But at the same time gender relations within classes shifted too. Women workers' massive participation in the propagation of war, publicly heralded as it had been, invested their new roles as voting citizens with added meaning. Despite the barring of married women from some jobs and the perpetuation of the family wage ideology in the 1920s and 1930s, the expectations of young women workers in particular had been slightly elevated. Their direct knowledge of the personal autonomy imparted by decent wages, and the social autonomy of their relative mobility during wartime, gave women who had been munitions workers a new index by which to measure their own subordination in the work place and in the family.

78. Bernard Waites, *A Class Society at War: England 1914–1918* (Leamington Spa: Berg, 1987), 235.